ROADSIDE
HISTORY
OF S COLORADO

ROADSIDE HISTORY OF COLORADO

REVISED EDITION

James McTighe

Johnson Books: Boulder

In memory of Mary, my wife,
without whose confident encouragement
these pages might be blank

ISBN 1-55566-054-1

LC Catalog Card Number: 89-84757

5 6 7 8 9 10

Cover Design: Robert Schram
Cover Photographs: Robert Schram

Printed in the United States of America by
Johnson Publishing Company
1880 South 57th Court
Boulder, Colorado 80301

Acknowledgements

A certain intoxication comes when I imbibe the notion that this is "my book." The feeling is like one drink too many. I need only to retrace my steps in the making of *Roadside History of Colorado* to realize its folly.

In the first place, who but my old friend and colleague Robert E. Owen introduced me to the trove of stories associated with historical sites? And did not Lynne Rienner, herself a publisher, urge me to present my idea to an important trade publisher, Johnson Books? Would this unique format be offered on these pages had not Johnson's editorial director Michael McNierney prompted me to modify my proposal?

Once I had a contract to write the book, I found fortune in a well-administered and congenial gold mine beneath Norlin Library on the University of Colorado's Boulder campus, where Sandy Volpe and her colleagues in the Western Historical Archives were of immeasurable help to me. Helpful too were Catherine Engel and Collette Chambellan of the Colorado Historical Society's Heritage Center reference library in Denver. Lois Anderton of Boulder's Carnegie Branch Library simplified my searches in the public library's historical collections. Jean Andrews helped me to screen the photographic archives of the Colorado Tourism Board.

Several officials of the National Park Service, commendably conscious of Colorado's past, guided me in my research on the historical sites within their reserves. Among them, my thanks to Vernon C. "Skip" Betts, naturalist on the headquarters staff of Rocky Mountain National Park; Don C. Hill, chief naturalist at the Curecanti National Recreation Area; and Robert C. Reyes, superintendent of the Florissant Fossil Beds National Monument.

ACKNOWLEDGEMENTS

I would like to acknowledge the help of the late Robert G. Athearn, from whose many fine published works I drew much information and insight, and upon whose precious time I unwittingly presumed in searching out some obscure detail when he was in his final weeks at the University of Colorado's history department. Let the record show that he was most gracious in aiding an utter stranger.

In the matter of obscure points I am grateful too to state wildlife official Robin Knox for an instant briefing on the biological antecedence of the axolotl, which (as you will see) had its part in the early settlement of Colorado. Also to be thanked are the numerous persons in museums, libraries, newspaper offices, service stations, railroad depots, and on the streets of hundreds of small towns around Colorado who helped me to locate many of these elusive sites when I was doing field research. I regret I cannot name them all.

Most especially, however, I must express appreciation for the fine art work volunteered by my talented son Tom; the excellent job of indexing done by his equally talented twin, Michele; the unrelenting assistance in field research lent me by daughters Monica, Catherine, and Chris, taking notes for hours and days on end in the far corners and crannies of the state; Martha who helped closer to home; Peggy, my auxiliary typist; and Patrick who kept the car running when a time or two it was on verge of collapse.

And thanks to Michael McNierney and Leslie Burger for seeing a bulky manuscript through to final form.

In this second edition I also want to thank Jean Zirkle for introducing me to Perry Park and helping with field research; the late Monica Shafer, a fine lady who lent me her uncle Dennis Sheedy's memoirs; Fev. David Ivey, who gave me a copy of the Cordova family memoir; Rose Northrup, who briefed me on Eldora; John Clarke and the staff at Eldorado Canyon State Park; Kit Carson County Social Services Director Norma Panratz of Burlington, and librarians Lois Anderton and Catherine Engel, who once again were most helpful to me.

Contents

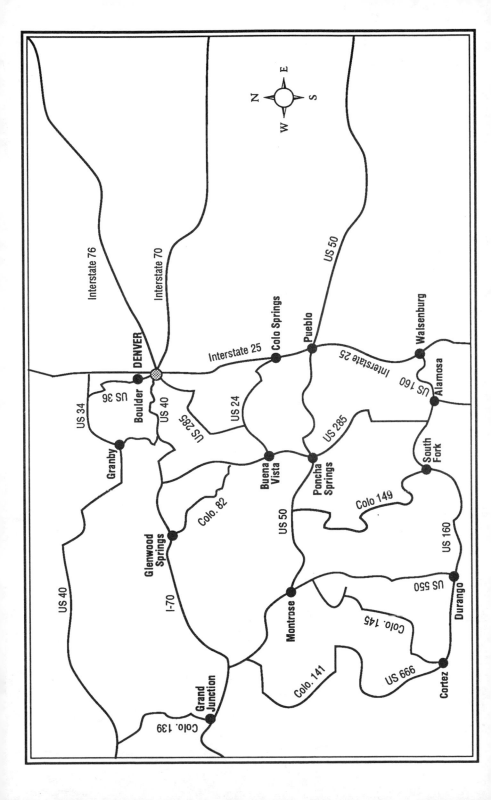

Introduction

One rainy November night in 1980, when my wife Mary and I were on a return visit to Washington, D.C., we had dinner with some old friends, Bob and Vivian Owen. A compulsive researcher, Bob had started a firm specializing in genealogical inquiries. Bob's idea of paradise is to possess a computer programmed to recapture every datum in the National Archives.

On the occasion of our visit, however, he revealed a new interest. He had assembled the complete texts of historical markers, with their precise locations along the highways of his home state, Wisconsin.

"Why bother?" I asked. "They're all right out there on the highway for all to see."

"How many motorists take time to read them?" he asked in turn. "How many pass these markers before realizing even that they are there?"

Many was the time that I had raced by a highway marker, wondered what it commemorated but determined not to take the time to find out. I am embarrassed even now at the ignorance haste has cost me over the years. Bob's idea was to publish the texts of markers so that motorists could anticipate them, know what they said and, if they should choose, stop and savor the sight. It was a good idea.

We discovered, however, that the idea was not original. Historical societies and highway departments in a number of states have published booklets with precisely that information. The Colorado Historical Society is one. These texts, however, tend merely to tease an interest in the often extraordinary persons and bizarre incidents haunting the places a traveler might pass. Markers are, inevitably, limited in the space needed to tell a story. Frequently, moreover, they aim more at conveying humor than information. Occasionally, they have been erected at the insistence of a local claque bent, for political reasons, on paying tribute to a dignitary of less than historic proportions. More often, I discovered, sites worthy of attention are not marked at all.

Roadside History of Colorado aims at remedying these deficiencies.

In Colorado, outside of National Parks and Monuments, less than two hundred historical sites are marked. This book, on the other hand, identifies several times that number, including many of those that are officially marked. Some markers, however, are passed over altogether for want of what I judge to be a worthwhile story. If you care to test this judgment, I urge that, when you come upon one, pull over and read the marker's text for yourself. Inherently indisputable is the old Latin adage, *De gustibus non est disputandum*, which, loosely translated, proclaims "each to his own taste."

What you will find in these eighty thousand words are stories about many fascinating persons of the past and some remarkable events that, until now, had been forgotten or only sketchily recounted in other publications. And, although nobody these days can dispute at least the durability of Latin adages, I sincerely hope you will find that the following stories do indeed suit your taste.

I make no pretense of being, in the strict sense, a historical scholar. Most of my sources are what academics would term "secondary." I think of myself as a journalist of the past. The only thing original in the information I will set before you is the method of organization, which may be unique; an occasional personal opinion that I could not resist injecting; and perhaps the breadth of the subject matter. The book covers centuries, even millennia, and nearly every aspect of human endeavor and foible that could take place in an area of 104,247 square miles.

Given the comprehensive nature of this work, there are bound to be some errors. I have rechecked the material repeatedly to weed them out, as have my editors and advisers. In any case, because the research is mine, the narrative is mine, and the selection of sources is mine, so also are the errors.

In format the narrative follows stretches of highway. It begins at one end and follows to an ofttimes arbitrary terminal, recounting the stories of the sites in the order in which they are passed. I have tried to fashion a degree of coherence in the telling of these stories for ease of reading, even though years may separate the events being dealt with. Despite narrative devices designed to make a smoother transition from one story to the next, each story at each site can stand alone.

At a slight disadvantage, of course, is the reader who happens to be traveling down the stretch of highway in a direction opposite to the narrative. In such a case, I suggest that you read the entire section from beginning to end—it will take about fifteen or twenty minutes—and, as each significant milepost is reached, the story for that site should be reviewed for the details you might not remember.

In the narration the direction taken for each of these routes has conformed to the flow of immigration in Colorado's past—east to west and north to south, with minor exceptions. Ironically, on modern highways this is contrary to the sequence of mileposts, as the state highway department has placed them. The numbering of north-south highways begins at the end nearest Colorado's southern border and ascends in number toward the north. On the east-west routes, numbering starts at the western border. On two-lane highways the mileposts are located on the east or the south side, but the number is printed on both front and back so that the milepost can be identified from either direction. For example, drivers traveling west or south must look to the opposite shoulder to find the milepost.

Vandals and snowplows have taken a toll of mileposts. Human error has mislocated a few. On the whole, however, the motorist will find them where they should be. In making my surveys of sites, however, I have found it useful to correlate the first milepost I come to on a given stretch of highway with the reading of my car's odometer. Thus, when

I need it, a little arithmetic will locate a missing milepost.

On federal reserves, notably Rocky Mountain National Park, there are no mileposts, so the traveler is obliged to fix his location after entering the reserve by means of the car's odometer, whose reading should be noted at the last milepost before entering the park. Fortunately, the National Park Service takes pains to identify the location of most historical sites within their domain.

Finally, perhaps in contrast with historical travelogues that focus on old structures remarkable for their architecture or ruins notable for their lingering semblance to the original, the narratives of *Roadside History of Colorado* in the main deal not with the inanimate but with the living, dead though they might now be, not with buildings so much as their builders. This is a book of testimonies, not tombstones.

I like stories, anecdotes that give spice to life. I like these stories. I hope you do, too.

1. The High Plains

To early travelers from the East, Colorado's high plains were only the last leg of a long approach to the place that really interested them—The Rocky Mountains.

"In regard to this extensive section of country," reported an army explorer in 1821, "we do not hesitate in giving the opinion that it is almost wholly unfit for cultivation, and of course uninhabitable by a people depending upon agriculture for their subsistence. . . . [The] scarcity of wood and water, almost uniformly prevalent, will prove an insuperable obstacle in the way of settling the country."

Maj. Stephen H. Long made this observation to John C. Calhoun, then President James Monroe's secretary of war. He had just returned from a scientific expedition along a route that in Colorado begins at the junction of I-76 and I-80, follows the South Platte River valley down to I-25 in present-day Denver, and continues down the Front Range to the vicinity of Raton Pass, where I-25 crosses into New Mexico.

"This region, however, viewed as a frontier, may prove of infinite importance to the United States, inasmuch as it is calculated to serve as a barrier to prevent too great an extension of our population westward, and secure us against the machinations or incursions of an enemy that might otherwise be disposed to annoy us in that quarter."

Although it took more than a century, Long was proved wrong on all counts. During his lifetime settlement was indeed sparse, and the plains served mainly as an avenue to elsewhere, a role they play even today for many tourists. But less than a hundred years later, the region had become an important part of the nation's prodigious bread basket. No Spanish invasion from Mexico ever materialized to test Long's concept of a military barrier, although in 1821 the idea was not preposterous. Ironically, the area became so secure that German prisoners of war were interned there during World War II.

Before the white man, of course, the high plains belonged to the buffalo and to the Plains Indians: in Colorado, the Cheyennes and Arapahoes in the north and the Kiowas in the south. In Long's survey of the arid, treeless prairies, he overlooked the awesome herds of buffalo which in the early days could blanket the landscape. The animals provided the Plains Indians with virtually every need, from clothing, to food, to shelter, to fuel for their fires.

The first white men to make an impact upon this delicately balanced environment were traders, itinerant merchants who introduced these people of the stone age to the world of iron kettles, guns, and steel knives. In exchange they took from the Indians their surplus buffalo robes and the pelts obtained from the beaver and other fur-bearing animals. Thus, from being the basis for the Indians' subsistence, the buffalo became a "cash crop."

As the demand for buffalo increased to satisfy the white man's home markets, the buffalo's vast range over the North American plains began to diminish. Rising European immigration pushed settlements farther west, displacing Indians from their traditional hunting grounds, first east of the Mississippi and then west of the great river that had formed the eastern boundary of the 1803 Louisiana Purchase. Eastern Indian tribes, such as the Cherokees, were moved to lands on the fringes of the Great Plains.

The celebrated editor of the old New York *Tribune*, Horace Greeley, prophesied in an 1859 visit to Denver:

Take away the buffalo, and the Plains will be desolate far beyond their present desolation; and I cannot but regard with sadness the inevitable and not distant fate of these noble and harmless brutes, already crowded into a breadth of country too narrow for them, and continually hunted, slaughtered, decimated, by the wolf, the Indian, the white man.

Trade with the Colorado Plains Indians flourished from the mid-1830s to the late 1840s. Trading posts or forts were established along the two major river valleys of the high plains, the Arkansas in the southern plains of Colorado and the South Platte in the north. In that period, however, white immigration bypassed the state's forbidding Rocky Mountain ranges and followed the Oregon and California trails up the North Platte to Wyoming's South Pass. The Santa Fe Trail ascended the Arkansas valley and turned south to New Mexico.

The Panic of 1857 inspired the wishful to give credence to rumors that there might be gold in the streams descending from Colorado's Rockies. "[We] make the first discovery of an absolute emigration of thousands toward the new El Dorado," reported one correspondent to his readers in the East, "apparently determined to recruit their *panic-stricken* fortunes. . . ."

Placer camps sprang up in the vicinity of present-day Denver only to shrink at early disappointments. But in the spring of 1859, California gold rush veterans uncovered important lodes high up in the mountains. The Colorado gold rush began in earnest.

Immigrant routes to Colorado multiplied. In addition to the traditional trails along the Platte and Arkansas rivers, the gold-seekers developed more direct, but more perilous, traces in between. One followed the south fork of the Republican River into Colorado and another wound along the Kansas River and up its Smoky Hill fork.

The outbreak of the Civil War in 1861 set in motion events that would have tragic consequences on the Great Plains.

The spark that ignited the Indian wars of this period was struck in Minnesota where the Santee Sioux, or Dakotas, in 1851 had forfeited the bulk of their hunting grounds from the headwaters of the Mississippi to the Missouri—twenty-four million acres—in exchange for annual stipends that would sustain the Indians on reservations. The 1862 annuities failed to arrive due to a mix-up in the federal bureaucracy where customary fecklessness was in this instance compounded by the dislocations of the Civil War. Fearing a second winter of starvation, the Dakotas took out their frustrations on white settlers who occupied the ceded hunting grounds. Although many of the perpetrators were caught and hanged, several bands of Dakotas managed to flee to the west bank of the Missouri where their cousins, the formidable Teton Sioux, or Lakotas, reigned.

An army pacification campaign prompted other Plains Indians to rise up against white incursions into their hunting grounds. The Cheyennes, Arapahoes, and Kiowas of Colorado were no exception. The Colorado high plains became dotted with battle sites like Sand Creek, Beecher's Island on the Arickaree River, Julesburg and Summit Springs.

When eastern guns were stilled at Appomattox, negotiations followed in the West to bury the hatchet. Peace in both quarters released pressures to push railroad lines from mid-continent all the way over the Rockies and the coast ranges to the Pacific. These pressures had been building since Col. John C. Fremont made highly publicized surveys of the Rocky Mountains in the 1840s. By 1854, before the steam locomotive had even been adapted to coal, Congress appropriated $150,000 and directed the army's Topographical Corps to dispatch four survey teams to locate suitable rail routes to the west coast somewhere between Montana and New Mexico. The pressure became relentless on the eve of the Civil War, when Greeley returned from his five-month trip to write:

> Men and brethren! Let us resolve to have a railroad to the Pacific—and have it soon. . . . It will prove a bond of

union not easily broken, and a new spring to our national industry, prosperity and wealth. It will call new manufactures into existence, and increase the demand for the products of those already existing. It will open new vistas to national and individual aspirations and crush out filibusterism by giving a new and wholesome direction to the public mind.

The Union Pacific, when it was completed in 1869, touched Colorado only at the old Oregon and Overland Trail waystation of Julesburg, where I-76 now enters Colorado from another overland transcontinental road, Interstate 80. But Colorado was not to be denied its chapter in the saga of the American railroad. Colorado Territory became the proving ground for the mountain-climbing narrow-gauge railroad, as well as the home of the first successful, privately financed railway in the West.

The arrival of the railroad fostered another industry— livestock raising— and, once again, the high plains became a highway, this time from south to north, as enormous cattle herds were driven from the plains of Texas up through Colorado to better pastures or to railheads for shipment to market. Domestic cattle herds came to fill the landscape of the high plains as wild buffalo herds had a few years earlier.

Charles Goodnight, the pioneer cattle drover of the high plains, once observed:

> The ordinary trail-herd in the years following the Civil War numbered about 3,000 head of cattle. . . . The oufit consisted of sixteen or eighteen men, each of whom had two good horses; a mess-wagon, drawn by four mules, which were driven by the cook; and a horsewrangler, who had charge of the horse-herd. We aimed to have as many experienced men as possible with our outfit. After a few years there had been developed on the trail a class of men that could be depended upon anywhere.

Immigration to Colorado and the settlement of its lands were given particular impetus by acts of Congress—the

1862 Homestead Act and the establishment of land grants to finance the building of railroads. The first offered title to 160 acres for the family that would settle on the land and develop it over a period of five years. The second granted to railroads, such as the Union Pacific, Kansas Pacific, and Denver Pacific, twenty square miles of land for every mile of track they laid in the West. Sale of railroad land, therefore, served to finance the building of the line.

The ever-observant Greeley, in his 1859 junket through Colorado, also noted:

> There seems to be as rich and deep soil in some of the creek bottoms, especially those of the South Platte, as almost anywhere. . . . [Thus], should the gold mines justify their present promise, farming, in the right localities at the base of these mountains, even by the help of irrigation, will yield—to those who bring to it the requisite sagacity, knowledge, and capital—richer rewards than elsewhere on earth.

Commercial and cooperative associations were organized in the east to establish agricultural colonies on these irrigable lands, the most notable among them being the Union Colony, brought together by Greeley's agricultural editor on the New York *Tribune*, Nathan C. Meeker. The colony was the beginning of the city of Greeley, located at the junction of U.S. 34 and U.S. 85, midway between I-76 and I-25.

With the irrigation of farm lands adjacent to snow-fed rivers, a remarkable transformation seemed to occur in the 1880s on the arid prairies farther east. But a quarter of a century earlier, the high plains had seemed to Greeley to be "the acme of barrenness and desolation" in which the grass was "less fit for food than physic."

Nonetheless, having completed its line to Denver along approximately the same route taken by Greeley, the Chicago, Burlington & Quincy Railroad informed its stockholders in 1887, ". . . the rain belt has moved westward to within less than eighty miles of Denver. . . . In our opinion the change is due to the extensive irrigation of land lying along the eastern base of the Rocky Mountains."

Persuaded that Major Long's Great American Desert had become the land of milk and honey, homesteaders moved in to farm the high plains. These "dirt farmers" had prospered only briefly when in the early 1890s drought returned to the high plains, and panic struck the nation's economy.

Dirt farmers made another attempt to cultivate the high plains after the turn of the century, armed this time with improved seed and more scientific methods for dry farming devised by the government's new agricultural extension service. Then came the Great Depression, and the drought of the mid-1930s produced the Dust Bowl.

Finally, after World War II, irrigation was brought to the high plains. Improved technology allowed farmers to perforate the enormous Oglalla Aquifer, which underlies the plains from Texas to South Dakota, and the Great American Desert suddenly bloomed.

The stories that follow take a closer look at the times and the places of some of the events that have given life to the history of the Colorado high plains.

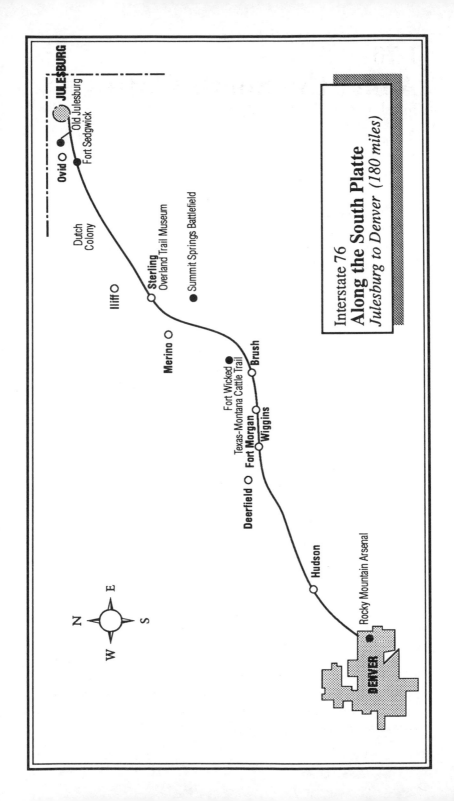

Interstate 76
Along the South Platte
Julesburg to Denver (180 miles)

I-76
Along the South Platte
Julesburg to Denver (180 miles)

Julesburg

An important Colorado crossroads at one time lay barely within the state's present borders. Now an unhurried town just across the South Platte River from Exit 180 on I-76, Julesburg is in its second incarnation as the junction of the Denver branch and the main line of the Union Pacific. Its previous life took place in a slightly different location and was a good deal more exciting, for then it was a major waystation on the Overland Stage and Pony Express lines.

In name, at least, Julesburg is a memorial to an early and ill-fated French trader who is otherwise rather uncertainly remembered as Jules Beni or Reni (or possibly Benoit). Building his post in the 1850s opposite the mouth of Lodgepole Creek on the South Platte's right or south bank, Old Jules catered to travelers who chose the upper crossing of the Oregon Trail as well as those headed south to the gold fields near Denver. Today the site can be seen by looking due north from I-76 at about **Milepost 173.**

Abandoning his position as station agent, Old Jules retired to a ranch in the vicinity but not, apparently, before provoking the ire of his former stage line supervisor, Joseph A. "Jack" Slade. Observing the loose protocol of the time, Slade confronted Jules and killed him, removing both of the Frenchman's ears. One he nailed to the door of the Pony Express station and the other he reportedly used as a watch fob. The brutal Slade eventually died at the hands of vigilantes in the gold fields of Montana.

In the brief and unprofitable history of the legendary Pony Express, Julesburg served as the eastern terminus of the division that extended to the Sweetwater River in central Wyoming. Fourteen-year-old William F. Cody, later known as "Buffalo Bill," signed on as a Pony Express rider at

Julesburg. He became one of the horsemen who provided express communications between mid-continent and the west coast from April 3, 1860, to October 24, 1861, when transcontinental telegraph service was inaugurated.

Julesburg was raided on February 2, 1865, by Sioux and Cheyenne warriors intent upon avenging the massacre at Sand Creek. The town's few citizens watched from the haven of Fort Sedgwick, a mile upriver, as Julesburg burned to the ground.

A short time later, however, the "new" Julesburg was raised at its present location to provide facilities for the Union Pacific railroad and the nation's first transcontinental rail passengers. Unlike the wagon and stage roads, the Union Pacific tracks followed the left, or north, bank of the South Platte as far as Julesburg, then continued west along Lodgepole Creek to Cheyenne, Wyoming.

Fort Sedgwick

The site of Fort Sedgwick lies just over a mile north of **Milepost 172,** between *County Road 28* and the South Platte. Originally called Camp Rankin, the fort was erected in the summer of 1864 under the command of young Capt. N. J. O'Brien, whose plucky Iowa bride made this their first home. Twelve companies of the 7th Iowa Cavalry were detailed to protect the overland trails to Denver and the west coast from marauding Indians. Until August 1868, wagon trains bound for Denver and the West were detained at Fort Sedgwick until wagonmasters had satisfied the post commander that their convoys were adequately manned and armed to withstand Indian attack. The post was officially abandoned in May 1871.

A curious high-tech crime occurred far out on the prairie west of Fort Sedgwick shortly after the Civil War. In a way it prefigured what we read today about computer crime perpetrated by hackers. At that time the Union Pacific railroad had just reached Julesburg, but telegraph lines had already been strung from Omaha to the Pacific.

One day in October 1867 three men got off the train from Chicago. They were all ex-employees of the Western Union Telegraph Company. The leader of the trio, George Cowdrey, had worked for the telegraph company for seven years, then left under a cloud. A second man, Frank Osborn, was a telegrapher in Chicago who had just been fired.

In operation only ten years, Western Union was under fire because of bogus wire reports giving false announcements of gold discoveries, the sinking of valuable merchant ships, the burning of railroad bridges on key through-lines. The reports had had profound effects on stocktrading on Wall Street. Western Union hired the supersleuth of the era, Allan Pinkerton, to investigate.

Meanwhile, the trio had headed west on foot following the telegraph line from Fort Sedgwick. After several days they stopped at a remote location midway between the North and the South Platte rivers, along what was then called Coopers Creek.

Cowdrey climbed the telegraph pole to attach some wires to a key on the ground. He listened to the traffic on the line, then, using the next dispatch number in the sequence, he transmitted a message purporting to originate in San Francisco, confirming a story that had appeared in the New York *Herald*:

> The special dispatch . . . was full and complete. It stated that the steamer *Great Republic* on the third of September, loaded with six hundred and forty tons of freight, and about $1,500,000 of Wells, Fargo & Co.'s treasures, and passengers and crew numbering about eight hundred souls, had been burned at sea; that the captain and officers were intoxicated at the time the fire originated. As near as I can ascertain, about one hundred and fifty of the passengers and crew were lost. The vessel being a total wreck, the crew mutinied, and, taking to the boats, carried off a large portion of the treasure.

The *Great Republic* was one of the largest of the Pacific Mail Steamship Company's score of ocean-going steamers.

With the *China*, the *Great Republic* sailed between San Francisco and Yokohama, Japan. The loss of either of them would be a significant blow to the company, because the firm's executives had opted not to insure them.

Cowdrey's phony report about the sinking of the *Great Republic*, however, failed to undermine confidence in the Pacific Mail's stock. Pinkerton had intercepted it in Chicago.

Unaware that their ploy had failed, the law-breakers in the wilds of Colorado faced another problem, one that suggests they were subject at least to Murphy's Law. They were captured by Indians.

Frank Osborn, however, managed to slip into the prairie darkness when their Indian sentry dozed off. Back in Julesburg he reported to another Pinkerton operative, for Osborn was an undercover informant in the telegraph scam.

After much searching, soldiers found Cowdrey and the other missing man where their captors had abandoned them, tied to some cottonwood trees along a creek bottom. They were in bad shape from exposure, hunger, and thirst. Arrested, they were shipped back to Chicago for trial.

The Dutch Colony

On thirty thousand acres of bottomland extending from Red Lion (**Exit 155**) to Proctor (**Exit 141**) along the left bank of the South Platte, a star-crossed colony of Dutch immigrants attempted in 1893 to make a new life in America. Organized by the Holland-American Land and Immigration Company of Utrecht, The Netherlands, two hundred adults and children passed through New York's Ellis Island immigrant station on November 26, 1892, on their way to the San Luis valley in Colorado. They were supposed to be the vanguard of two thousand Dutch immigrants.

Mismanagement and a fatal epidemic prompted fifty-two adults and twenty-three children to relocate on this irrigated tract of the South Platte. Purchasing the land for $450,000, the Dutch colonists moved from southern Colorado to this site on February 1, 1893. They quickly erected an office building and a hotel in the town of Crook (**Exit 149**) and put in their crops. Financial losses, compounded by the Panic of 1893, and the return that year of dry weather produced discontent that led to the colony's demise at harvest time. Some of the colonists moved to Greeley, Brush, and Fort Morgan. Others went as far away as Iowa, but the majority returned to the Netherlands. In 1894 the colony's abandoned buildings were razed and the lumber was reclaimed to meet outstanding mortgage payments.

Iliff

Across the river from **Exit 134**, the dusty little community of Iliff commemorates, without pretension, Colorado's biggest cattle empire. At the height of its power in the 1870s, the Iliff Cattle Company boasted fifty thousand cattle and claimed use of about three thousand square miles, extending from Greeley to the Nebraska line to the north banks of the South Platte. John W. Iliff, whose 1878 obituary proclaimed him the Cattle King of the Plains, was an immigrant from Ohio and originally more merchant than cattleman.

In the first wave of the 1859 gold rush, Iliff came to Denver with a wagonload of merchandise, which he soon parlayed into cattle purchased from hard-pressed immigrants and drovers of thousand-head Texas herds. He found ready customers in the army garrisons that had multiplied during the Indian uprisings of the middle-1860s, the peaceful Indians on nearby reservations, the crews of the railroad lines building in the territory, and, not the least, the flood of immigrants who came to prospect for gold or farm public land following passage of the 1862 Homestead Act.

Standing in the graveled intersection of two streets in today's Iliff is a monument of more universal memory in America. Under shelter of four posts and a roof and facing the fire station is an authentic town pump.

Another enterprising merchant who prospered in the wake of Iliff and other cattlemen was a gentleman remembered only as "Wild Horse Jerry." He dealt, as his name would suggest, not in cattle but in horses. His source of supply was the wild herds that roamed the same grasslands claimed by the Iliff Cattle Company. Many of the horses were blessed with the good blood lines of animals that had escaped years before from emigrants on the Oregon and gold rush trails.

After finding the wild herds in late April or early May, Jerry would drive them relentlessly along a route where he had staked out fresh mounts for himself and his collaborators. When his prey were exhausted, he would force them into corrals, where they could be roped and tethered to logging chains. Jerry sold his prizes to Texas wranglers on their way through these grasslands to Wyoming and Montana or to local cattle outfits such as the Iliff Company.

While millionaire Iliff's surname graces the school of theology at the University of Denver, Wild Horse Jerry's has been lost to anonymity—even though, at $150 to $200 for each horse captured, he clearly did not do badly.

The Overland Trail Museum

Just west of **Exit 125** on the outskirts of Sterling is the Overland Trail Museum, a nicely appointed establishment that offers exhibits of stage line memorabilia and artifacts relating to early ranching and pioneer life. In the museum gardens are plots of the various grasses that have been forage for plains animals from buffalo to sheep.

The Summit Springs Battlefield

Five miles south of **Exit 115** on *Colorado 63* and five miles east on *County Road 60* lies the site of the battle of Summit Springs, the last contest between the U.S. cavalry and the Indians on Colorado's eastern plains. It was an event that would provide substance for drama, legend, and lie.

In the hot summer of 1869, a thousand-member village of Cheyenne Dog Soldiers under Chief Tall Bull left their reservation to rampage among white settlements that had cropped up on the Great Plains. When Tall Bull's band attacked a Swedish colony in central Kansas and kidnapped two women, the 5th U.S. Cavalry rode out from Fort McPherson, near present-day North Platte, Nebraska, to try to run them down. Accompanying Brevet Maj. Gen. Eugene A. Carr's regiment were 150 Pawnee Scouts, Indian irregulars organized and commanded by Maj. Frank North and his brother, Luther, a captain. Also with the 5th Cavalry was the seemingly ubiquitous Buffalo Bill Cody, now a twenty-three-year-old army scout.

After the Dog Soldiers had fled westward onto the Colorado high plains, Tall Bull employed a favorite Indian tactic—he split his band into three groups, dispatching

William F. "Buffalo Bill" Cody poses with some Indians who performed in his Wild West Show. *Colorado Historical Society.*

them in different directions to confuse their pursuers. General Carr chose to divide his command as well. The main cavalry contingent took one trail, Cody and Carr's second-in-command another, and the Pawnee Scouts the third.

Early Sunday afternoon, July 11, 1869, one of Carr's scouting parties discovered the Cheyenne encampment. The Pawnee scouts rejoined the main group to lead the attack. There was no time to summon the other troopers with Cody. Taking the Dog Soldiers by surprise, the attackers forced some of the Cheyenne warriors to flee on foot to the shelter of neighboring sand hill coulees.

When the attackers paused to regroup among the abandoned lodges, a panic-stricken woman emerged suddenly from Tall Bull's lodge and clutched one of them about the knees. She spoke no English, but she was white. Mrs. G. Weichel had been kidnapped from the Swedish settlement. The body of her companion, Mrs. Susannah Alderdice, was found nearby, the skull crushed with the blow of a tomahawk. Days before, Mrs. Alderdice's infant had also been killed when his crying threatened to betray the location of the Indian village.

Meanwhile, Frank North and his brother accosted the Cheyenne leader, Tall Bull, where he had taken cover with his wife and daughter in a ravine. In a exchange of fire, North killed the Indian.

Later, western novelist Ned Buntline published a fictionalized version of the battle, which depicted the colorful Buffalo Bill Cody as the protagonist of the engagement and the slayer of Tall Bull, although Cody was miles away when the battle took place. In 1898 Cody, already an international legend of the Old West, felt compelled to endorse the fanciful account in a book of which he was the co-author, *The Great Salt Lake Trail*. By this time, moreover, the story had become so garbled that Cody erroneously referred to Tall Bull as a great Sioux chieftain. Until well into the twentieth century, Cody employed a reenactment of the Summit Springs battle as the grand finale for his internationally traveled Wild West Show.

Eventually asked why he had never contradicted the false version of Tall Bull's slaying, the laconic Frank North, still Cody's close friend, explained: "I was not in the show business."

Merino

Merino, a town on the west bank of the South Platte River west of **Exit 115**, was originally called Buffalo. When a road-building crew of the Union Pacific reached the town in 1882 while laying the Julesburg-to-Denver line, one of the builders was so impressed with the sight of sheep covering the surrounding hills that the town's name was changed to that of a popular breed.

Fort Wicked

Fort Wicked, otherwise known as Godfrey's Station of the Overland Stage route, lay two and a half miles south of Merino on the right bank of the river, due west of **Milepost 112**. Thanks to the doughty Holon Godfrey and his equally doughty wife and two daughters, Fort Wicked was the only stage stop between the forks of the Platte River and Denver that was not destroyed by Indians in the 1864-65 war. In one sustained engagement, the fifty-two-year-old New Yorker and his family held off attacking Indians for two full days before troopers from Fort Morgan arrived to lift the siege (see *U.S. 50* itinerary).

Brush

At the headwaters of Beaver Creek fifty miles south of **Exit 90** at Brush, the Texas-Montana cattle trail entered the watershed of the South Platte at the divide separating it from that of the Arkansas River. Following Beaver Creek, thousands of cattle annually forded the South Platte River near Brush from the post-Civil War years to the 1880s.

The town itself was the creation of the Lincoln Land Company, a subsidiary of the Burlington Railroad, which reached this point in 1882. Named for Jared L. Brush, an area cattleman and one-time state lieutenant governor, the community became a refuge for some of the Dutch immigrants who in 1893 abandoned the Holland-American Immigration & Land Company colony downriver.

Fort Morgan

The Lincoln Land Company and its railroad parent also founded Fort Morgan at **Exit 80.** The military post from which the city was to take its name was established during the Civil War as Camp Tyler. In 1865 the name was changed to Fort Wardwell and finally to Fort Morgan. Troops from this post relieved the siege of Fort Wicked.

A charter member of Greeley's Union Colony, Abner S. Baker, developed an irrigation ditch in the early 1880s to encourage agriculture in the vicinity. He had the town site surveyed in 1884 and cannily deeded alternate town lots to the Lincoln Land Company to ensure that the Burlington Railroad would pay due attention to the needs of the town.

The site of the military post is a quarter-mile south of **Exit 80** on Riverview Avenue.

The wandering journalist of the West, Rufus B. Sage, in late August 1842 reported an encounter with a remarkable individual whom he found on an island in the middle of the Platte River, somewhere north of **Exit 75.** The island was a camp of furtraders in the employ of Bent and St. Vrain (see below). They were guarding a stockpile of furs that they had intended to float down the Platte to the Missouri and St. Louis. Low water in the river, however, had stalled the move.

"The camp," said Sage, "was under the direction of a half-breed, named Chabonard, who proved to be a gentleman of superior information. He had acquired a classic education and could converse quite fluently in German, Spanish, French, and English, as well as several Indian languages. His mind, also, was well stored with choice reading, and enriched by extensive travel and observation."

"Charbonard" was in fact Jean Baptiste Charbonneau, the son of the famous Sacajawea, Bird Woman, who guided Meriwether Lewis and William Clark for their famous exploration of the West for President Thomas Jefferson. The child was born on February 11, 1805, as the Lewis and Clark expedition lay in winter quarters at Fort Mandan, in today's North Dakota, preparing to continue their journey to the Pacific.

Clark was so taken with the infant Baptiste that he sought to adopt him after the expedition had returned. As superintendent for Indian affairs in St. Louis and governor of Missouri Territory, Clark did arrange for the Charbonneaus to come to St. Louis, where Baptiste began his education.

In 1823 twenty-five-year-old Prince Paul of Wurttemberg visited Louisiana Territory on a scientific expedition. As he prepared his return to Europe, Prince Paul persuaded William Clark to allow him to take Baptiste Charbonneau, then 18, with him. Charbonneau spent the next six years receiving a European education.

He returned with Prince Paul in 1829 and joined the American Fur Company. Over the next fifteen years he worked as a mountain man. When the trade in beaver pelts collapsed in the 1840s due to a change in fashions in Europe, Charbonneau became a hunter for Bent's Fort on the Arkansas, guided an Army topographical expedition down the Canadian River, and was a guide for Colonel Phillip St. George Cooke and the famous Mormon Battalion, accompanying them from Santa Fe to San Diego, California, during the Mexican War of 1846-48. In California he was named the mayor of San Luis Rey under the U.S. occupation of this Mexican territory. Eventually he returned to his mother's people, the Shoshone Indians, at their reservation on the Wind River of Wyoming, where he died in 1885.

Dearfield

Just before World War I a rather unusual agricultural colony took root about seven miles west of **Exit 66** on *U.S.*

34. An Ohio-born son of slaves inspired by Booker T. Washington's *Up From Slavery* sought to promote a colony for blacks. Backed by Governor John T. Shaforth, for whom he had worked as a messenger, O. T. Jackson and seven black families in 1914 filed for land at this site along the South Platte's right bank.

One of the colonists, a Denver physician J.H.P. Westbrook, observed, "These are to be our fields, and because they are ours and we expect and hope to develop them into substantial homes, they will be very dear to us." They decided to call the place Dearfield.

By 1921 the colony comprised seven hundred people, and the land they occupied was valued at $750,000. Unfortunately, the 1919-23 farm depression, which caused foreclosure of almost 500,000 farms nationwide, undermined Dearfield's financial resources.

At the end of World War II, this ad appeared in the Greeley *Tribune*: "On acct. of poor health and not possible to get competent help the townsite of Dearfield, Highway 34, 30 miles east of Greeley is for sale on reasonable terms . . . about 240 acres in all, fixtures & furniture at invoice prices." Today there are no blacks in Dearfield.

Rocky Mountain Arsenal

Rocky Mountain Arsenal, located two miles south of **Exit 16**, on *Colorado 2* just north of Denver's Stapleton Airport, was built as a chemical weapons plant in 1942, during World War II. As many as fifteen thousand workers have been employed there at one time.

I-70 East
The Smoky Hill Trail
Kansas to Denver (175 miles)

Interstate 70 crosses into Colorado from Kansas in the heart of buffalo country. Today there are no buffalo to be seen, but a little more than a century ago a traveler reaching this point might find himself in an ocean of black—tens of thousands of lumbering creatures milling from one horizon to the other. Even then, the buffalo were seeing the dawn of their demise, but their concentration became greater for a brief time as the encroaching frontier reduced their grazing lands.

Pressure on the frontier intensified in 1862, when, in May, Congress passed the Homestead Act and, in July, the Railroad Act. The first offered acreage to the landless at token cost if they would develop farms. The second prompted railroads to span the continent and, in the tractless prairies, develop towns to accommodate both the railroads and the surrounding homesteaders.

At the close of the Civil War in the mid-1860s the Union Pacific started building westward from the Missouri River. It started from Kansas City on a line that would bisect Kansas and buffalo country—the prized hunting grounds of the nomadic Plains Indians. As the railroad progressed toward Denver, towns proliferated along its course and 160-acre homesteads radiated outward from the towns.

Laying track at a rate of a mile a day, the thousands of railroad workers who pressed into the wilderness had to be fed. A "catering" firm called Goddard Brothers put scores of hunters under contract, the most notable among them William Frederick Cody. In his seventeen months on the job, Cody roamed these plains, killing buffalo to feed the railroad crews. From the outset, it seems, he had the decency—or the audacity—to count. A total of 4,280 buffalo died at his hand, earning him the nickname, "Buffalo Bill."

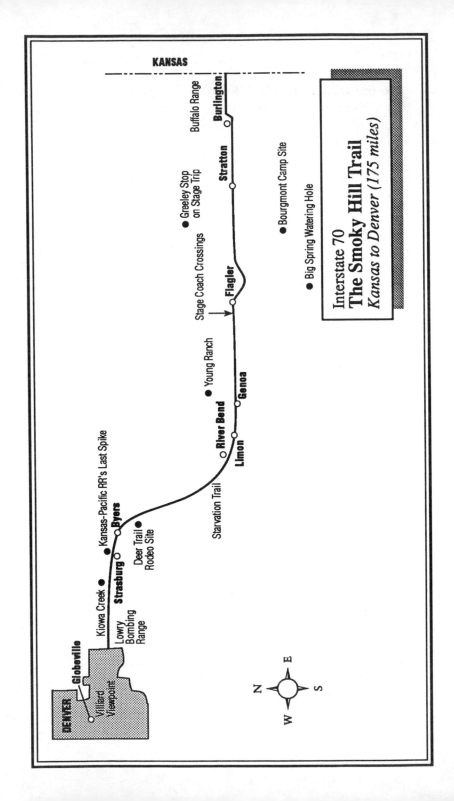

KANSAS

Buffalo Range

Burlington

Stratton

Greeley Stop
on Stage Trip

Bourgmont Camp Site

Stage Coach Crossings

Flagler

Big Spring Watering Hole

Young Ranch

River Bend

Genoa

Limon

Starvation Trail

Kansas-Pacific RR's Last Spike

Byers

Deer Trail
Rodeo Site

Kiowa Creek

Strasburg

Lowry
Bombing
Range

Globeville

DENVER

Villard
Viewpoint

Interstate 70
The Smoky Hill Trail
Kansas to Denver (175 miles)

N
E
W S

In the winter of 1871-72, Buffalo Bill Cody returned to this vicinity (around present-day Burlington) on the now completed Kansas Pacific Railroad in the entourage of Grand Duke Alexis of Russia. Prowess gained in the employ of the Goddard Brothers enabled Cody to assist the Romanov gadfly and his friends in the slaughtering of some two hundred buffalo.

By 1881 the buffalo was nearly extinct.

Burlington

In 1928 three Kit Carson County commissioners paid the handsome sum of $1,250 to bring some rather strange animals to the region. They purchased an elegant carousel from Denver's Elitch Gardens amusement park and moved it to the Kit Carson County fairgrounds in Burlington just north of **Milepost 438**. For twenty-three years the carousel had regaled Denver's children with forty-six hand-carved and handsomely painted animals that included such exotic creatures as a seahorse, lion, tiger, camels, and giraffe with a snake entwined on its neck. Made by the Philadelphia Toboggan Company in 1905, the carvings were almost medieval in their intricacy and detail. The animals pranced in rows of three to the booming sound of a Wurlitzer military band organ, whose perforated paper rolls produced the sounds of a fifteen-piece band.

However handsome the carousel, frugal citizens stung by the farm recession of the 1920s thought the purchase folly. The three commissioners were voted out of office. The Great Depression descended on Burlington. For six years Kit Carson County had to forego the annual fair at which the carousel would have been featured.

When the fair was resumed in 1937, organizers discovered that the organ's paper rolls had been devoured by mice. The carousel itself was scrubbed and put in operation to the mundane accompaniment of recorded music. Not until 1976 was the original organ fully restored and put back into use.

Today, remarkable not only for its organ but for the painstaking restoration of its original paint, the Kit Carson County carousel is listed in the National Register of Historic Places. The exhibit is open to visitors from Memorial Day to Labor Day.

The Homestead Act prompted settlers to transform into tilled fields land that had been grazed since prehistoric times. Seduced in the mid-1880s by abundant rain, farmers came to believe that the Great American Desert was a myth.

Cheyenne Wells

Drought returned in 1889 and 1890. When the financial panic of 1893 was compounded by another drought on the eastern Colorado plains, followed by yet another dry year in 1894 and a grasshopper plague in 1895, the Colorado Board of Agriculture sought to stop the exodus of bankrupt farmers from the high plains. With land donated by the Kansas Pacific Railroad, the board set up, in 1894, an experimental farm near Cheyenne Wells, thirty-eight miles south of **Exit 437** at Burlington. There J. W. Adams developed the now widely practiced technique of contour farming. Said Adams a generation before the Dust Bowl of the 1930s, "Diversified farming is the most successful. . . . When grain fails it will usually make feed [for cows]. . . . Great care should be taken to protect the land from blowing, as this not only ruins growing crops, but injures the soil. . . ." Unfortunately, as we know, to this day not everyone farming the unpredictable prairies heeds Adams' advice.

Even in the 1890s scientific farming was not for everyone. An Australian "rain fakir," with the improbable name of Frank Melbourne arrived in this region in 1892 with a promise to deliver a half-inch of rain within seventy-two hours to those farmers who would pay six cents for each acre so blessed.

Remarkably, in at least one instance, the rain came as promised, but, as one observer noted at the time, "Before enough rain fell to quench the thirst of a grasshopper, the rain ceased." Someone else had the wit to realize that the dates Melbourne selected coincided exactly with those of a St. Louis almanac publisher. In 1894 a debunked Melbourne was found in a Denver hotel room, a suicide.

The Smoky Hill River

The region just south of **Exit 419** was once described by a European traveler as "the most beautiful land in the world." Etienne Veniard de Bourgmont, an officer in the French Army, made the first visit on record to this part of Colorado in 1724. Bourgmont led an expedition up the Smoky Hill River from the forks of the Kansas River at Junction City, Kansas, to its headwaters, which lie about fifteen miles south of this spot. Bourgmont encountered Padouca Indians, a tribe unknown now, whose descendants may be Comanches or Apaches.

In 1843, on his second expedition to explore routes to the Pacific, Fremont also traced the Smoky Hill to its source.

As the shortest route from the east to Denver the Smoky Hill valley was tempting to gold-seekers. The river itself originates in an arid ridge of high land that runs from Cheyenne Wells to the vicinity of Denver and divides the waters of the Platte-Missouri drainage from those of the Arkansas River. Imposing the logic of the straight line, ill-prepared travelers trudged across this spine of land, sometimes with no better vehicle than a wheelbarrow. Consequently it became known as the Starvation Trail.

Denver City's *Rocky Mountain News* reported on May 7, 1859: "Two footmen have just arrived via the Smoky Hill route. They appear to have suffered severely from hunger and thirst. They report having passed some ten or fifteen dead bodies unburied, and many new-made graves. These men say they lived for nine days on prickly pears and one hawk."

Anxious to supply gold prospectors, several Kansas towns collected funds to finance the survey and building of a road to Denver that would guide travelers to wood, water, and grass. The task was begun by one of the more venturesome entrepreneurs of the Colorado gold fields, William Green Russell, of Auraria, formerly of Lumpkin County, Georgia. When he had done his survey and pocketed the several-thousand-dollar fee, he also managed to strike it rich in Clear Creek Canyon on the Front Range.

Butterfield Overland Despatch

No sooner was the Smoky Hill road laid out than the hazards of the Civil War severely diminished travel. At war's end in 1865, however, a former Denver merchant, David A. Butterfield, decided to create a stagecoach and freight wagon line from Kansas City to Denver along the Smoky Hill. He hired Lt. Julian R. Fitch of the U.S. Army Signal Corps to conduct the survey. Fitch had participated in Russell's 1860 project.

For Fitch the Smoky Hill route had no rival. It was much shorter than that through the Arkansas Valley, "whilst from Julesburg to Denver [along the South Platte], a distance of two hundred miles, the emigrant or freighter has a dead pull of sand. . . ."

The Butterfield Overland Despatch had fourteen stations in Colorado, running from Cheyenne Wells to Denver over a distance of about 180 miles.

New York *Tribune* correspondent Bayard Taylor reported in June 1866:

At Cheyenne Wells we found a large and handsome frame stable for mules, but no dwelling. The people lived in a natural cave, extending some thirty feet under the bluff. . . . Here we saw the last of the Smoky Hill fork. The road strikes across a broad plateau for twenty miles, and then descends to the Big Sandy [Creek], a branch of the Arkansas. . . . At the stage station, we found two men living in a hole in the ground, with nothing but alkaline water to offer us. At Grady's Station, 18 miles farther, there was but one man, a lonely troglodyte, burrowing in the bank like a cliff-swallow. . . . The hard "hack" bumped and jolted over the rough roads; we were flung backward and forward, right and left, pummelled, pounded and bruised, not only out of sleep, but out of temper, and into pain and exasperation. . . .

Such vicissitudes demanded an etiquette. To meet this need someone devised what was called the Ten Commandments of the Butterfield stage line:

1. The best seat is the forward one, next to the driver.
2. If the stage teams run away or are pursued by Indians, stay in the coach and take your chances. Don't jump out, for you'll be either injured or scalped.
3. In cold weather abstain from liquor.
4. But if you are drinking from a bottle, pass it around.
5. Don't smoke a strong cigar . . . spit to the leeward side.
6. Don't swear . . . or lop over on neighbors when sleeping.
7. Don't shoot firearms for pleasure.
8. Don't discuss politics or religion. Don't point out sites where Indian attacks took place.
9. While at stations, don't lag at wash basins or privies. Don't grease hair with bear grease or buffalo tallow.
10. Don't imagine you are going on a picnic.

Big Spring Watering Hole

About twenty miles south of **Exit 405** the source of Big Spring Creek served as a watering hole for the huge herds of cattle on the Texas-Montana trail as they prepared to trek across the divide to the South Platte watershed.

Texas stockmen were prompted to consider the hazards of driving cattle across the trackless high plains during the Civil War after the Union capture of the port of New Orleans in April 1862 interdicted their shipping lines to Confederate consumers. Texan Oliver Loving had driven a herd to Denver as early as 1860. After the war they drove their cattle north to hungry gold seekers in western Montana, to railroad building crews, and to military posts then multiplying in the West. Ultimately, drovers were forced to skirt the tilled fields of angry farmers, who were edging westward through Kansas, to reach railheads from which to ship their livestock to eastern markets.

Kit Carson

About twelve miles southeast of the Big Spring watering hole, the town of Kit Carson came into being when the Kansas Pacific Railroad reached that point in late 1869. The town was named to commemorate the famous frontiersman, who had died a year earlier. Kit Carson's citizens saw the first trainload of cattle leave Colorado for eastern markets. By 1872 the town had become a major cattle shipping station, sending 162 carloads eastward that year.

Conflict between cattlemen and farmers developed in Colorado as early as 1864 when the territorial legislature voted to exempt farmers from fencing their land, whereas "all persons owning or having charge of stock will be required to herd or confine same during the season of growing crops."

One western cattlemen's organization tried unsuccessfully to get Congress to set aside a two-hundred-mile corridor from Texas to Canada to permit the unhindered trailing of cattle.

In 1875 the Colorado State Grange, obviously not under the domination of dirt farmers, resolved that "Government lands in Colorado, east of the Rocky Mountains, which are not situated under irrigation ditches now constructed, or within one mile of running streams or living water, ought not to be sold, but should by act of congress, be set apart for perpetual free pasture, to be used in common by the people of Colorado. . . ." This of course did not happen.

Leavenworth and Pike's Peak Express

Near **Exit 395** one of the shifting routes of the Smoky Hill Trail intersected another, shorter-lived stage route known as the Leavenworth and Pike's Peak Express (L&PPE) line, which left the forks of the Kansas River in central Kansas and went northwest along the south bank of the Republican River, whose headwaters lie just north of **Milepost 386.** When he reached this vicinity on an L&PPE coach in early June 1859, Horace Greeley, the famous editor of the New York *Tribune*, observed,

Water is obtained from an apology for a river, or by digging in the sand by its side; in default of wood, corrals (cattle-pens) ["corral" was a word yet unknown to his readers] are formed at the stations by laying up a heavy wall of clayey earth flanked by sods, and thus excavating a deep ditch on the inner side, except at the portal, which is closed at night by running a wagon into it. Tents are sodded at their bases. . . . Such are the shifts of human ingenuity in a country which has probably not a cord of growing wood to each township of land.

Hell Creek

On September 22, 1894, a twenty-five-year-old cowboy named Perry Davis paused a couple miles north of **Exit 376** on Hell Creek en route with his comrades on a horse drive from the Montana-South Dakota border to the panhandle of Texas. On that day he left this poignant note in his diary: "Red's birthday. . . . Make the acquaintance of the Young family, who were very sociable southern people, there being three small children, a young miss just entering her teens, and a Miss Myrtle, a beautiful girl of nineteen summers. Invited to call the next day. Go back and tell Edd what I had seen, and he said don't tell the other boys, and we would go over the next day as we were intending to lay over."

This interlude was by far the exception on their eight-hundred-mile drive across the plains. Typical hardships were lack of water or bad water. "We fill our barrel . . . where there is a [slough] filled with bugs, dead turtle, and sheep sign. . . ."

The cowboys pilfered hard-to-come-by fence posts from farms in route in order to use them for firewood. Near Brush (see I-76 itinerary), "Picked up a couple of fence posts; granger follows me and uses very harsh language. He wants the post back and two dollars for his trouble. I told him I'd be hanged if I'd do it. . . . I thought I could knock him out . . . but if I had stayed with him a few minutes longer there wouldn't have been enough left of me to grease a flintlock gun. I said, 'Say, partner, if you will just wait a while I will get your post and two dollars for your trouble.'"

Hell Creek is one of the sources of the Arikaree River, which originates just north of **Milepost 373**. The river is named for a tribe of Indians—the Arikaras or Rees—whose traditional home was on the Missouri River in North Dakota. Punished by the U.S. Army in 1823 for attacking a party of fur traders bound up the Missouri, the Arikaras migrated to this area for a few years to find haven with their cousins, the Pawnees.

The Battle of Beecher's Island

On September 17, 1868, a group of fifty scouts was besieged on an island in the Arikaree River, about eighty-five miles northeast of **Milepost 373**. Organized and commanded by Col. George A. Forsythe, the scouts had been recruited among civilian volunteers on the frontier willing to help combat roving bands of renegade Indians who were harassing homesteads and settlements. Heavily outnumbered and under nearly constant attack, Forsythe, his second-in-command, Lt. Fred Beecher, and the fifty irregulars managed to hold out for ten days. Volunteer couriers slipped through to Fort Wallace, a post set up to guard the Smoky Hill Trail in western Kansas, and the all-Negro 10th Cavalry

Regiment was dispatched to their rescue. When the siege was finally lifted, on September 27, seventy-five Indians had been killed and many wounded. Forsythe's command suffered five dead, including Lieutenant Beecher. Located about fifteen miles south of Wray on a gravel road, the site is now known as Beecher's Island.

Starvation Trail

Near **Exit 352**, a celebrated wagon road, known as the Starvation Trail, turned west to negotiate the last, taxing leg of the journey to Denver, striking Cherry Creek near present-day Parker. The route was used by the Leavenworth & Pike's Peak Express, by freighters on the old Smoky Hill route, and by hapless Fifty-Niners who wanted to get to the gold fields by the shortest possible route. Henry Villard, a correspondent for the Cincinnati *Daily Commercial*, reported on July 17, 1859, the story that earned the route its name.

On May 4, 1859, the story went, Daniel Blue, an emigrant from Illinois, was delivered by an Arapahoe Indian to Station 25 of the L&PPE, located about fifteen miles due west of this point on East Bijou Creek. He was brought to Denver City by L&PPE superintendent B. D. Williams, and then he told the grisly story reported by Villard.

With his two brothers, Alexander and Charles, and two other men, Daniel Blue had left his home in Illinois in February. Taking the Smoky Hill route from Kansas City, they were joined by nine other men in Topeka. They had one horse among them.

After about sixteen days on the trail five of the party chose not to continue. The remaining nine slogged on but lost their packhorse after three or four days. Two more dropped out. The party had a single shotgun at this point, because their other weapons had been thrown away. Three more dropped out. Only a man named Soleg from Cleveland remained with the three Blue brothers.

As Soleg lay dying of exhaustion on Beaver Creek, still

seventy-five miles from Denver, "he authorized and re-
quested us," said Daniel Blue, "to make use of his mortal
remains in the way of nourishment." For the next eight days
they did just that. Then Alexander Blue died and managed
to sustain his siblings for another ten days. Finally, Charles
Blue succumbed, leaving only Daniel Blue to tell the tale.

The German-born Villard, incidentally, went on to become an important railroad magnate. Eventually he backed
the inventions of Thomas Edison and presided over the
Edison General Electric Company until 1893 when it became today's General Electric.

Deer Trail Rodeo

On Independence Day, 1869, the first truly American
rodeo took place just off **Exit 328** at Deer Trail. At that point
it was a campsite on the Texas-to-Cheyenne cattle trail, but
the place had been a stagecoach waystation. Gathering to
match skills were cowboys from three trail outfits—the
Hashknife, the Mill Iron, and the Camp Stool. Bets were
placed by contenders and onlookers and, for the first time,
there was an elaborate set of rules.

Thus was launched an industry that today pays out about
$10 million annually to journeyman competitors, whose
prototype remains the rugged cowhand of these plains. For
those conditioned by decades of western movies it may be
difficult to believe that the "champion bronco buster of the
plains" at this unprecedented rodeo was an Englishman
with the rather prissy name of Emilnie Gardenshire. Riding
for the Mill Iron outfit, Gardenshire managed to stay on the
Hashknife's killer bronc, Montana Blizzard, for a full fifteen
minutes. The Englishman won a suit of clothes.

Byers

Byers, at **Exit 316**, was founded in 1886 by a former army
scout, Oliver P. Wiggins. The town's name was later
changed to honor the memory of the newspaper publisher,
William N. Byers, who founded the state's oldest daily

newspaper, Denver's *Rocky Mountain News*. Arriving with the first wave of gold-seekers in 1859, Byers later moonlighted as an agent for a land development company that was a subsidiary of the Union Pacific.

William N. Byers, founder of the *Rocky Mountain News* and a moonlighting land agent, appears at rear right with some early day hunting companions. *Colorado Historical Society.*

Strasburg

The last spike in the Kansas Pacific's line into Denver was driven near **Exit 310** at the present town of Strasburg. In order to meet a contract deadline, which called for the line's completion by August 15, 1870, two railroad crews—one working from Denver and the other from the eastern terminus of the line—laid more than ten miles of track in less than ten hours. It was the speediest example of tracklaying in America's railroad history to that point.

Kiowa Creek

Near **Milepost 305** the ample but generally waterless Kiowa Creek passes under I-70 on its way to the South Platte

River. Its volume is deceptive, because like so many of the
nearly dry streams on the high plains, Kiowa Creek has its
moments of glory.

One of those moments occurred on May 21, 1878, when a
cloudburst struck the South Platte-Arkansas divide about
forty miles to the south. It gorged the bed of Kiowa Creek
at its head so that when the flood reached this point it had
attained immense volume and power. At that moment,
unfortunately, a Kansas Pacific freight train was passing as
well.

The bodies of fireman Frank Selden and brakeman John
Piatt were found the next day a mile and a half downstream.
It was not until four days later that the body of engineer John
Bacon was recovered ten miles downstream.

Cars from the train were scattered, half buried in the
sandy bottom of the subsided stream for miles to the north of
the right-of-way. The oddest result of this disaster was that
searchers failed to find any sign at all of the locomotive, even
after probing the shoals of the creek with long steel rods.

A century later, novelist Clive Cussler, in January 1989,
led another party down Kiowa Creek with long steel rods
in search of the missing locomotive. Bob Richardson, director of the Colorado Railroad Museum, has contended, however, that the locomotive was recovered and in 1886 was
still in service with the Union Pacific railroad.

Lowry Air Force Base

Due south of **Exit 295** lies a sixty-four-thousand-acre tract
that once was an air force bombing range administered by
Lowry Air Force Base in Denver. Lowry AFB was established in 1938 on 960 acres of a former sanatorium, land that
lies now in the heart of the metropolitan area.

View of the Mountains

Perhaps it was near **Milepost 278** that reporter Henry
Villard made this observation in May 1859: "I have seen the
Alps of Switzerland and Tyrol, the Pyrenees and Ap-

penines, yet their attractions appear to dwindle into nothing when compared with the at once grotesque and sublime beauty of the mountain scenery upon which my eyes feasted before descending into the valley."

Globeville lies north of **Exit 275** along Brighton Boulevard. It was a company town, named for the Globe smelter, an enterprise of the late nineteenth century that processed much of the gold and silver ore and other metals taken from the Rocky Mountains. Because of the smelter Globeville was itself a human melting pot of numerous immigrant groups who worked at the smelter.

The man who developed the Globe smelter into a going concern was himself an immigrant. Dennis Sheedy was born in Ireland in 1846 of stock their poorer countrymen called "lace curtain Irish." His father, a small landowner, lost his holdings during the Potato Famine of the 1840s and brought his wife and twelve children to Massachusetts.

After clerking for his older brother, Dennis himself came west during the Civil War at the age of seventeen to apprentice himself to one of Denver's pioneer merchant barons, William B. Daniels. Born with a sharp business sense and, of course, Irish luck, Sheedy soon left Daniel's tutelage and Denver for the new gold fields of Virginia City, Montana. Though still in his teens he had acquired a nest egg of some proportions which he left with Daniels.

He bought into a mining stake in Montana that in time struck gold. He sold that and decided to stick to a business he knew better, merchandising. Parleying one venture after another into a tidy profit, Sheedy managed to outwit rivals and the insidious underground of robbers, charlatans and highwaymen that pervaded the lawless mining West at that time.

He took a sabbatical from his highrisk ventures long enough to go to Chicago to study at a business school. Upon graduation, however, he lost no time in returning to the West. From Montana he went to Idaho, Utah, California, Arizona Territory, and finally to Texas where he plunged into the cattle business. There he bought thousands of cattle and trailed them to railroad terminals, such as Abilene, Kansas. In time Sheedy acquired huge ranches along the North Platte river at Chimney Rock and Scotts Bluff, Nebraska, as well as in Wyoming where he was a director of the Wyoming Stockgrowers Association.

By 1882 Sheedy, now 36 and wealthy, had married, so he decided to settle in Denver, his first home in the West. He bought into the Colorado National Bank and was promptly elected a vice-president. Within a few years he watched as a small smelting company foundered in bankruptcy, heavily in debt to Sheedy's bank. Asked to save the enterprise Sheedy became its president, changed the name to Globe and made up his mind to learn the business of smelting.

"Up to this time I knew nothing of smelting or ores . . . I realized that to accomplish anything I must master the details of the industry, and there followed three years of incessant study, part of the time under a tutor."

Sheedy enlarged the smelter, managed to defuse labor problems, established the town on Globeville, and in less than ten years had trebled the company's gross receipts.

South of **Exit 275** down Brighton Boulevard to the heart of Denver's business district, is another enterprise Sheedy rescued, a dry goods store that went bust in the 1893 Panic that devastated the Colorado economy when Federal price supports for silver were dropped. Another debtor of the Colorado National Bank, McNamara Dry Goods Company, was transformed in 1894, with Sheedy as president, into the Denver Dry Goods Company. The Denver came to occupy a full block in the city's commercial center, stretching from 16th to 15th street on California. The Denver survived for nearly a century as one of the elegant department stores of the West until 1987 when it was purchased and dismantled by May D&F. The "D" in D&F stands for Daniels, Sheedy's old merchandising mentor.

US 50 East
The Santa Fe Trail
Kansas to Pueblo (151 miles)

The Chisholm Trail

High and dry, the plains of eastern Colorado presented to the passage of man or beast no obstacles that could prevail over simple endurance. Having seen sterner environments—on the Staked Plains, for example—the longhorns of Texas certainly possessed that quality. Even before the Civil War, they had been driven north over the Chisholm Trail, named for Cherokee cattleman Jesse Chisholm, who brought cattle from far down the Arkansas River to Fort Scott in eastern Kansas.

As farmers staked out homesteads in Kansas moving the frontier of tilled fields gradually westward, the cattle trail, like water bowing before a prow, moved ahead of it. By the mid-1870s the trail had bowed to the Kansas-Colorado border where it crosses the Arkansas valley. There, at approximately **Milepost 467** on *U.S. 50*, the Chisholm or Texas-Montana Trail forded the Arkansas at a now-defunct frontier town known appropriately as Trail City.

"It was the toughest town God ever let live; nothing there but saloons and gambling houses, hotels and corrals. Here the Colorado stockman would meet the Texas drovers who came up with the trail herds." The speaker, Edward Bowles, was just a boy then, in the late 1870s. From their four-thousand-acre ranch west of Wray, in northeastern Colorado, he accompanied his father to Trail City where "we would buy maybe a thousand or two or three [of Texas longhorn steers] whatever we could pick up of yearlings that looked good to us."

The Bowles herd averaged about eight or nine thousand head. The yearlings, bought from passing Texas drovers, were kept on the Bowles range over two winters and then

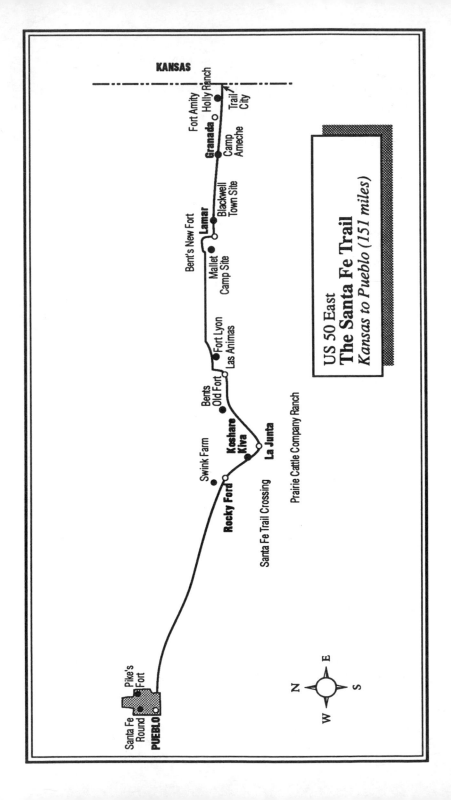

were sold, generally for four to five times their purchase price.

The Arkansas Valley Roundup

The treeless, barrier-free high plains offered boundless acres of forage for resident herds. "Our cattle would run from the Arkansas on the south to the Platte," said Bowles. "We were out from April to November. . . ." This circumstance produced a local phenomenon characteristic to the trail drive—the roundup. Twice each year, in spring and fall, the Colorado cattlemen would conduct joint roundups to collect their stock for branding or marketing. Each ranch would assign a crew proportionate to the number of cattle the ranch had on the public range, and each crew was accompanied by a chuck wagon and cook. Crew members were allowed a string of six to eight horses apiece.

The spring roundups in the Arkansas valley started from Hiram S. Holly's ranch in this vicinity. They brought together several thousand horses and as many as fifty chuck-wagons.

By the early 1880s, however, the irrigable Arkansas valley had drawn homesteaders to crowd out cattlemen who lacked title to the land they were using, even though they had fenced much of it. The federal government intervened in behalf of the nesters, as homesteaders were derisively called, and obliged ranchers without deeds to dismantle their fences. Until 1885, for example, the "SS" ranch of Hiram S. Holly enclosed an area estimated to be twenty square miles west from the Kansas border and north of the Arkansas River. When the ranchers eliminated their fences, homesteaders put up their own to protect crop and hay land. With the invention of the barbed wire manufacturing machine in 1874, nesters could more readily afford to use wire that was designed to discourage livestock encroachment.

In time, the "SS" ranch came into the possession of the Holly Sugar Company, and its irrigable acres were devoted to the cultivation of sugar beets.

Fort Amity

In 1898 thirty families of unemployed slum dwellers from Chicago and cities in Iowa arrived and began cultivating a thousand-acre holding west of Holly, around **Milepost 460.** The project implemented an aspiration of Gen. William Booth, the British-born founder of the Salvation Army. Under the supervision of Booth's daughter, British Consul Emma Booth-Tucker, Col. Thomas Holland had selected heads of families who possessed needed skills. Transported to property that had been purchased by the Salvation Army, each family was assigned an initial ten-acre plot, with livestock and poultry—all of it granted on long-term, relatively low interest loans. Colonists could also reduce their indebtedness by working on common projects, for which they received credit at the rate of two dollars per day. The colony was called Fort Amity.

Growing sugar beets, which were sold to the sugar factory upriver at Rocky Ford (**Milepost 369**), the colony prospered for a few years until, due to seepage, the crop land became alkaline. Because of the deteriorating soil the Salvation Army abandoned the colony project around 1910, and its members were sent to a similar enterprise in California. Later, in private hands, the crop land was successfully reclaimed.

The somewhat feckless spouse of the late but still notorious woman outlaw, Belle Starr, gave Fort Amity dubious celebrity at one point before its demise. On July 9, 1908, Henry Starr, assisted by Kid Wilson, held up the Bank of Amity. Later caught and convicted, Starr served his sentence but, apparently undaunted by his tarnished reputation, returned to nearby Holly to run a restaurant. Like the cattle trail, the outlaw trail evidently had its charms, for Starr later left Holly to resume his life of crime.

Granada

In 1875, five years after Denver had been linked to the nation's railroad networks by the Kansas Pacific and Denver

Pacific lines, the Atchison, Topeka and Santa Fe Railroad remained stalled at **Milepost 453**. Since 1873 Granada had been the jumping-off point for the wagon trail to Santa Fe. Three wagons, each demanding the pulling power of sixteen oxen, were required to transport the contents of a single railroad car. Like Trail City down the road, Granada was a "tough town," populated by railroad workers, gamblers, freighters, and buffalo hunters.

Granada's early population may have been fearsome, but many years later, fear imposed a different kind of population on the area. Less than a year after the Japanese attack on Pearl Harbor in December 1941, President Franklin D. Roosevelt ordered the relocation of thousands of Japanese-Americans from their homes on the Pacific coast to internment camps in the nation's remote interior. A tract of eleven thousand acres was set aside just south of **Milepost 452** to accommodate several thousand detainees.

The Granada Relocation Camp, "Amache," was closed in July 1945, a month before the atomic bombing of Hiroshima and Nagasaki brought the war with Japan to an end.

Big Sandy Creek and the Sand Creek Massacre

Big Sandy Creek empties into the Arkansas River just north of **Milepost 443**. Skirting the south slope of the divide separating the Platte-Missouri from the Arkansas watersheds, the stream was salvation to many traveling the Smoky Hill Trail. After passing the headwaters of the Smoky Hill or Republican rivers, wagonmasters and stage drivers learned to head straight for this Arkansas tributary, even when they had to deviate from a more direct course to Denver. One well-traveled route followed the creek northwest from about Kit Carson to River Bend, a distance of perhaps fifty miles, where the creek turns west to find its source.

The Big Sandy was also witness to tragedy. One late fall day in 1864 the still-controversial Sand Creek Massacre occurred on its banks about thirty-three miles north of here. The incident took place after a long, hot summer of depredations by assorted and not always well identified Indian marauders. The first and most alarming incident was the massacre of the Hungate family south of Denver (see I-25M itinerary). Indians had attacked isolated farms and ranches as well as lightly armed wagon trains and stage stations, often savagely brutalizing their victims.

A small band of Cheyenne and Arapahoe warriors, with their wives and children, appeared in Denver in September 1864. Both tribes were presumed to have harbored the culprits of the summer's attacks. This band arrived, however, under the leadership of Cheyenne chief Black Kettle, who sought out Governor John Evans to sue for peace. No one knew if or to what extent the men with Black Kettle had been guilty of harassing whites, but the indignation of the community remained at such a fever that Evans would not authorize an amnesty for Black Kettle's band. Dismayed, the Cheyenne chief led his people to Fort Lyon, then located near the site of Bent's New Fort (see below). Black Kettle asked the post's commander for U.S. government protection. Whether sanctuary was formally extended to Black Kettle's band or not remains unclear, but the Indians were asked to locate their winter camp away from the lightly manned military post where facilities were deemed to be inadequate to accommodate them.

The village moved on to the banks of the Big Sandy, the eastern boundary of a large Indian reservation set aside by the territorial legislature. There two hundred warriors with their women and children—about five hundred in all— prepared to wait out the winter.

But popular wrath blurred distinctions. Enraged by Indian misdeeds, settlers and their leaders focused their anger on these Indians, whose location was known. In the misty morning chill of November 29, 1864, a regiment of volunteers, activated for the occasion, heeded Col. John M. Chivington's command to attack. The Indian village erupted in panic and confusion.

"I, at daylight this morning," Chivington told the *Rocky Mountain News*, "attacked a Cheyenne village of one hundred and thirty lodges, from nine hundred to one

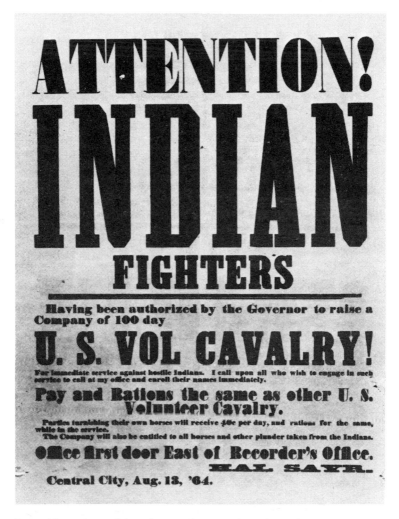

ATTENTION!
INDIAN
FIGHTERS

Having been authorized by the Governor to raise a Company of 100 day

U. S. VOL CAVALRY!

For immediate service against hostile Indians.   I call upon all who wish to engage in such service to call at my office and enroll their names immediately.

Pay and Rations the same as other U. S. Volunteer Cavalry.

Parties furnishing their own horses will receive 40c per day, and rations for the same, while in the service.
The Company will also be entitled to all horses and other plunder taken from the Indians.

Office first door East of Recorder's Office.

HAL. SAYR.

Central City, Aug. 13, '64.

A recruiting poster solicits volunteers for a cavalry regiment that was organized by the territorial government following the Hungate massacre near Denver. *Colorado Historical Society.*

thousand warriors strong. We killed Chief Black Kettle, White Antelope and Little Robe, and between four and five hundred other Indians. . . ." In fact, Black Kettle had escaped, and an on-site count of the slain Indians totaled 123, a majority of whom were women and children.

Chivington's "victory," presented to Colorado's settlers as a crushing blow to the warmaking potential of the Cheyennes and Arapahoes, inspired short-lived complacency.

As terrorism seems ever to beget terrorism, so another even more intense cycle of Indian attacks descended upon Colorado's settlers. All of the stage stations (twenty or more) between Denver and forks of the Platte were destroyed—except for Godfrey's Station, known afterwords as "Fort Wicked" for the fierce defense put up there (see I-76 itinerary). On February 2, 1865, within sight of a military fort, the town of Julesburg was burned to the ground. At least two thousand Cheyennes, Arapahoes, and Sioux had joined forces to avenge Sand Creek. What Chivington's raid had meant to extinguish, it fueled instead.

Ten miles south of the battle site, the town of Chivington today commemorates its namesake's brief but fateful excursion into this area.

Lamar

In 1739 an Indian village stood near the present site of Lamar. Two French-Canadian brothers, Pierre and Paul Mallet, arrived here in the course of a meandering tour of exploration. They had gone from the Lower to the Upper Missouri River and back down across the Platte River, where they paused long enough to give the stream its current name. When they reached the future site of Lamar on the Arkansas River, the Mallets were halfway to becoming the first to trek the Santa Fe Trail.

The Indians they identified as "Laitanes" might be the same whom travelers in the early 1800s had called Ietans. Given the phonetics of the various languages involved, the Indians in both cases might be the "Utahs" or Utes of today. In any case, it was a "Laitan" prisoner, an Arikara who had wandered incautiously from his village on the Upper Missouri, who aided them. The Arikara guided the Mallets from the Laitan village to Raton Pass (see I-25S itinerary), the gateway to Spanish New Mexico and Santa Fe.

Stimulated no doubt by generous grants of public lands to railroads that would develop the West, the founding of towns became a rather bizarre growth industry from 1869 to 1890. As with any enterprise, of course, success can come honestly or questionably, and in the history of town-founding, there may have been no example more devious than that which occurred at **Milepost 435** to bring about the city of Lamar.

I. R. Holmes, a gentleman who had a hand in the rise of Garden City, Kansas, perceived, in 1886, a golden opportunity. As the establishment of a federal land office had sparked the growth of Garden City, so should it stimulate an urban settlement on the vast eastern plains of Colorado, thought Holmes. Throughout the Arkansas valley of Colorado, only Pueblo was at that time blessed with a land office.

Constrained only by the location of unclaimed land along the railroad right-of-way, Holmes bought a site three miles from the town of Blackwell, whose ghost today hovers in the vicinity of **Milepost 438**. He could not, however, persuade A. R. Black, who held title to Blackwell, to move the Santa Fe station to Holmes's newly acquired site. Regulations, moreover, forbade establishing another station so close to the first.

But Holmes had already had the foresight to name as president of his new company an official of the Santa Fe Railroad's land department. His next move was to arrange for Black to be summoned to Pueblo over the weekend of May 22, 1886. Thanks to the timely intercession of the president of Holmes's company, the Santa Fe obligingly dispatched a construction train to Blackwell. Secretly the crew dismantled the Blackwell station house, moved it to Holmes's town site, and reassembled it. When Black returned on Monday, May 24, and discovered the relocated railroad station, he also found the sale of city lots around it to be brisk.

Equally astute in dealing with Washington's bureaucracy, Holmes recognized that President Grover Cleveland's interior secretary, the official responsible for public land management, was a gentleman of no small vanity. So the new town was named in reverence of the Cabinet member and former Senator from Mississippi, the Honorable L.Q.C. Lamar. Scarcely six months later the land office opened its doors in the new town.

Like doting parents, Holmes and Lamar's founding fathers wanted further distinction bestowed on their fair city: Lamar should become the county seat. But, because the courthouse in Las Animas was not as transportable as the railroad station house, they turned to other devices. They persuaded the state legislature to carve a new county from the parent Bent County, which they named Prowers for a deceased Bent county pioneer and state legislator (see below).

From 1886 to 1889, Lamar boomed. Its prosperity lured enough rowdies to require the services of such marshals as gunman Bat Masterson and Ben Daniel. In 1889, however, came drought. The boom ended, but Lamar was saved by its proximity to Arkansas valley irrigation ditches.

Bent's New Fort—Fort Lyon

William Bent, the builder of the earliest and best-known fur trading fort in Colorado forty miles west of Lamar (across the Arkansas River from **Milepost 387**), established a second fort, known as Bent's New Fort, just south of **Milepost 426**. It was built in 1853 at Big Timber and was an outpost for trade with Plains Indians attracted by the abundance of trees along this stretch of the river. The fort was sold to the army in 1859. Known originally as Fort Wise, the army post was renamed Fort Lyon in 1862.

A prim and proper twenty-three-year-old Army wife, Mary Sanford, accompanied her husband, 1st Lt. Byron Sanford, from the mining town of Gold Hill to Fort Lyon at the outset of the Civil War, when the 1st Colorado Regiment of Volunteers was activated by the Union. In the wintry depths of February 1862, she confided to her diary:

Well, I have done something I never expected to do. I played cards, but trust the motive will make it right. I have been considerably exorcised [sic] over the Captain [Sanborn], Lieut. Bonesteel and by [my husband] going to the sutler's to play for cigars, and sometimes, I hear, for wine. I expostulated with them, time and again, when Captain Sanborn said, "Mary, if you will learn to play the game of cribbage, I'll promise not to go there again. You know we have no amusements and have to do something."

. . . It is a mathematical game and I confess, [I] find it pleasant, but it is seldom I yield my scruples and I shall only play in our own quarters. . . .

When, a few days later, a Confederate force of Texas Rangers came north through New Mexico to test Union strength in the West, Lieutenant Sanford's regiment was called from Fort Lyon to reinforce Fort Union, New Mexico. Wives accompanied the regiment as far as Hull's Ranche, near today's Pueblo, where the soldiers turned south to confront their adversaries. The wives were escorted to Camp Weld in Denver (see I-25M itinerary).

A Union commander who was highly commended for his military prowess in the resulting campaign was none other than the soon-to-be notorious John M. Chivington.

At Fort Lyon, possibly in charge of that infamous sutler's store was a man about Mary Stanford's age, John Wesley Prowers. Prowers had come to the fort as an eighteen year old in the company of Robert Miller, the Indian agent assigned to the region. In Bent's employ Prowers worked as a wagon master, making as many as twenty-two lengthy treks across the plains, and as sutler to Fort Lyon's garrison.

About the time Mary and her husband arrived at Fort Lyon, Prowers was married to Amy, the daughter of Cheyenne Chief Ochinee.

In 1863 Prowers went into business for himself with such enterprise that within a few years he had gained a prominence that would merit a posthumous memorial in the county now bearing his name. He launched a farm and livestock breeding operation at a little town two miles south of Las Animas on Colorado 101, where he was the famous Kit Carson's neighbor. In time he possessed 400,000 acres, including forty miles of river frontage.

To protect not only his crops but the bloodlines of the purebred Herefords and other shorthorn cattle he had introduced to the territory, Prowers fenced about eighty thousand acres. The move of course signaled the beginning of the end of the open range and the decline and even disdain of the old Texas longhorn on Colorado's eastern plains. The venerable beasts that were being trailed up from Texas were scrawny compared to the bulky Herefords. Frequently, moreover, they brought a fatal disease known as "Texas fever," which threatened local herds. Finally, dismissing the longhorns as "Spanish cattle," Colorado stockmen, by some manifestly extralegal process, managed to "naturalize" their own Herefords.

Ironically, today many Colorado cattle breeders are crossing their angular Herefords with the sleek Longhorn (now a recognized breed) in order to beget calves that can be delivered with fewer complications.

Before he died at the age of forty-six on Valentine's Day, 1884, John Wesley Prowers had established the region's first slaughter house to deliver dressed beef rather than beef-on-the-hoof to eastern customers. He also had been named vice-president of the Bent County Bank, and he had served as Bent County's representative to the state legislature.

When an 1866 flood undermined Fort Lyon's foundations, the U.S. Army decided to move the fort twenty miles west to a site across the river from Las Animas, one mile south of **Milepost 405**, on Bent *County Road 15*. There a mortally ailing Kit Carson arrived, after a trip to Washington, in the spring of 1868. Suffering from an aneurism of the aorta, the consequence of an 1860 hunting accident, Carson in vain had sought a cure on the east coast.

Returning by way of the nearly completed Union Pacific's transcontinental line—already on its way from Omaha to an 1869 linkup with the Central Pacific in Utah—Carson stopped off to see an old mountaineer friend, Mariano Medina, at Namaqua (see *U.S. 34* itinerary), near today's Loveland, before proceeding to his deathbed at the Fort Lyon military infirmary.

The two had served together as scouts for Col. John Charles Fremont. Medina was born in Taos, New Mexico, where subsequently Carson himself lived and married Maria Josephina Jaramillo, then fifteen years old. When Carson succumbed on May 23, 1868, their seventh child, Josephita, was not yet six weeks old.

In a gesture of friendship for the deceased Carson, Gen. William Tecumseh Sherman, the Union commander who had "marched through Georgia" in the Civil War, arranged for Carson's oldest child, William to attend Notre Dame University in Indiana.

Today Fort Lyon houses a national cemetery and a major veterans' hospital.

Prairie Cattle Company

As life grew more complicated on the Colorado plains, big business came to the cattle industry, much of it based on foreign capital. The Colorado cattle company that, in the long run, controlled the most acreage, handled the most cattle, and survived the longest was an outfit called the Prairie Cattle Company, which was organized in Great Britain in 1881 and was not dissolved until World War I. Their range ran from the Arkansas River at the mouth of the Purgatoire River, below **Milepost 403**, south to the New Mexico border, and in some places fifty miles eastward from the Purgatoire. The range comprised an estimated thirty-five hundred square miles, accommodating in the early 1880s nearly fifty-four thousand cattle.

Las Animas

Las Animas, the capital of Bent County, is located at the mouth of the Purgatoire River. Its name is derived from the now largely forgotten Spanish designation for the river, *Las*

Animas Perdidas en Purgatorio—The Lost Souls in Purgatory. If not the name itself, the sense of the name was soon lost in passing through an English ear to an English tongue. Colorado cattlemen referred to the river as the "Picketwire."

Bent's Old Fort

Construction of Bent's Old Fort, fourteen miles west of Las Animas on *Colorado 194* and north of **Milepost 387** on *U.S. 50*, was begun in the early 1830s by William Bent in partnership with his older brother, Charles, and Ceran St. Vrain, all experienced St. Louis traders.

William Bent had specialized in the Indian trade, operating originally as an itinerant buyer and seller of goods among the plains and mountain tribes. Charles and St. Vrain had concentrated on the burgeoning trade with New Mexico, which had come about with Mexico's secession from Spain in 1821. It was due to the New Mexico trade that the famous Santa Fe Trail was instituted around 1827. Bent's Fort, or Fort William as it was called, was situated where the Santa Fe Trail crossed the Arkansas River to head south toward Raton Pass along the divide between the Purgatoire River and Timpas Creek. Today *U.S. 350* and the Santa Fe Railroad right-of-way depart from **Milepost 379** to follow approximately the same trace as the old trail.

The Bent and St. Vrain enterprise seems to have thrived from its inception until the 1846-48 war with Mexico. In that campaign the War Department requisitioned a portion of the fort's facilities for support of U.S. Army elements occupying New Mexico. Such heavy use resulted in overgrazing of prairie meadows around the fort, exhausting much of the wood supply in the neighborhood, and introducing disease. A cholera epidemic intermittently raged up and down the Missouri valley in these years, and the disease apparently reached the fort in 1849, forcing William Bent to abandon the installation.

Another misfortune involved Charles Bent, who had been named governor of New Mexico in 1846, following its occupation by U.S. forces. He was assassinated on January 19, 1847, by a mob of rioting Pueblo Indians, who attacked him in Taos. Also killed was his mistress of eleven years and mother of his five children, Ignacia Jaramillo, older sister of Kit Carson's wife.

Shortly after establishing the trading fort, William Bent had married the daughter of a prominent Southern Cheyenne leader. Owl Woman's father was Grey Thunder, a medicine man. Eventually, in recognition of Bent's good relations with the Indians, the fort was made the Indian Agency for much of the Colorado region.

The old fort was destroyed, either by Bent himself or by Indians after he had abandoned it, but recently it was restored by the National Park Service as a monument to its own history. Authentically reconstructed of grass-reinforced adobe clay, the replica is furnished and staffed by Park Service personnel in period garb, much in the fashion of other National Historic Sites such as Williamsburg, Virginia.

On May 19, 1869, William Bent died at his ranch, two miles east of Las Animas, the seat of the county named for him. Ironically, at least one of his sons, Charles, was rumored to have sided with his Cheyenne kinsmen after the Sand Creek massacre and to have participated in raids on white settlements.

Koshare Kiva

Koshare Kiva, a museum commemorating the cultures of the various Indian tribes of this region, is located in La Junta at 18th and Santa Fe streets.

Rocky Ford

George Washington Swink, a man reared on the well-watered loam of Illinois, decided at age thirty-five to resolve a mid-life crisis. In 1871, he took temporary leave of his family and boarded a Kansas Pacific train that dropped him at Kit Carson, Colorado Territory. Accompanying an ox-drawn wagon train headed south, he walked sixty miles to the Arkansas River, arrived at a point about three miles north and west of Rocky Ford, **Milepost 369**, where a rocky shoal served as a ford when the river was high. He bought an interest in the mercantile store that served the small community and, with the arrival of his family, prepared to settle down again.

He filed a homestead claim and a timber claim, the latter under a new provision of the Homestead Act that encouraged tree-planting on the barren plains. His claim, as it turned out, would result in the first land title issued under the timber claim amendment— Patent No. 1, November 3, 1887, signed by President Grover Cleveland. But it was not tree-growing that gave Swink his fame or his fortune.

Perceiving that plants grew readily, with adequate water, in the valley soil, Swink persuaded his neighbors to help in the digging of the first cooperative irrigation ditch in the Arkansas valley. That year, 1874, he planted an experimental plot of vegetables and grains. He discovered that vine crops, especially cantaloupe, did exceptionally well.

When the Santa Fe Railroad reached Rocky Ford in 1877, Swink made his first attempt at a cash crop of cantaloupes. After experimenting with varieties of the melon, in 1880 Swink finally found one worth offering to eastern markets. He turned his first profit in 1882, when his Rocky Ford cantaloupes began to gain favor in the better hotels and restaurants of Kansas City, St. Louis, and even New York City. By the turn of the century, Rocky Ford growers were shipping as many as ten million melons annually to New York City alone.

Swink died at the age of seventy-four in 1910. He had been a long-time mayor of the town he put on the map, a state senator for southeastern Colorado, and the father, not only of the Rocky ford melon industry, but of eleven children as well.

Fountain Creek

During Thomas Jefferson's second administration, Capt.

Zebulon Pike was dispatched on an expedition that in many ways was the complement of the more famous Lewis and Clark venture two years earlier. As Lewis and Clark surveyed the northern reaches of the 1803 Louisiana Purchase, Pike was to explore the southern sector of Jefferson's important acquisition.

Pike and his companions left St. Louis, Missouri Territory, on July 15, 1806, and ascended the Arkansas River by its south bank, following a trail left by the Spaniard Don Facundo Melgares. Pike reached what is now Colorado on November 12. At a point midway between Las Animas and La Junta, they first saw the mountains. On November 17 they reached the present site of Rocky Ford, **Milepost 369**, and by November 23, Fountain Creek (**Milepost 316**).

Remarkably, despite the likely hazards of this venture into the unknown, only twenty-three men accompanied Pike. Among them was a civilian, Dr. John H. Robinson, and an interpreter, Antoine Francois Vasquez. Vasquez was the brother of Louis Vasquez, the St. Louis trader who built Fort Vasquez on the South Platte (see I-25N itinerary). His association with Pike so impressed Antoine Vasquez that he christened his son Pike.

Their modest force was threatened by a war party of sixty Indians when they reached Fountain Creek, prompting Pike to build the first fort in the region. It was a small, three-sided log breastwork, about five feet high, which backed onto the Arkansas River. It proved sufficient to deter aggression.

Union Station In Pueblo

In April 1879, during the Royal Gorge War (see *U.S. 50W*) supporters of the Denver & Rio Grande's William Jackson Palmer cornered Santa Fe agent Bat Masterson and his gunmen in a Pueblo roundhouse. The site is now Pueblo's Union Station at Union and "B" streets. Masterson gave up without a fight. He was moonlighting on this occasion from his job as sheriff of Ford County (Dodge City), Kansas. A few years later, he would become marshal of another town important to the Santa Fe Railroad—Trinidad, Colorado Territory (See I-25S itinerary).

At a less tense moment, on July 26, 1869, the same William Jackson Palmer, founder of the Denver & Rio Grande, wrote from Pueblo to his fiancee back East:

. . . Nothing [is] is more attractive perhaps in the whole range of the Rocky Mountains. . . . [Here] the air is fraught with health and vigour, and . . . life would be poetry—an idyll of blue sky, clear intense atmosphere, fantastic rock, dancing water, green meadow, high mountain, rugged canyon, and distant view of the kind that gives wing to the imagination and allows no foothold for it to halt upon, short of infinity.

I-25 North
Route of the Rails
Wyoming to Denver (89 miles)

Lindenmeier Archaeological Site

In 1924, three amateur archaeologists from Fort Collins uncovered some stone arrowheads a few miles west of **Milepost 297** on the horse ranch of William Lindenmeier, Jr. This was not unusual; arrowhead collecting on Colorado's ranges is as commonplace as stamp collecting elsewhere. Even the man who made the discovery, Judge C. C. Coffin, did not consider his find to be anything remarkable. Six years later it turned out to be one of the archaeological discoveries of the century.

A year after Judge Coffin had picked up his arrowheads on the Lindenmeier ranch, a black cowboy, George McJunkins, found some more stone projection points on a Cimarron River ranch near Folsom, in northeastern New Mexico. McJunkins's find prompted a visit by the director of the Denver Museum of Natural History, who established that the Folsom points had killed a giant bison, an ancestor of the Great Plains buffalo, which had been extinct for about 10,000 years.

In time Judge Coffin was informed that his "arrowheads"—more likely spearheads, because the paleo-Indians of America had not yet acquired the bow and arrow—were of the same type and period.

The discovery established human habitation in North America far earlier than had been previously believed. It was a time, in fact, when this part of the country contained not only a giant ancestor of the buffalo, but camels and giant sloths as well. So startling was this new discovery that Washington's Smithsonian Institution funded six years of excavating at the Lindennmeir site in the 1930s.

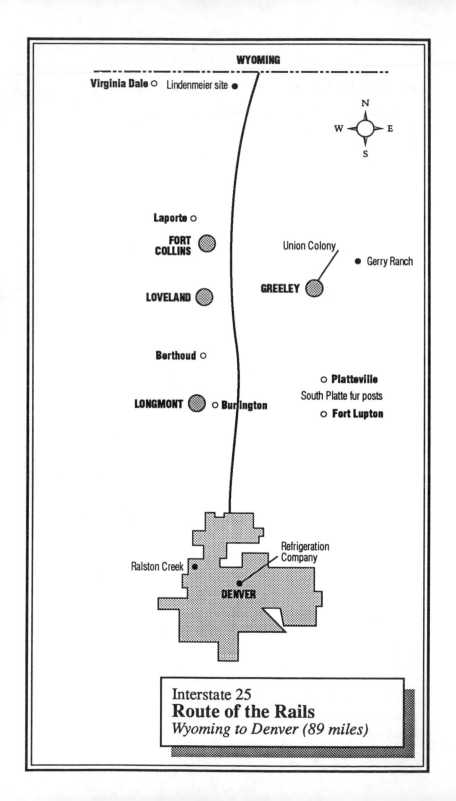

WYOMING

Virginia Dale ○ Lindenmeier site ●

N
W ←✦→ E
S

Laporte ○

FORT COLLINS ⊚

Union Colony

● Gerry Ranch

LOVELAND ⊚

GREELEY ⊚

Berthoud ○

○ **Platteville**

South Platte fur posts

LONGMONT ⊚ ○ Burlington

○ **Fort Lupton**

Ralston Creek ●

Refrigeration Company

DENVER ●

Interstate 25
Route of the Rails
Wyoming to Denver (89 miles)

The Overland Stage

Colorado's 1864-65 Indian wars may have been foreshadowed in the Minnesota Massacre of 1862 when the Santee Sioux rose up against white encroachment in a rage of hostility that quickly spread to their Teton Sioux kinsmen on the northern plains. The transcontinental Overland Stage line until then had been running from Julesburg (see I-76 itinerary) to South Pass in western Wyoming by way of the North Platte River valley. The stretch from Julesburg to the Sweetwater River in central Wyoming was Sioux country, and their depredations forced the Overland to detour.

The new route went from Julesburg to Denver and back north via the Cherokee Trail, which paralleled today's I-25 from Denver to Fort Collins, **Exit 269**, before angling to the northwest along a path that coincided roughly with modern U.S. 287.

The sinister Joseph A. "Jack" Slade, erstwhile supervisor of the Julesburg-to-Sweetwater division of the Overland (see I-76 intinerary), was called upon to establish a waystation along this detour. He built one near the Wyoming border at a point about twenty miles west of **Milepost 294**.

Better known as the ruthless killer of "Old Jules," Slade, in an incongruous show of sentiment, named the new station Virginia Dale, in honor of his wife. Suspicions prevailed that Slade was secretly abetting bands of outlaws, euphemistically known as "road agents," who attacked overland stage and freight wagons from their lairs in "Robbers' Roost," a region of the Laramie mountains to the northeast of Virginia Dale station.

Pressured by the U.S. Army, the Overland Stage company fired the rogue Slade, who decamped with his beloved wife for the Montana gold fields, newly discovered in 1864. At Virginia City Jack Slade again surrounded himself with a retinue of cutthroats and gunmen. To rescue terrorized townsfolk from Slade's menacing, vigilantes seized Slade and two of his bullies when, of all things, Slade had come to town to get a prescription filled. The three were summarily lynched.

Fort Collins

Fort Collins, at **Exit 269**, was the site of a military installation, Camp Collins, erected during the Indian wars of the mid-1860s to protect the Overland mail route that had by this time detoured through the region. Manned originally by two companies of the 11th Ohio Volunteer Cavalry, the post was named for the commandant of Fort Laramie, Col. W. O. Collins. Abandoned in 1872, after Indian hostilities had diminished and the mails had been transferred to the newly completed railroads, an agricultural colony was established on the site at the instigation of one of the officials of the Union Colony in Greeley (see below).

Much earlier, in the spring of 1844, a twenty-year-old Missouri Frenchman, Antoine Janis, arrived in this area. "On the first of June, 1844, I stuck my claim in the valley, intending the location selected for my home should the country ever be settled. At the time the streams were all very high and the valley black with buffalo. . . . [After the gold fever of 1858] I moved over from Fort Laramie and settled on it. . . . One hundred and fifty lodges of Arapahoes moved there with me. . . . "

The town, a few miles west of present-day Fort Collins on *Colorado 14*, was called Colona by Janis and his colleagues. Renamed Laporte in 1862, a name it retains, the town was Larimer County's seat until 1868 when it was eclipsed commercially and politically by Fort Collins. In addition to town-building, Janis and his brothers moonlighted in the gold rush years as mountain guides (see below, Fort Lupton).

The Fremont Expedition

For the dashing Col. John Charles Fremont, an absence of mountain guides caused anguish at the outset of his 1843 expedition to seek out a suitable route through the Colorado Rockies for a proposed transcontinental railroad. In his official report, Fremont complained: "Immediately at the foot of the mountains, I could find no one sufficiently acquainted with them to guide us to the plains at their western base; but the race of trappers, who formerly lived in their recesses has almost entirely disappeared—dwindled to a few scattered individuals—save one or two of whom are regularly killed in the course of a year by the Indians."

In his exploration, Fremont intended to follow the Cache la Poudre River, which emerges from the mountains a few miles west of Fort Collins and Laporte. Despite the presence of the estimable guide Kit Carson (see *U.S. 50, U.S. 160* and *U.S. 34* itineraries), Fremont seems to have mistaken his route. Instead of following the main body of the river, Fremont took its north fork, pursuing a route approximating that of *U.S. 287* to the Laramie River plain of today's Wyoming.

The first to have followed Fremont's intended route seems to have been the baron of the Rocky Mountain fur trade, Gen. William H. Ashley, and his trappers on their way to the first trappers' rendezvous in the Green River valley in the fall of 1824.

The name of the Cache la Poudre River dates from the era of the fur trade. In French it means "the powder's hiding place," referring to gunpowder buried by mountain men for future retrieval.

The Union Pacific Railroad and its Rivals

The route between Cheyenne and Denver presently followed by I-25 was first used by the railroads. Cheyenne came into being largely as a consequence of its status as a main station on the Union Pacific line. It did not take Denver businessmen long to realize that a link to the transcontinental railroad would pay early dividends. The impudence of a businessman from the rival town of Golden (see I-70 itinerary), W.A.H. Loveland, spurred them to action.

Loveland had organized the Colorado Central & Pacific Railroad in 1868, shortly after the Union Pacific reached Cheyenne from its starting point at Omaha, Nebraska. Loveland planned to bring a branch line down from Cheyenne to Golden, fifteen miles west of Denver, with only a spur to serve the state capital. Unfortunately, Loveland was unable to find the capital with which to launch his enterprise.

Former governor John Evans (see *U.S. 285* itinerary) quickly rallied Denver's merchants and launched the Denver Pacific Railroad, which reached Denver from Cheyenne on June 22, 1870. Helping to build the Denver Pacific, incidentally, was Gen. William Jackson Palmer, soon to begin his own pioneering rail line, the Denver & Rio Grande (see I-25M).

Foiled for the time being, Loveland tied his still modest Colorado Central & Pacific Railroad into the Denver Pacific right-of-way in order to share its facilities between Denver and Cheyenne.

The maneuvering among the sundry railroad interests in the West in the 1870s came to resemble a Napoleonic battle plan. Bonaparte, in this case, seems to have been gold speculator Jay Gould. Gould began with the Missouri Pacific Railroad, which served Pueblo. In the late 1870s he also gained control of the Kansas Pacific and the Denver Pacific. His archrivals, owners of the Union Pacific, were confronted with the need to use Denver Pacific facilities to tap the now lucrative Denver market. So, in 1877, they decided to fund Loveland's long dormant project to provide the Colorado Central with an independent right-of-way to Cheyenne. The route chosen was approximately that now followed by I-25. (The Denver Pacific right-of-way coincides with that of *U.S. 85*.) With the completion of the new line, the Union Pacific leased the Colorado Central trackage for its own use in 1879.

The following year, however, the canny Jay Gould forced Union Pacific stockholders into a situation that obliged them to purchase the Missouri Pacific, Kansas Pacific, and, albeit a redundancy for their purposes, the Denver Pacific—all at high prices.

The building of the Colorado Central branch line established the city of Loveland, **Exit 257**, honoring the railroad's founder (see *U.S. 34* itinerary).

Greeley

In 1869, the year the National Prohibition Party came into existence, an ad appeared in the New York *Tribune* soliciting persons who would help to establish a "colony" in the West. The promoter was the *Tribune*'s own agricultural editor, Nathan C. Meeker. "The persons with whom I would be willing to associate," Meeker declared, "must be temperance men, and ambitious to establish good society. . . ."

Both Meeker and his boss, Horace Greeley, had visited the Colorado piedmont, so it was not surprising that "Union Colony No. 1" was located on the delta of the Cache la Poudre and South Platte rivers, twenty-one miles east of **Exit 357**, at the junction today of **U.S. 34** and **U.S. 85**.

Greeley, himself an informal booster of the colony, had observed a decade before the project was launched, "This region, though inferior in soil, and less smooth in surface, is not dissimilar in its topography to Lombardy [in northern Italy], and, like it, will in time be subject to systematic irrigation. . . . The enterprise should pay well."

In April 1870, the colonists purchased and filed on a total of seventy-two thousand acres. A mere two months later an irrigation ditch nine miles long, six feet wide, and three feet deep watered the fields of the colony. The colonists struggled through their first year of cooperation, bickering over policies and practices. Some left and others came. After a visit to Greeley, George A. Hobbs wrote in the Genesee (Illinois) *Republic*: "It is a snare, a delusion, a fraud, a cheat, a swindle, a graveyard, in which are buried heaps of bright hopes and lots of joyous anticipation. . . . If they can't stay where they are but must go somewhere else, for pity's sake don't ever dream of such a mad and foolish thing as striking out for the great colony of Greeley, C.T."

On the colony's first anniversary, however, the *Rocky Mountain News* declared emphatically, "Success has placed its imprint not only upon the organization itself, but has illustrated the correctness of the idea, and fully demonstrated its claims as the most practical and efficient method of peopling the great west . . . ." The Denver paper's enthusiasm may have been slightly colored by the wishful thinking of its publisher, William N. Byers, who, moonlighting as the agent of the railroad land development subsidiary, had sold Union Colony its land.

Not lost, of course, was Meeker's initial sense of righteousness. On the same day that the *Rocky Mountain News* proclaimed the Greeley experiment a success, the colony's own newspaper pointed the finger at a similar experiment in southern Colorado that had foundered (see *U.S. 50* itinerary): "It is generally understood that the German Colony, of Wet Mountain Valley has failed. What the real cause may have been we cannot say [but] we understand that they established a Brewery early, which, of itself, is enough to ruin any Colony."

Elbridge Gerry, "The Paul Revere of Colorado"

Ten miles east of Greeley, Crow Creek empties into the South Platte River. Here in the early 1860s the middle-aged grandson and namesake of a signer of the Declaration of Independence, Elbridge Gerry, began a horse ranch. Born on July 18, 1818, in Massachusetts, this Elbridge Gerry had been a hunter and mountain man before settling down with his wife, Big Woman, the daughter of the Oglala Sioux Chief Swift Bird, and their six children.

Elbridge Gerry became the "Paul Revere of Colorado" when he rode sixty-five miles to Denver to warn of Indian plans to begin hostilities. *Colorado Historical Society.*

On August 19, 1864, Gerry became "the Paul Revere of Colorado." On that day two Cheyenne Indians came to warn Gerry to remove his livestock from the vicinity of the South Platte River, because, they said, a thousand Indians planned to attack settlements and ranches in the region. Gerry rode sixty-five miles to Denver to warn Governor John Evans. As a result, Evans was able to mobilize militia and diminish casualties with the onset of the Indian Wars of 1864-65.

For his part, Gerry forfeited immunity to Indian attack. A war party of Cheyennes raided his ranch two days later, stealing sixty horses and mules. A year later a Brule Sioux band took twenty-one horses and, after that, his in-laws, the Oglalas, struck, taking eighty-eight horses. Gerry eventually retired to the railroad town of Evans, two miles south of Greeley on U.S. 85. The town was named, of course, for Governor Evans, who later became the president of the Denver Pacific Railroad, which passed through Greeley and Evans en route from Cheyenne to Denver.

Berthoud

Another railroad town, five miles west of **Exit 250**, is Berthoud, whose name was changed from Little Thompson to commemorate Capt. Edward L. Berthoud, the chief civil engineer of the Colorado Central Railroad. In 1861, while in the employ of a wagon road company, the Central Overland California & Pike's Peak Express, Berthoud discovered a pass over the Continental Divide. The pass also bears his name (see U.S. 40 itinerary)

Fort Lupton

Nine miles east of I-25, between **Milepost 248** and **Exit 235**, fur traders in the mid-1830s built a string of four competing trading posts along the South Platte River bottoms. Among the first of these was Fort Lancaster, established in the summer of 1836 by a young West Pointer who had lately resigned his commission. Lancaster P. Lupton had visited the area a year before in the official expedition of U.S. Army

Col. Henry M. Dodge. Lupton was so taken with the environment, that he decided to return and try his luck as a trader among the Indians.

Fort Lupton, as it came to be called, was located a mile northwest of the present town of Fort Lupton, due east of **Exit 235**. Lupton had elected to challenge two veteran St. Louis traders, Louis Vasquez (see *U.S. 50* and I-25M) and Andrew W. Sublette, who had erected Fort Vasquez just seven miles north of Lupton's emporium the previous fall. (A reconstruction of Fort Vasquez can be found on the site of the original near *U.S. 85*, one mile south of Platteville.)

By the summer of 1837 two other forts had been built along the south bank of the South Platte, the farthest only fifteen miles from Fort Lupton. Between Fort Lupton and Fort Vasquez, Pratte, Chouteau & Company, a St. Louis offshoot of the powerful John Jacob Astor's trading empire, sponsored Peter A. Sarpy and Henry Fraeb in the founding of Fort Jackson. Down river, the dominant trading company on the Arkansas River, Bent and St. Vrain, established Fort St. Vrain as a satellite trading post of the well-known Bent's Fort (see *U.S. 50* itinerary). Competition was so fierce among the traders that the owners of Fort Jackson were forced to sell out to Bent and St. Vrain within a year.

In the winter of 1841-42, two employees of neighboring posts were involved in a competition of a more deadly sort near the derelict Fort Jackson. Traveling journalist Rufus B. Sage recorded the romantic story of a duel between Henry Beer and Valentine "Rube" Herring for the affections of Herring's comely but coquettish Mexican wife.

> Backed by a number of friends, and anxious to obtain the lady from her husband, the former had provoked a quarrel and used very insulting language to his antagonist. . . . A challenge was promptly accepted. The preliminaries were arranged in confident expectation of killing Herring, who was considered a poor marksman. . . .
>
> The weapons selected by Beer were rifles, the distance

fifty yards, the manner off-hand, and the time of shooting between the word fire and three. . . . At the word "fire," the ball of Beer's rifle was buried in a cottonwood a few inches above the head of his antagonist — at the word "three" the contents of Herring's rifle found lodgement in the body of Beer, who fell and expired in a few minutes.

A half-century later, the original story had ballooned to legend. A newspaper recalled the incident as a rivalry between Lt. Lancaster Lupton and one Palette St. Vrain for the affections of an Indian maiden named Touch-the-Sky. That version had St. Vrain being stabbed to death "almost on the eve of his wedding day" by Lupton, "who fled the country."

In the early 1840s the introduction of the silk hat to the fashion world knocked the bottom from the market in beaver felt, the effects of which were most keenly felt in the region perhaps the most removed from the world of high fashion— the South Platte River. After trying several strategies in an effort to make a go of it, Lancaster P. Lupton in 1845 abandoned his trading fort. After a couple of years with Rube Herring and others on Hardscrabble Creek in the Arkansas valley (see *U.S. 50* itinerary), Lupton and his frontier buddies joined the 1849 California gold rush. He died in California, mourned by his Cheyenne Indian wife and their eight children.

The economic hard times finally resulted in the abandonment, in 1845, of the last of the four trading forts, Fort St. Vrain, by the redoubtable firm of Bent and St. Vrain.

The remains of the derelict forts were restored to use to provide shelter for gold seekers and other travelers on their way to Denver City and Auraria in 1858. This advertisement appeared in an 1858 guidebook published for would-be emigrants: "Miners' ranche of Miles, Stocky and Co. Antoine and Nicholas Janes [Janis], mountain guides, St. Vrain's fort, Colonia Territory. Having eighteen years experience in the mountains, are prepared to give information relative to any portion of the country in the vicinity of the mines, or to accompany prospecting parties. Terms reasonable."

On the site of St. Vrain's fort today is the first helium-cooled nuclear power plant in the United States, Fort St. Vrain. Plagued by technical problems compounded by mismanagement, the plant was closed in 1988. The utility's directors decided to cease nuclear power operations in June 1990.

Burlington

Halfway House, an Overland Stage station so called because it divided the distance between Denver and Laporte, was about seven miles west of **Exit 240**, in the vanished town of Burlington. Twenty-two-passenger Concord coaches—four rows of four-seat interior benches, four topside seats behind the driver, and two places by his side—drawn by matched six-horse teams, stopped at Burlington during the 1860s for meals and refreshment on their way to places of greater moment.

Burlington expired by the end of the decade—a casualty, along with the Overland Stage, of the completed Denver Pacific Railroad and a victim of its vulnerable location on the flood plain of the St. Vrain River.

Longmont

Almost a year to the day after the organizers of Union Colony No. 1 gathered in New York, a similar group convened in Chicago. Calling themselves the Chicago-Colorado Colony, they took their inspiration from the Greeley experiment and, in 1871, acquired rights to seventy thousand acres in the valley of the St. Vrain River around Burlington. Recognizing the existing townsite's susceptibility to snowmelt flooding, the new colonists decided to build their town facilities on the higher ground of the St. Vrain's north bank. The splendid view of Long's Peak from that point inspired a name for the new town—Longmont.

The first building on the site was a twenty-four-by-sixty-foot barracks, which provided temporary accommodations for new settlers until they could build on their own land. The barracks was eventually relegated to the status of a livery stable.

Perceiving the advantages of the new location, Burlington's residents soon moved themselves and their buildings across the river to high ground as well. One perplexing disadvantage materialized, however. Wells dug for drinking water came up either alkaline or salt-laden. Potable water had to be carted from the mouth of St. Vrain canyon ten miles away.

Cherokee Trail

Gold was discovered in Colorado about two and one-half miles west of **Exit 215**, where Ralston Creek enters Clear Creek. Oddly, the discovery was not made during the official gold rush of 1858-59, but during the California gold rush a decade earlier. The discoverer, moreover, was not some grizzled old prospector, but a Cherokee Indian.

One of the so-called Five Civilized Tribes, the Cherokees had been displaced from their ancestral home in Georgia by the administration of Andrew Jackson. They were moved across the Mississippi to what is now eastern Oklahoma and, in 1850, was known as the Cherokee Nation. Some of the Cherokees were experienced miners. They had worked the mines of western Georgia and North Carolina before being forced to emigrate west.

Not surprisingly, therefore, several companies of Cherokees decided to join in California's quest for gold. The route they took from the Cherokee Nation to the Pacific coast became known, in Colorado, as the Cherokee Trail. They came up the Arkansas River, using the already well-established Santa Fe Trail (see *U.S. 50* itinerary), to the east bank of Fountain Creek near today's Pueblo, then turned north to the South Platte divide (see *I-25M*). From that point a young Cherokee, John Lowrey Brown, recorded in his diary:

June 18. Today we crossed the dividing ridge between the Arks and the Platt. Traveled twenty-five miles.

Camped on a bold running clear stream of water [Cherry Creek]. Waters of the Platt. Good grass and wood. Camp 41.

June 19. Very hard storm this evening, hale from the size of a birds to a hens egg. Continued down above mentioned creek twenty miles. Good grass, water and timber. Camp 42.

June 20. Ten miles today. Took a left hand trail down the creek, which was made by Capt. Edmondson about two weeks ago. About ten oclock came to the South Fork of the Platt river. Made a raft and commenced crossing the waggons. Camped on the bank of the Platt. Camp 43.

June 21. Finished crossing at two oclock. Left the Platt and traveled six miles to creek. Good water, grass, and timber. Camp 44. We called this Ralstons creek because a man of that name found gold here.

June 22. Lay bye. Gold found. . . .

Despite their find, the Cherokees continued on to California. Their route approximated that of I-25 as far as Fort Collins. There they went up the northern tributaries of the Cache la Poudre, probably along much the same route described above as that taken by Colonel Fremont. Out on the Laramie plain they turned west for California.

Memory of this find among those who had returned to the Cherokee Nation from California stirred efforts to mount a new prospecting expedition to Colorado. Finally, in 1858, a company of Cherokees and whites returned to the Ralston Creek vicinity. They were joined by another party of Georgians headed by William Green Russell of Auraria, Lumpkin County, Georgia (see I-25M and I-70).

Thus began the Colorado gold rush.

1st Commercial Refrigeration

A stunning innovation in refrigeration began in Denver in 1889 when three clever entrepreneurs established the Colorado Automatic Refrigeration Company, east of **Exit**

210B in downtown Denver at 1722 Blake Street. This was thirteen years before the first building in the U.S. was air-conditioned. Buildings were being heated at that time with steam piped through underground conduits from a central steam plant. The founders of the Colorado Automatic Refrigeration Company sought to transmit cold much the same way.

They built a thirty-ton ice machine to pump liquid ammonia through one-inch street mains that shunted ammonia to their customers along the route. The ammonia lines entered a room from the ceiling into a large coil that permitted the ammonia to expand into its natural state as a gas. The expanding ammonia absorbed heat in the room, chilling the air.

One customer called the system "absolutely perfect . . . something a butcher needs to use only one week to make him feel that he is rescued from one of the greatest evils of the butcher's business, namely, the price, trouble, labor, and dirt, attendant upon handling natural ice."

By 1902, however, Willard Haviland Carrier had installed the first real air conditioner in a Brooklyn printing plant. Remotely piped-in refrigeration seems to have disappeared about the same time. In the last documented use of the system, a plant like the one in Denver was closed down by the Atlantic City Cooling Company in 1906. The Colorado Automatic Refrigerating Company seems to have operated only from 1889 to 1895 at the latest.

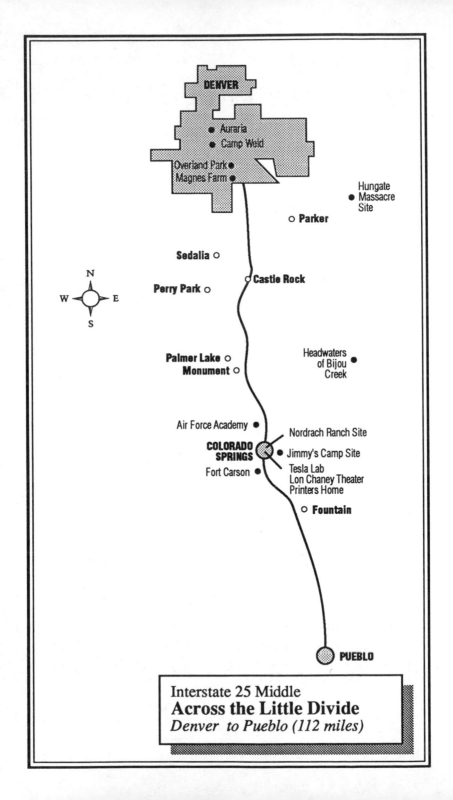

DENVER

Auraria

Camp Weld

Overland Park
Magnes Farm

Hungate
Massacre
Site

○ **Parker**

Sedalia ○

Perry Park ○   ○ **Castle Rock**

Palmer Lake ○   Headwaters
of Bijou
Monument ○   Creek

Air Force Academy ●

Nordrach Ranch Site

**COLORADO
SPRINGS**   Jimmy's Camp Site

Fort Carson ●   Tesla Lab
Lon Chaney Theater
Printers Home

○ **Fountain**

PUEBLO

Interstate 25 Middle
Across the Little Divide
Denver to Pueblo (112 miles)

N
W   E
S

I-25 Middle
Across the Little Divide
Denver to Pueblo (112 miles)

Auraria vs. Denver City

The mouth of Cherry Creek, flanked now by Speer Boulevard, **Exit 212**, marks the point at which urban Denver began. The first organized town at this site was Auraria, whose formal existence began on November 1, 1858, on the south bank of Cherry Creek.

The town was launched under the auspices of a group of Georgians headed by William Green Russell, whose resolute leadership transcended such eccentricities as a long braided beard. The new community's namesake was Russell's home in Lumpkin County, Georgia, the scene of a less-remembered gold rush in the 1820s.

Libeus Barney, builder of Denver's first entertainment hall, the Apollo, second from left, once said he found more gold sweeping up after dances than he ever could prospecting. *Colorado Historical Society.*

Within a week of Auraria's birth, a rival company of prospectors from Leavenworth and Lecompton, Kansas Territory, arrived and at the urging of their leader, William Larimer, an experienced town promoter, organized Denver City, across the creek. Larimer's party chose to honor a former governor of Kansas Territory, James W. Denver. Kansas Territory at that time included much of Colorado.

Auraria resident Libeus Barney reported to his hometown newspaper, the Bennington (Vermont) *Banner*, on October 4, 1859:

> . . . Being separated only by the dry bed of Cherry Creek, about twenty rods wide, the stranger arriving in town would imagine the two cities one; but a short acquaintance would undeceive him, for there exists between them a bitter spirit of rivalry; each striving with no little effort for the superiority, and, as a nursery of almost every vice, as a hotbed of an unprincipled and dangerous sporting fraternity, we most cheerfully concede to our neighbor the palm.

William N. Byers, whose *Rocky Mountain News* was established with the organization of the rival towns, sought to remain evenhanded in the competition. He erected the building housing his print shop on stilts in the middle of Cherry Creek. Unfortunately an 1864 flood destroyed this Solomon-like monument. The *Rocky Mountain News* continues in existence, presumably out of reach of flood waters, at 400 West Colfax street in Denver.

The two towns finally merged on April 5, 1860.

Denver's Basilica

A Gothic-style cathedral, described by one Denver newspaper at its dedication in 1912 as Denver's "most beautiful church," stands two miles east of **Exit 210.** Elevated by Rome in 1979 to the status of minor basilica, the church of the Immaculate Conception is one of only twenty-nine Roman Catholic basilicas in the U.S.

In his nearly forty years as rector, a crusty Irish-American priest named Hugh L. McMenamin masterminded the building and funding of the twin-spired edifice on the corner of Logan and Colfax avenue, a block from Colorado's capitol. Father Mac tapped the pockets of many of Denver's Irish-Catholic mining and merchandising magnates, such as Dennis Sheedy of the Denver Dry, J.J. Brown, husband of the famous "Unsinkable" Molly, John K. Mullen, for whom Catholic Mullen High School is named. He also collected "pew rent" of the less affluent at the rate of twenty-five cents for adults and ten cents for children.

Father Mac made his presence felt in the secular world as well, according to Professor Thomas Noel of the University of Colorado in Denver. "A dignified, wiry man rushing about in his flowing purple robes and long white hair [he was made a prelate in 1933], he became a favorite Denver character, noted for pornography raids, storming into the nearby State Capitol to denounce the Ku Klux Klan, his avid support of the Denver Symphony Orchestra. . ."

For his efforts the 1,500-capacity Basilica is now listed on the National Register of Historic Places, noted especially for seventy-five stained glass windows crafted at the Royal Bavarian Art Institute in Munich, Austria.

Camp Weld

Two miles south, on the east bank of the South Platte River near **Exit 210**, lies the site of Camp Weld, a Civil War military post that was the staging installation for Colorado volunteer units serving in Union forces. The camp was named for Colorado Territory's first secretary of state, Lewis Ledyard Weld, a graduate of Yale Law School. Ironically, despairing at the anarchy in this gold camp community, Weld was one of eight Denver attorneys who foresook the practice of law (see *U.S. 285* itinerary).

As territorial secretary Weld shared a suite of three rooms above the New York Store at what is now Larimer and

Fourteenth streets with the territorial governor, William Gilpin. Both were appointed by President Abraham Lincoln on March 22, 1861. Regrettably, the spirit of legal improvisation that had pervaded the community managed also to filter into the second story of the New York Store. Gilpin was sacked as governor for having written unauthorized drafts on the U.S. Treasury to pay for the construction of Camp Weld and for the outfitting of Colorado's Union troops. John Evans of Illinois was named to replace Gilpin on March 24, 1862.

In 1863 Weld went east to volunteer for service in the Union army. Specifically requesting an assignment with Negro units, Weld was commissioned a captain with the 7th Regiment of U.S. Colored Troops. He eventually attained the grade of lieutenant colonel while serving with the 41st Colored Infantry. A month later, in January 1865, he succumbed to a fever that had resulted from exposure to the elements on the battlefield at Appomattox.

Overland Tourist Park

When the automobile came of age, the City of Denver purchased Overland Park on the east bank of the South Platte River, two miles west of **Exit 205** (University Boulevard). In 1921 it was converted for the use of what then were called "gypsy motorists"—tourists. The Exposition Building at the park was remodeled to provide a grocery, a soda fountain, and a laundry. By 1925, seventy-six thousand motorists had taken advantage of this camp and two others later set up by the city.

The "Father of Sugar Beet Growing"

Along the same stretch of the South Platte River, approximately three miles west of **Exit 203**, a farmer from Ottawa, Illinois, established himself in the summer of 1860 as the "father of sugar beet growing" in Colorado. Peter Magnes brought with him fruit trees, currant bushes, grape vines, and "seeds of all kinds," but the crop that seemed to thrive in

A piedmont farmer prepares his sugar beet field for the 1908 growing season. The region's first sugar mill began operations in Loveland in 1901. *Boulder Historical Society.*

the soil of his South Platte bottom land was the sugar beet, itself only lately introduced from Europe.

The *Rocky Mountain News* was so impressed with Magnes's results that the editor entoned in the November 3, 1866, edition:

The past seasons have demonstrated that the soil of Colorado has no superior in the world for producing the sugar beet. It is a singular fact that there are no manufactories for making sugar from this vegetable, on this side of the Atlantic, notwithstanding the superior excellence of the product and great demand for it. We are of the opinion that its manufacture here would prove a good paying investment, besides saving to the country a large amount of the capital that now goes east for the purchase of this staple.

Within sixty years, there were seventeen "manufactories" for sugar in Colorado.

The Hungate Massacre

At midday on June 15, 1864, a tragic event occurred eighteen miles east of **Exit 195**. Its consequences would affect residents of Colorado for years to come.

Ward Hungate and his hired hand saw smoke that day rising from the vicinity of the cabin and buildings of the ranch Hungate managed for Isaac P. Van Wormer on Running Creek (now Boxelder Creek). Suspecting an Indian attack, Hungate raced to aid his wife and two daughters. The hired hand, fearing the same thing, fled to Denver.

Alerted to the danger but unable to persuade others to accompany him to his ranch, Isaac Van Wormer drove out alone in a horse and buggy. He found the building razed and Hungate's body nearby, mutilated and punctured with eighty bullet wounds. After a lengthy search Van Wormer finally found the bodies of Mrs. Hungate and her children in the ranch well.

Van Wormer returned with the bodies to Denver where, according to the Denver *Commonwealth*, they were to be put on display. The atrocity so aroused the settlers that Governor John Evans felt the need to mobilize a militia to patrol the countryside. The ensuing chain of events, culminating five months later in the Sand Creek massacre (see *U.S. 50* itinerary), is known now as the Indian Wars of 1864-65 (see I-25N and I-76 itineraries).

Parker

Five or so miles south of the site of the Hungate killings, the old Smoky Hill Trail crossed Running Creek on its way to Twenty-Mile House at Parker. (Parker Road joins I-25 at **Exit 193**.) At Parker, travelers and stagecoaches on the so-called Starvation Trail (see I-70 itinerary) struck Cherry Creek and the last twenty-mile leg of a six-hundred-mile trek that had begun in Leavenworth, Kansas.

Reporting to his Vermont readers, Libeus Barney said in May 1859; "Reports come in thick and fast of the suffering and starvation of the Smoky Hill emigrants. I have conversed with a number of men who tell me they have lived for two weeks on no other sustenance but prickly pears; and others tell of living for days on a dead ox found by the road-side in an advanced stage of decomposition and without water for two or three days in succession."

And Horace Greeley told his New York audience at about the same time: ". . . The very mothers who bore them would hardly recognize their sons now toiling across the Plains, and straggling into [Denver] hideously hirsute, recklessly ragged, barefoot, sun-brown, dust-covered. . . ."

1st U.S. Forest Ranger

The nation's first U.S. forest ranger was a cowboy, born and reared on a ranch west of Sedalia, six miles northwest of **Exit 183**. Forestry, however, may have been in his blood, for William Richard "Billy" Kreutzer was the son of a German immigrant who had been trained as a tree nurseryman and whose father was a forester in Bavaria.

Congress in 1891 had authorized the president to set aside "timber land reserves" across the country. Restricting use of public lands, however, was a sore point at the time, particularly in the West. The controversy kept congress from appropriating funds to implement the forest reserve act until 1897.

Kreutzer won his appointment from Colonel W.T.S. May, a Civil War veteran and Denver attorney who was appointed Forestry Superintendent of Colorado under the act by President William McKinley.

". . . The U.S. Forest Reserves were in charge of the General Land Office [of the Interior Department], which knew nothing about forestry," wrote Gifford Pinchot, the nation's first Chief Forester when the U.S. Forest Service was established in 1905, to the Department of Agriculture. "[It's] fundamental purpose was to turn all public resources

in its charge over to private ownership as fast as possible
. . . Into this Land Office mismanagement . . . by political
appointees . . . came Bill Kreutzer, a youngster of twenty,
result, intelligent, enterprising, with a real interest in the
forests and the mountains, and a genuine determination to
do the right thing."

Kreutzer's first assignment was to ride the range of the
Plum Creek Timber Reserve, which included the family
ranch. He was to put out forest fires in an area that spread
from the Arkansas–South Platte divide to the South Platte
river west of Denver. As itinerant fire warden, he carried
a pup tent, blanket roll, a Dutch oven, two frying pans,
coffee pot, beans, flour, and bacon.

Kreutzer found that he faced three primary problems in
trying to do his job of forest management:

—To persuade those who lived and worked in the forests
to cooperate in putting out fires. Westerners of the time
viewed forest fires as a natural phenomenon, at least until
it directly threatened their property.

—To halt unauthorized timber cutting in the reserves.
Wood, like water, was there to be used. Sometimes some
freelancing entrepreneurs would cut reserve trees into railroad ties and sell them to the railroads that operated between Colorado Springs and Denver.

—To convince ranchers to submit to government management of livestock grazing on public lands. As the cattle and
sheep industries burgeoned in the West, popular forest
meadows suffered severely from overgrazing. The Forest
Service sought to get ranchers to apply for grazing permits,
at modest or even no fees, to ensure that herds were rotated
among grazing areas, so that depleted grass lands could
recover.

Local resistance to this enforced change of habit provided
Kreutzer with numerous adventures in his forty-one-year
career. From Plum Creek to his other early-day assignments
in Battlement Mesa and Gunnison national forests, Kreutzer
was always armed when he rode his circuit.

Castle Rock

In early July 1820, the expedition of Maj. Stephen H. Long left the valley of the South Platte and started to climb the divide along the Rampart Range that separates the waters of the Platte from those of the Arkansas River to the south. Scientist Edwin James, the chronicler of the expedition, commented on the then utterly vacant terrain near **Exit 182**: "In the vallies, toward the east, were many lofty insular hills with perpendicular sides and level table-like summits. . . . One . . . was called the Castle rock, on account of its striking resemblance to a work of art. It has columns, and porticoes, and arches, and, when seen from a distance, has an astonishingly regular and artificial appearance."

Fifty years later Silas W. Madge, whose ranch lay two miles south of "the Castle rock," took a little closer look at the stone in the vicinity. He sent a sample to Denver to be assayed. The assayer found no precious metals, but he observed that it was "good building stone." By coincidence the Denver & Rio Grande Railroad had lately passed through Castle Rock on its way to Colorado Springs. At Madge's prompting they installed a siding, duly dubbed "Douglass." By 1873 Madge's newly opened quarry had produced six hundred tons of building stone. A year later the quantity had risen to three thousand tons. By 1870 the local press had proclaimed the erstwhile rancher to be the "Father of the Lava Stone Industry."

An unabashed booster of the hometown operation, the Castle Rock *Record Journal* on February 8, 1888, made this rather ungracious criticism of another Front Range city: "The stone of the west wing of the capitol building at Lincoln, Nebraska, is crumbling, and the building is sinking. It is unnecessary to say that the building was not constructed of stone from the Castle Rock quarries. It was a Ft. Collins product."

Castle Rock "lava stone" can be found in the older portions of Denver's Union Station (**Exit 212**) and the old Den-

ver City Hall (**Exit 210**), as well as some buildings on the
campus of Colorado College in Colorado Springs.

Isabella Bird

Fortyish Isabella Bird, an upperclass Englishwoman (see
U.S. 36 itinerary), rode her horse from Denver up this
route one snowy day in late October 1873. As night drew
on, she remained as she had been when she left Denver—
alone. She looked for a place to stay. Later she wrote to
her sister in England: "You must understand that in Colorado travel, unless on the main road and in the larger settlements, there are neither hotels nor taverns, and that it
is the custom of the settlers to receive travellers, charging
them at the usual hotel rate. . ."

She had a letter of introduction to John D. Perry, whose
ranch lay some six miles west of **Exit 172**. Perry, himself a
recent "settler" from St. Louis, was the president of the
Kansas Pacific Railroad, whose line from Kansas City to
Denver had been completed just three years earlier (see
I-70E itinerary).

"Mr. Perry was away, but his daughter, a very bright-
looking, elegantly dressed girl, invited me to dine and remain. They had stewed venison and various luxuries on the
table, which was tasteful and refined, and an adroit, col-
oured table-maid waited, one of the five attached negro
servants who had been their slaves before the [Civil] war."

A mere five years earlier the environment was not quite
so genteel. Ardis Webb recounts the reminiscence of a
young girl who lived through an 1868 Indian attack on
homesteaders near what is now Perry Park: ". . . The
women laid down in the wagon and an Indian fighter that
lived with them kept shooting every time an Indian got
close enough. One man held the lines [of the team of horses]
and the other whipped [them] with a black snake whip.
The man in the wagon kept shooting when the Indians got
in shooting distance. I saw this man the next day. He wore
a black coat and a wide brim black hat. He had several

holes in his coat, top of sleeves and top of shoulders and several in his hat and not one bullet had drawn blood."

Palmer Lake

The actual divide is not surmounted on I-25 until one reaches the El Paso County line at **Exit 163**. Two and one-half miles west and a half-mile south of this exit is Palmer Lake, originally known as Divide Lake, a turn-of-the-century resort town whose current name memorializes the celebrated founder of the D&RG Railroad, Gen. William Jackson Palmer.

Denver-Palmer Lake Bicycle Path

When the bicycle era came to Denver in the 1890s, local enthusiasts, many of them members of the League of American Wheelmen, pressed for the construction of a ten-foot-wide bicycle path from Denver to Palmer Lake, a distance of fifty miles. Palmer Lake, moreover, sits about eighteen hundred feet higher than Denver. Century Runs, mass races of twice that distance, were the fashion in the halcyon Gay Nineties, when "democracy held sway, and class distinctions bowed before the sportsman's ability."

Unfortunately, the diversion of wheelmen and wheelwomen, whatever their abilities, peaked about the time the automobile was introduced at the turn of the century. Almost another hundred years would pass before the bicycle again became a popular sporting vehicle.

Bijou Creek

Cherry Creek heads about eight miles east of Monument, **Exit 161**, and ten miles beyond that lies the head of West Bijou Creek. Luke Tierney, a member of the 1858 Leavenworth prospecting party who became a journalist, reported in *History of the Gold Discoveries on the South Platte* that the Leavenworth party had made a startling observation when it passed through this section: ". . . Near a rivulet called Bijou's creek . . . was a pond, about thirty feet in diameter, densely thronged with a singular fish known as the Torpedo. It is of a greyish color, has four feet like an alligator, four talons or fingers on the two fore feet, and five on the hinder ones, with one continued fin from tip to tip. Its bite is said to be incurable."

"Bijou" was the nickname of Joseph Bissonette, who was Stephen H. Long's guide in 1820. The Torpedo most likely is the prairie cousin of the Loch Ness monster. (The creature may not be imaginary. Colorado wildlife official Robin Knox indicates that a mutant form of tiger salamander, known as the axototl, seems to fit Tierney's somewhat lurid description. Found in ponds throughout the region, the axototl is usually eight to twelve inches in length, but, like the salamander, it is nonvenomous.)

Monument

The town of Monument had its origin in 1874 when it was platted by the D&RG's local station agent, Henry Limbach, known as "Dutch Henry," and Gen. Charles Adams. An absentee owner, Adams had settled in Manitou Springs, outside of Colorado Springs, following a varied and colorful career. A youth when he arrived in the United States from Germany, Adams joined the Union army and, after the Civil War, served as a cavalryman during the Indian wars. Named a brigadier general of the Colorado militia, he served also as an Indian agent, a special agent of the U.S. Postal Service, and finally, a diplomatic minister to Bolivia.

In 1879, in a tense moment during hostilities with the Ute Indians in western Colorado, Adams made a dangerous trip into Ute country to negotiate the release of some white hostages (see *Colorado 13* itinerary).

The First Narrow-Gauge Railways

The D&RG trains that ran from Denver down the foothills and into the mountains (see *U.S. 160* and *U.S. 50* itineraries) were the first narrow-gauge railways in the West. Specifically designed to General Palmer's specifications by the Baldwin Locomotive Works of Philadelphia, the engines—each of the early ones named for an Indian chief—were remarkably small and lightweight but powerful. One, the Montezuma, was only thirty-five feet four inches long and nine feet nine inches to the top of its smokestack, weighing a mere twelve and one half tons.

"She was perfectly balanced, not top heavy, and took the curves like a piece of tangent track," said William Walk, the Montezuma's engineer. "Yet she never so much as spilled a drop of water from a glass set in any of the windows of the cab."

Except once, perhaps. Shortly after the engine was put into service on July 3, 1871, it was standing at a siding near Monument when one of those hurricane-strength chinook winds known to the Colorado Front Range whistled down from the mountains and blew the Montezuma from the track.

U.S. Air Force Academy

Set up against the foothills of the Rampart Range west of Exit 156 is an institution of relatively recent history, the United States Air Force Academy. The counterpart of much older service academies maintained by the army and the navy in the east, the Air Force Academy was authorized by Congress in 1954. The first class of cadets matriculated at Lowry Air Force Base in Denver (see I-70 itinerary) the following year. Construction of facilities at the 17,900-acre site was not completed until August 1958. Approximately twenty-five hundred cadets constitute the student body.

Appropriate to their lofty calling, the academy's cadets selected the falcon as their mascot, which as it turns out, fits neatly into the ecology of the Arkansas-South Platte divide. Native to this region is a small brown and white prairie falcon, or hawk, whose local prominence has given name to the town of Falcon, only thirteen miles east of the academy.

Nordrach Ranch Sanitarium

In the northeast section of Colorado Springs, at 2525 North Chelton Road, a private home occupies a site that in the first decade of the twentieth century contributed to medical history. Originally the location of the mansion of a Colorado Springs banker, it became the headquarters of a novel sanitarium for treatment of victims of tuberculosis, the Nordrach Ranch.

From its early settlement, of course, the Colorado Front Range had been touted as a haven for the unhealthy. Numerous celebrated individuals came here for a cure of some sort, among them the inventor of the Stanley Steamer (see *U.S. 34* itinerary). The crisp, clear air was reputed to be especially beneficial for treatment of lung diseases. In the period following the founding of Colorado Springs in 1871, consumptives flocked to the city until, by 1900, an estimated 60 percent of the population comprised migrants in search of a cure.

Eventually alarmed that their town had become a well of contagion, city fathers obliged the ill to move beyond the city's limits. The Nordrach Ranch came into being at what was then the city's outskirts under the direction of an innovative young physician named John E. White. Dr. White adopted a form of treatment that involved persistent overfeeding and prolonged exposure to fresh, even winter air. Patients were required to limit their shelter, winter and summer, to specifically constructed canvas tents. "He filled us so full of food and froze us so badly," said one survivor, "that it scared the hell out of the bacilli, and we were cured!"

A 1907 fire and White's departure in 1910 combined with an especially severe December in 1913 to force the sanitarium's closure.

Jimmy's Camp

The site of an early-day murder became a much-frequented overnight stopping place for travelers passing across the high plains divide. Called Jimmy's Camp, the site recalls a deed whose circumstances are lost in uncertainty.

An 1842 traveler, Rufus B. Sage, noted that the murder took place "several years since." The famous author of *The Oregon Trail*, Francis Parkman, was reminded of it in 1846, as were the Fifty-Niners who came to the gold fields over the Arkansas trails. The site lies in a sheltered glen watered by a spring about ten miles east of **Exit 142**, midway between *U.S. 24* and *Colorado 94*.

The victim was an Indian trader of small stature and Irish ancestry. His last name has been variously reported as Daugherty, Dockerty, and Boyer, his first name Jim, Jimmy, and Jamie.

Jimmy annually brought a wagonload of trade goods to this site from some fort on the Arkansas, probably Bent's Old Fort (see *U.S. 50* itinerary), and the Indians came to barter their furs and robes for what he had to offer, in the manner of the era.

"He came once too often," said one old-timer in an 1882 reminiscence. "On this occasion he scarcely built his fire ere a party of six guerrillas from Old Mexico pounced upon him and murdered him, and then carried away his valuable goods. The Indians, coming into camp soon after and finding him murdered, pursued the murderers, and on overtaking them, avenged his death by hanging them by their toes to the limbs of trees. These are matters of history, as related to the writer by old Jim Beckwourth." (For the story of Jim Beckwourth's violent end see *U.S. 285* itinerary).

An Eccentric Genius

One night in 1899 electricity flashed from a copper ball on a tower three hundred feet above a long low building that sat behind a high fence with signs warning "Keep Out! Great Danger!" The site then lay in what was a remote area of Colorado Springs about 1.8 miles east of today's **Exit 142**. As an eerie violet light glowed around the structure, there was a loud thunder-like clap. Colorado Springs was plunged into darkness.

Inside the building a lank man with piercing grey eyes was dressed in evening clothes and rubber boots. He was furious that the city power company had turned off his electricity, for he was in the midst of a dramatic electrical experiment. In fact, however, his experiment had blown out the city's electrical generators.

The "mad scientist" was a forty-three-year-old native of Croatia named Nikola Tesla. He had already developed a method for producing alternating current whose principle remains in use today (see *Colorado 62-145* itinerary). Beyond question, eccentric Tesla was, nonetheless, a real genius. He anticipated the development of radio and television and was among the first to predict radio communication with beings on other planets. So important were his inventions and discoveries in the field of electricity, he was slated to share the 1912 Nobel Prize for physics with Thomas A. Edison. Tesla, however, disdained sharing the prize with anyone. He had worked briefly with Edison early in his career and had developed a dislike for him.

An 1884 immigrant to the United States, Tesla worked in New York until 1899, when, backed by John Jacob Astor and other magnates, he elected to build a laboratory near Colorado Springs to continue his experiments with a sole assistant, Kolman Czito. The lab site today is a quiet urban neighborhood on North Foote avenue two blocks east of the Colorado School for the Deaf & Blind.

He was given free electricity by the Colorado Springs electric company until he burned out their facilities. Tesla left Colorado to return east before a year was out. He died in New York in 1943 at the age of 86. A plaque in Tesla's memory has been erected by the city in Memorial Park on Pikes Peak avenue near the intersection of North Foote.

Lon Chaney Theater

Just to the west of the site of Tesla laboratory is the Colorado School for the Deaf & Blind. It is the modern successor of the Colorado Institute for Education of Deaf

Mutes, which was founded in 1874 by a couple who had raised three deaf mute children, Jonathan and Mary Kennedy. Their daughter, in turn, married someone with a similar disability. On April 1, 1883, the couple gave birth to a son who was to become a Hollywood legend. Down Pikes Peak avenue five blocks west of the School for the Deaf & Blind, on Carpenter at Boulder Avenue, the city of Colorado Springs honors its native son with the Lon Chaney Theater in the city auditorium.

Chaney left Colorado Springs at the age of 19 to tour with an opera company. Later in Hollywood he became acclaimed for his skill as a makeup artist as well as an actor. *Encyclopedia Brittanica* commissioned him to write the section on theater makeup in their fourteenth edition.

Twenty years after Chaney had left home, his parents would not have recognized him as he starred as the original Quasimodo in the 1923 movie, *The Hunchback of Notre Dame.* Elaborate disguise also figured in his role as the phantom in the 1925 *Phantom of the Opera.* He was known as the "man of a thousand faces."

Chaney died on Aug. 26, 1930, of lung cancer. He was 47.

America's 1st Union

East of the Colorado School for the Deaf & Blind at Pikes Peak and Union is the century-old Union Printers Home. Established in 1892 by the country's oldest trade union, the International Typographical Union, the home cares for nearly 150 aged or infirm printers. Like the Nordrach Ranch Sanatorium, the Printers Home was built in Colorado to treat tuberculosis, an occupational hazard for printers.

The ITU itself was organized in 1852 as the nation's first trade union. An early aim of the organization was to win protection of its members from environmental hazards associated with the trade.

"Conditions were very, very bad for printers," one union official told the *Rocky Mountain News.* "Tuberculosis was rampant. We worked with hot lead type, and the fumes

from those leads damaged people's lungs and led to tuberculosis."

Colorado Springs was headquarters for the ITU's eighty
thousand members and 491 locals until January 1, 1987,
when the ITU was merged with the Communications Workers of America, whose headquarters are in Washington,
D.C.

The Printers Home remains on a two-hundred-acre park
overlooking the city. Until the merger with the CWA, ITU
members were assessed six dollars annually for its support.
The home is now funded precariously by investments.

Fountain

The city of Fountain, **Exit 128**, takes its name from the
creek but owes its existence to the railroad, although not in
the same way as such "railroad towns" as Colorado Springs,
which were creations of railroad interests. Fountain was
settled in 1870, nearly two years before the D&RG Railroad
passed through on its way to Pueblo. In 1888, a freight car
loaded with powder blew up and leveled the buildings in the
community. Compensation paid by the D&RG enabled the
town to rebuild.

I-25 South
The Mexican Mountain Trails
Pueblo to Raton Pass (100 miles)

Fountain Creek

The mouth of Fountain Creek, three-quarters of a mile east of **Exit 98**, served as a crossroads for frontier travelers from the earliest days of the Santa Fe trade, following Mexican independence in 1821. It offered the essential elements of wood, water and forage. Travelers from Santa Fe and Taos on their way to Fort Laramie on the North Platte passed this way along the eastern face of the Rockies over what was known as the Trappers' Trail. Travelers coming up the Arkansas valley turned north at Fountain Creek on their way to the forts along the South Platte River (see I-25N itinerary).

As a stopping place on the Taos Trail, it offered a rugged but shorter route between the Arkansas and New Mexican trading centers, eliminating some miles from the Santa Fe wagon route that turned south from Bent's Old Fort to cross Raton Pass and skirted the southern end of the Sangre de Cristo mountains to approach Santa Fe from the south.

Not surprisingly, the Fountain Creek site was a natural one for a fort. The first to be built here was the rudimentary breastwork thrown up by Zebulon Pike and his comrades in 1806. The next was a more substantial structure erected by one of the pioneers of the Santa Fe Trail, Jacob Fowler, in 1821.

Several American traders, striking out on their own after leaving the employ of William Bent, moved up here to build a fort in 1842. This fort was still in existence on Christmas Day, 1854, when Chief Tierra Blanca brought a band of his Mohuache Utes to the post and feigning friendship, gained entry to the place. They killed most of the seventeen inhabitants and kidnapped a woman and her two sons. One fatally wounded victim, whose jaw was shattered in the

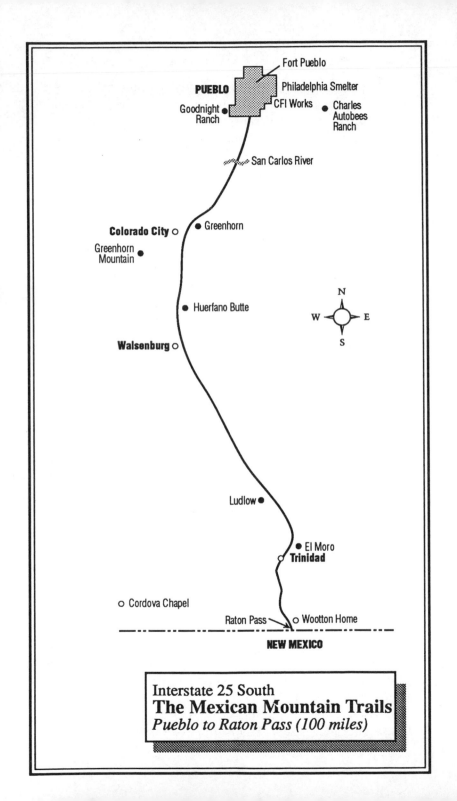

Fort Pueblo

PUEBLO

Philadelphia Smelter

Goodnight
Ranch

CFI Works

Charles
Autobees
Ranch

San Carlos River

Colorado City ○ ● Greenhorn

Greenhorn
Mountain ●

● Huerfano Butte

Walsenburg ○

N
W ○ E
S

Ludlow ●

● El Moro
○ Trinidad

○ Cordova Chapel

Raton Pass ○ Wootton Home

NEW MEXICO

Interstate 25 South
The Mexican Mountain Trails
Pueblo to Raton Pass (100 miles)

melee, managed through hand signals to inform rescuers from the Marcelino Baca ranch, two miles down the Arkansas River, of what had transpired.

Gen. John Garland, the military commander of the New Mexico district for whom Fort Garland was eventually named (see *U.S. 160* itinerary), ordered his troops into the field against Tierra Blanca's band. A contingent under command of Col. Thomas T. Fauntleroy, commandant of Fort Union in New Mexico, tracked down the Utes and rescued the kidnapped youths. The woman was killed. The rescuing contingent included Kit Carson and a company of volunteers under Lt. Col. Ceran St. Vrain, the Bent brothers' partner.

Pueblo

Four years later, following the reported discovery of gold on Front Range streams (see I-25N itinerary), the town of Fountain City was established on the east bank of the creek, comprising at its highpoint about thirty log and adobe cabins. In 1859 a rival town was laid out on the west side of the creek, mimicking, it seemed, the experience of Auraria and Denver City to the north. Originally called Independence, this new settlement in time acquired the name Pueblo, as the 1842 fort had been designated. Pueblo soon became the preferred site and residents of Fountain City abandoned their location for lots on the Pueblo side.

Rocky Canon Ranch

In 1869, one of the West's earliest and greatest cattlemen decided to locate a ranch across the Arkansas from the Pueblo settlement, about three miles west of **Exit 97B**. Charles Goodnight, native of Illinois and transplanted Texan, was already the trailblazer for the huge cattle drives that were bringing Texas cattle north across the high plains to customers from New Mexico to Montana—prospectors, military installations, Indian reservations.

He had started just after the Civil War from his home in Cross Timbers, Texas. His route was circuitous, to avoid the troublesome Kiowas and Comanches in northwest Texas: it followed the abandoned Overland Stage route southwest across the so-called staked plains (*el llano estacado*) to the Pecos River and thence north over Raton Pass to Denver and eventually Cheyenne.

The first drive left Cross Timbers on June 6, 1866, under the direction of Goodnight and his partner, Oliver Loving, a veteran drover. The first Goodnight-Loving trail herd was sold to John Wesley Iliff in Denver for $12,000. It was the purchase that launched Iliff's career as the Cattle King of the West (see I-76 itinerary). In 1868 Goodnight delivered $40,000 worth of cattle from Bosque Grande, New Mexico, to Cheyenne at Iliff's request.

Goodnight in 1870 brought his bride to his newly established residence, Rocky Canon Ranch, across from Pueblo. He built a huge stone barn that was still standing a century later and a stone corral that survived almost as long. He also brought in apple seedlings for the region's first orchard and dug an irrigation canal that watered the grasses for his three thousand cattle.

When the land development subsidiary of the Denver & Rio Grande Railroad, Central Colorado Improvement Co., arrived in 1872 to begin South Pueblo, Goodnight invested heavily. The financial panic of 1873 hurt him, however, and he was forced to sell a parcel of land in South Pueblo to meet his mounting debts. Two years later, when that same parcel was sold again to become the site of today's Colorado Fuel & Iron Company's steel mill, **Milepost 96**, it commanded more than twelve times what Goodnight had received.

Goodnight returned to the business he knew best—cattle driving. He sold his Rocky Canon Ranch in 1875 and, two years later, left Colorado altogether on another pioneering venture. Financed by Irish-born, Denver-based stockbroker John Adair, Goodnight drove a herd of blooded bulls from Pueblo to the Texas panhandle to launch a huge ranching operation at Palo Duro Canyon. This enterprise would set the pattern for others, such as the Prairie Cattle Company (see *U.S. 50* itinerary).

Philadelphia Smelting and Refining Company

A foreign-born peddler, Meyer Guggenheim, defied the conventional belief that luck determined fortunes to be made in Colorado. Dogged diligence made him and his seven sons into millionaires. A keystone of his fortune was located in Pueblo, bearing the unlikely name of Philadelphia Smelting and Refining Company.

Guggenheim, son of a tailor in the Swiss ghetto town of Lengnau, came to the United States with his father in 1849. Settling in Philadelphia, Meyer sold notions and lotions door to door in the mining communities of Pennsylvania. Devising innovations that improved sales of his products, Guggenheim prospered to the point of becoming a manufacturer and importer of Swiss machine-made lace.

A cash-short acquaintance from Philadelphia persuaded Guggenheim in 1879 to buy a half-interest in the A.Y. and Minnie silver mines in far-off Leadville, Colo. Already producing modestly, the mines showed even greater promise because of their proximity in California Gulch to the bonanza Little Pittsburg mine. Unfortunately, no sooner had Guggenheim bought into the venture than the mines became flooded, requiring a further investment in pumps.

Not one to take things for granted, Guggenheim visited the mine before funding the purchase of pumps. Within months of their installation, however, the A.Y. mine alone was producing $200 to 400 in silver daily, plus the lead that accompanied it. In time these mines also struck a bonanza lode (see *U.S. 24W* itinerary).

The price mine operators were able to get for their ore depended considerably on what smelter operators chose to pay for the ore, or charge for their services. So the astute Meyer Guggenheim seized an opportunity in 1886 to integrate his operations. He bought a share of the Globe smelter, which was operating at the time on a site just north of Denver.

Within two years the wisdom of that move proved itself so emphatically that Guggenheim was prepared to build the world's biggest smelter. Surveying prospective sites,

Guggenheim and his seven sons chose Pueblo for its access to coal, coke, and lime, all essential to smelting. There were in this period two other smelters at the mouth of Fountain Creek.

In a classic exhibition of commercial coquetry, the Guggenheims whetted the city's enthusiasm for the project to such an extent that Pueblo provided land for the plant without cost, put up a $25,000 bonus (of which Governor Alva Adams, then a Pueblan, kicked in $500 from his own pocket) and suspended taxes on the new business for its first ten years of operation. The plant site provided was due east of **Exit 97A**, north of the current CF&I plant.

Overcoming construction delays, cost overruns, and a decline in silver prices, the Philadelphia Smelter and Refining Company's plant went into successful operation in 1889. Shortly after the plant got under way, workers went on strike to demand a reduction in the workday from twelve to eight hours. After holding out for two months they lost. Guggenheim had granted without quibble, however, an earlier demand by furnace workers for shorter hours in the heat of summer.

The Guggenheims gained favor with labor in 1899 when they refused to join the Colorado-based national smelter trust, American Smelting and Refining Company, which sought to close down a number of smelters due to a sharp decline in the silver and metals markets. Outmaneuvering their rivals, the Guggenheims forced an amalgamation of their firm with the trust on terms that left them in control of the entire operation. By this time, moreover, the Guggenheims were world-class mining magnates.

"Topers' Trail"

His name has been spelled almost as many different ways as there were persons to write about him. And there was much to write about his long and turbulent life. Charles Autobees's last thirty years, however, were spent in relative tranquility about eighteen miles east of **Milepost 95**, where, in 1853, he settled down to the humdrum life of frontier ranching near the mouth of the Huerfano River.

Born in 1812 in St. Louis of ambiguous parentage, Autobees began his career as a trapper in the Oregon Territory at the headwaters of the Missouri and Columbia rivers. There, in a couple of close scrapes with the Blackfoot Indians he escaped with his life. He later fathered a child by a Flathead Indian woman. After three or four years, hoping to compound his fortunes, he decamped for Taos, New Mexico, with a group of other trappers. His plan to pack trade goods from Taos back to the upper Missouri was foiled, however, when someone stole his string of horses. Bidding his buddies farewell, Autobees hired on with Simeon Turley as a distributor of an infamous frontier rotgut known as "Taos Lightning."

Turley, an older man and himself a Missourian, had arrived in Taos in 1830. He started his distillery, twelve miles north of Taos on the Rio Hondo, the following year, using wheat and corn he grew and milled himself. He allowed his Taos Lightning to earn its reputation locally at first, but with Autobees's arrival, he began to pack it off to distant trading posts where resident hucksters bartered it to Indians for peltries and robes.

To these outposts Autobees would conduct caravans of donkeys carrying 4.5-gallon barrels of Turley's booze. In the winter of 1841-42 Autobees was reportedly as far north as Fort Lupton dispensing the stuff. There he was alleged to have witnessed the famous duel between Rube Herring and Henry Beer (see I25-N itinerary). If so, his rotgut may have lubricated the circumstances that led to it.

Autobees was so successful that Turley established a subsidiary depot. In 1842 he leased a portion of Fort Pueblo, a trading post just built by George Simpson, Joseph Doyle, and Alexander Barclay, former employes of William Bent. Autobees's caravan of casks thenceforth made the climb from Taos over Sangre de Cristo Pass and down the Huerfano Valley, **Milepost 59**, to Pueblo, the route already known as the Taos and Trappers' trails. Inexplicably, history has failed to credit Autobees with having established the Topers' Trail.

On occasion, after depositing his whiskey in the storerooms of Fort Pueblo, Autobees would load a wagon with the trade goods his previous delivery had gained and drive on across the prairies to Independence, Missouri, to sell them.

As Autobees's business prospered, he acquired, in 1837, another child, Mariano, in liaison with Serafina Abila. When, in 1842, Jose Maria was born, Autobees was persuaded to have the permanency of the relationship ratified by a Taos priest. Three more children were born to their union.

The birth of their fourth child, Manuella, in 1846, coincided with the hostilities of the Mexican War between the United States and the government that was Autobees's host in Taos. The war caused circumstances that resulted in the killing of Taos Lightning distiller Turley and the burning of his distillery and added another close scrape to Autobees's seemingly charmed life.

The angry mob of Indians and Mexicans who stormed into Taos on January 19, 1847, to kill Governor Charles Bent and other Americans identified with the occupying forces went on to put Turley's distillery under siege. The sole American to escape the Taos Massacre, Charles Towne, had managed to warn Turley before racing on to Santa Fe. At the time of the attack Autobees fortuitously was himself enroute to Santa Fe. He later joined a company of volunteers that helped put down the rebellion.

Autobees chose that summer to visit the valley of the St. Charles River, **Milepost 87**, with the aim of starting a farm and ranch.

Vigil–St. Vrain Grant

The independence of Texas in 1836 caused a dispute over sovereignty in the region that now comprises Colorado south of the Arkansas River. The Republic of Texas claimed it but was unable to wrest control from the Republic of

Mexico. As sentiment grew to admit Texas to the Union as a state, New Mexico's governor, Manuel Armijo, began awarding large grants of Colorado land to American merchants in Santa Fe and Taos on condition that they develop settlements in these regions. Among those receiving a grant in 1843 were Ceran St. Vrain, partner of William and Charles Bent, and Cornelio Vigil, a resident of Taos. Vigil was later killed in the 1847 Taos Massacre.

The Vigil-St. Vrain grant was bounded on the northwest by the St. Charles River, on the north by the Arkansas River, and on the east and south by the Purgatoire and its headwaters. The Treaty of Guadalupe Hidalgo, which in 1848 ended the Mexican War and ceded much of today's southwest to the United States, acknowledged the property rights of Mexican citizens within the ceded territories.

One-sixth of the Vigil-St. Vrain grant was signed over to Charles Bent and his descendants, so the daughter of the deceased New Mexico governor, Estafana Bent, and her husband, Alexander "Zan" Hicklin, arrived in 1859 to take up five thousand acres. They erected their adobe home just east of **Exit 74** on the banks of the Greenhorn River.

In 1847, George Frederick Ruxton had passed through here. He wrote in one of his books about the West; "This valley will, I have no doubt, become one day a thriving settlement, the soil being exceedingly rich and admirably adapted to the growth of all kinds of grain." But such prosperity was not in the cards for the Hicklins.

Mismanagement and the early death of Zan Hicklin in 1874 left Estafana Bent Hicklin with several teenaged children, an unsure grasp of business matters, and some avaricious neighbors. Allegedly trying to jump the Hicklins' claim to the land, one neighbor provoked an encounter with Estafana's two sons, Alexander, Jr., 19, and Thomas, 16. Unarmed, Alexander was shot and killed, and Thomas was badly wounded. An effort to lynch the killer was thwarted, and he was eventually tried in Pueblo and imprisoned. Things did not improve for Estafana. She eventually lost her land and died in 1927, destitute.

The Greenhorn River

The Greenhorn River, **Milepost 73.5**, takes its name from an eighteenth century Comanche chief named "Cuerno Verde" by his Spanish protagonists. In 1779 the governor of New Mexico, Juan Bautista de Anza, pursued Cuerno Verde and his band to the foot of Greenhorn Mountain, eleven miles west of **Milepost 68**, where in the ensuing battle the now famous "Green Horn" fell.

The Taos Trail

The famous Taos Trail from Pueblo departs from I-25 at the Huerfano River, **Milepost 59.5**, to cross over Sangre de Cristo Pass into the San Luis valley (see *U.S. 160* itinerary) and then down the Rio Grande del Norte to the home of Turley's distillery and the great American trading fraternity of the mid-nineteenth century.

Huerfano County

The Huerfano River gets its name from lonely Huerfano Butte, east of **Milepost 59**. This landmark was named by an unknown Spanish traveler around 1800 and, within a generation, was regularly called "Huerfano" ("orphan") in Spanish reports. In 1861 Huerfano was the name given to one of the original seventeen counties marked off in newly created Colorado Territory. It covered the entire southeastern portion of the current state, embracing on three sides a large Indian reservation, which lay north of the Arkansas River in the heart of the high plains.

Walsenburg

Walsenburg, at **Exits 52** and **49**, began as a New Mexican settlement called Plaza de los Leones, "Plaza of the Lions," probably in honor of an early settler named Leon. With the arrival of some settlers of German ancestry, Plaza de los Leones was renamed Walsenburg after one of their number who was an early storekeeper in the community.

Ludlow

One of the tragedies of the twentieth century occurred scarcely one mile west of **Exit 27** at the coal-mining camp of Ludlow. It was another of those "massacres" that seem to dot the calendar of western history, only this time the Indians were not involved. The antagonists confronting one another on April 20, 1914, were the Colorado Fuel & Iron Company; coal mine operators under the financial control of eastern interests, which included John D. Rockefeller, Jr.; and the United Mine Workers Union, whose most celebrated official for the occasion was 71-year-old Mother Jones—Irish-born Mary Harris Jones.

Miners at Ludlow had gone out on strike on September 6, 1913, demanding, among several things, company recognition of the UMW. The company retaliated by forcing the miners' families from company-owned housing. To shelter those evicted against a threatening winter the UMW established a tent city a couple of miles from the town. Both company guards and strikers were armed. Resulting hostilities prompted Governor Elias M. Ammons to declare

State militia and company guards survey the tent camp of striking coal miners at Ludlow. *Colorado Historical Society.*

martial law in the region, enforcing it with Colorado National Guardsmen.

Stalemated, the strike persisted into the winter, provoking vacancies in the peace-keeping forces as a consequence of expired enlistments and desertions. Strikers claimed that the openings were filled by double-dipping company guards, paid both by the state and the company. Meanwhile, in defiance of Governor Ammons's ban on picketing, Mother Jones had organized a series of demonstrations involving miners' wives. On Ammons's orders she was deported from the region and eventually interned in a hospital. One of her protegees, Mary Thomas, a Ludlow wife, organized a march in Trinidad to demand Mother Jones's release. The mounted militia, sabres drawn, charged among the women, causing a number of injuries.

National publicity brought congressional hearings to Denver at which both John D. Rockefeller, Jr., and Mother Jones testified. Although Rockefeller professed willingness to concede most of the strikers' demands, he remained adamantly opposed to formal recognition of the UMW as the workers' official bargaining agent. Despite this, Mother Jones congratulated Rockefeller for his attitude, proclaiming him a badly misunderstood young man.

Conciliatory gestures in Denver, however, had little effect on the course of events in Ludlow, 185 miles away. Two hundred seventy-five tents housed about eight hundred miners and dependents in a compound that was surrounded by militiamen who, in at least one instance, had a machine gun mounted and trained on the encampment. On April 19 officials accosted camp leaders to demand the arrest of Louis Tikas, a Greek immigrant who was one of the strike leaders. Denied, they returned the next day and, in a confrontation whose origins are obscure, fired the machine gun into the tent city, killing Tikas and eighteen others. The clash caused a fire among the canvas shelters, resulting in the deaths of two women and eleven children. The encampment was razed. The outcry from this forced Governor Ammons to request the dispatch of federal troops.

Trinidad

Coal mining had become an important industry in the Trinidad region when the railroads arrived. The first was General Palmer's narrow gauge Denver & Rio Grande, which reached El Moro, three miles northeast of **Exit 15** on *Colorado 239*, in 1876. As he had in the case of Colorado Springs (in 1871) and South Pueblo (in 1872), General Palmer paused in his railroad-building to create a rival town to Trinidad—El Moro—through the subsidiary South Colorado Coal & Town Company. Coal mines were opened and coke ovens set up to provide industry and employment. The pause to regroup may have been the undoing of Palmer's long standing ambition to build his railroad from Denver to El Paso, Texas, and Mexico City.

The coal industry of Trinidad burgeoned with a second railroad. Santa Fe Railroad interests opened mines near Starkville, **Exit 11**. In 1900 the redoubtable smelting trust, American Smelting & Refining Company, also became a coal operator in the region.

A man who had figured prominently in the affairs of the Santa Fe, and in fact had a conspicuous if minor role in the Royal Gorge War, was the sheriff of Ford County (Dodge City), Kansas. Moonlighting from his Ford County duties, Bat Masterson had raced off on at least two occasions to bring armed goon squads to Pueblo and Canon City at the behest of Santa Fe Railroad officials (see *U.S. 50* itinerary).

Now that the Santa Fe had reconciled its interests with the Denver & Rio Grande, gaining rights to Raton Pass and conceding them to Royal Gorge and Leadville, Masterson left Dodge City and showed up in Trinidad in 1882 to accept the new mayor's nomination as city marshal.

In a year's tenure his most notable achievement was to block the extradition of John Henry "Doc" Holliday, D.D.S., to Arizona to stand trial for murder. The charge stemmed from a fray in which Holliday had participated with the notorious Wyatt Earp, a sequel to the famous shootout at the O.K. Corral in Tombstone. Masterson acted at the behest of Earp, his close friend, despite a personal antipathy toward the consumptive and reckless Holliday (see I-70 itinerary).

Cordova Chapel

Trinidad was founded by a New Mexican, Felipe Baca, who passed through the Purgatoire River valley in 1859 during a trip to bring trade goods from New Mexico to the mining camps around Denver. Baca encouraged family and friends to resettle in the valley.

Some twenty-six miles up the river another New Mexican clan headed by Jesus Maria Cordova settled somewhat later. Acting on the imperatives of his Roman Catholic culture, Cordova in 1878 built an imposing adobe chapel which still stands between the Colorado & Wyoming railroad line and Colorado 12. Dedicated to Our Lady of Mount Carmel, the building featured sixteen-inch adobe walls, twelve-inch ceiling timbers hewed from native lumber, and a floor of planking that was taken up periodically to inter deceased family members.

As a private chapel, the church was used mainly for funerals of family members and for a special celebration on July 16, the feast of Our Lady of Mount Carmel. Accompanied by guitar and violin, "a procession around the church was always held" on the eve of the feast, recalls one family member. "To light the way for the evening procession, pitch wood was fashioned into . . . luminaries . . . [and the Cordovas] furnished firecrackers for the celebration during the evening and day processions."

"In the winter time catechism classes for the younger [family members] were conducted [by] the older children . . . During the month of May all the people of the village . . . assembled . . . to pray the rosary . . . When hail storms approached[,] the tolling of the bell seemed to drive the storm away on many occasions . . . and the valley crops were saved."

The removable planking was eventually replaced by a permanent floor that sealed graves beneath the church. The plastered walls were also sealed with a permanent yellow stucco. The open eaves were closed as well, denying access to nesting pigeons, and the wooden roof was covered over with galvanized metal.

Uncle Dick Wootton

Yet another formidable figure in the history of the area was a man who might have been called "the Colossus of Raton Pass." Instead they called six-foot-four-inch, 240-pound Richens Lacy Wootton "Uncle Dick." For thirteen years, from 1865 until the Santa Fe Railroad arrived, Uncle Dick Wootton collected a toll for all the creatures that passed over the twenty-seven-mile road he had built through Raton Pass.

On one notable occasion he confronted Charlie Goodnight in Raton Pass as the Texas drover was trailing several thousand head of cattle from his New Mexico base camp to Denver. Wootton demanded ten cents a head. Goodnight refused, retreated, and eventually discovered a more accommodating pass for cattle, Trinchera Pass, at the head of Trinchera Creek, twenty-two miles east of I-25 on the Colorado-New Mexico border.

Born May 6, 1816, in Mecklenburg County, Virginia, Wootton at the age of twenty hired on with a Bent, St. Vrain wagon train headed down the Santa Fe Trail from Independence, Missouri. Under Ceran St. Vrain's instruction Wootton learned quickly. Within two years he had organized a company of seventeen free trappers for a hunting expedition into the Rockies. The next winter he put together another band that trekked to the headwaters of the Missouri, to the Columbia, down the west coast to Los Angeles, back up the Colorado River to Utah, and finally to Bent's Fort.

Under contract with Bent to supply buffalo meat to the fort, Wootton anticipated the 1842 settlement of Fort Pueblo. In 1840 he built a corral there to breed buffalo calves.

In January 1847, once again at Pueblo, Wootton joined a company of volunteers organized by Ceran St. Vrain to help put down the Taos rebellion. In 1854, at the time of the Fort Pueblo massacre, Wootton was ranching less than twenty miles downstream on the Arkansas River at the mouth of the Huerfano River in a joint venture with Joseph B. Doyle. Their ranch was spared by the Utes.

In late 1858 Wootton left Taos for the South Platte-Cherry Creek region, supposedly to trade with the resident Cheyennes and Arapahoes. Finding the argonauts of the early Cherry Creek gold rush instead, he stayed to set up the first store on the site, later adding a saloon, loan office and a hotel. In the loft of Wootton's cabin, on April 23, 1859, William N. Byers printed the first issue of the newspaper that would become the *Rocky Mountain News*.

In time, Wootton's Denver enterprises foundered and his second wife died in childbirth, so he moved to Pueblo where he farmed east of Fountain Creek. But disaster followed him there: an 1864 flood washed out his crop, his third wife died, and he lost a store due to local opposition to his sympathy with the secessionist South.

The Raton Pass toll road prospered, however, and Wootton was able to stay until 1878, when the Santa Fe Railroad tendered him a fifty-dollar-per-month pension in exchange for the use of his right-of-way.

Wootton died at age 77 in 1893, the year of the panic that devastated Colorado's silver-based economy.

US 36
Steaming with Stanleys
Denver to Estes Park (63 miles)

Samuel Hawken, Gun Maker

At the height of the gold rush, on June 30, 1859, a sixty-seven-year-old veteran of the War of 1812 showed up at the mouth of Cherry Creek. Why he chose to chance the hazardous journey across the prairies from his home in St. Louis no one knows. He had made his reputation as an artisan long before and had lived for thirty-five years in St. Louis. No one could have suspected him of wanderlust.

When he arrived, he set up shop and, in time, inserted this ad in the *Rocky Mountain News*:

"Gun Maker—S. Hawken, for the last thirty-seven years engaged in the manufacture of the Rocky Mountain rifle in St. Louis, would respectfully say to the citizens of Denver, Auraria, and his old mountain friends that he has established himself in the gun business on Ferry street between Fourth & Fifth, next door to Jones & Cartwrights, Auraria, and now prepared to manufacture his style of rifles to order. Repairing done on short notice."

Some of the most famous of the mountain men had indeed carried the Hawken rifle, among them Jim Bridger, and the weapon might easily be dubbed "the rifle that won the West." Samuel Hawken eventually retired on a farm near St. Louis and died at age ninety-two.

Broomfield

Broomfield, **Milepost 48**, became a stop in the early 1900s on David H. Moffat's Denver & Salt Lake Railroad. Known previously as Zang's Spur, named for a local rancher who

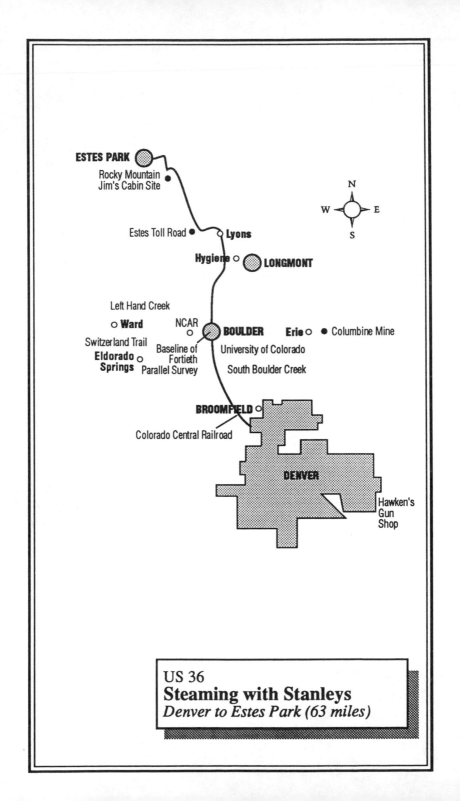

US 36
Steaming with Stanleys
Denver to Estes Park (63 miles)

had enjoyed the services of a rival railroad, Broomfield was renamed by D&SL officials who were inspired by a nearby field of broom corn.

Not an illicit crap game, but a group of oil field workers are shown in this early glass plate photo preparing dynamite for use in a wellhead. *Boulder Historical Society.*

Near **Milepost 46** the Colorado Central Railroad crossed U.S. 36 on its way, in 1872-74, to its railhead at Longmont (see I-25N). Passengers coming from Longmont south to Golden or Denver were asked to disembark in this vicinity and to walk up to the heights of Rocky Flats south of this point, because the train's engine could not make the climb with much of a load. At the top they got aboard again and continued their trip.

National Center for Atmospheric Research

As motorists clear the summit of Davidson Mesa at **Milepost 41**, below them the city of Boulder stretches eastward from the mountains. To the west on a conspicuous tableland attached to the Flatirons lies a curious complex of pink adobe-like buildings. Except for the prominence that comes from its elevation, the structure seems to blend with its landscape.

The building housing the National Center for Atmospheric Research (referred to locally as NCAR, pronounced "N-Car") is one of the early triumphs of Cantonese-born architect I.M. (for Ieoh Ming) Pei. A more recent one is the crystal triangle entrance to the Louvre Museum which opened in 1989 in Paris. Pei, who is a graduate of the Harvard School of Design, took inspiration for NCAR from two principal sources, the work of the Anasazi Indians at Mesa Verde (see *U.S. 160* itinerary) and Walter Orr Roberts.

Roberts, a Boulder resident at the time, was picked in 1960 to be the first head of NCAR. An astronomer and physicist, he had been head of the University of Colorado's High Altitude Observatory for twenty years. In the 1950s he turned to meteorology, however, to study the relationship between sunspot activity and weather on earth. His work in this area commended him to the University Corporation of Atmospheric Research, a consortium of fifty-four universities, which underwrote the creation of NCAR.

Roberts had insisted that NCAR be located in Boulder, if he was to head it, and he chose the mesa site for the building Pei was commissioned to design. Roberts retired in 1974 and was named president emeritus of NCAR.

Noted in recent years for the theory of "nuclear winter" developed by its scientists, NCAR offers noontime tours Monday through Saturday for summertime visitors. In winter there is one tour weekly on Wednesday at noon. NCAR is located at the top of Boulder's Table Mesa Drive, three miles west of **Milepost 39**.

South Boulder Creek

South Boulder Creek, known originally as the Bonita Forks of the St. Vrain River, crosses *U.S. 36* at **Milepost 40.** The noted New York editor and failed presidential candidate Horace Greeley, en route from New York City to San Francisco on June 21, 1859, hired a wagon and driver to take him from Denver to Fort Laramie to catch the Overland Stage.

> I left Denver at 3 p.m., crossed the Platte directly at Denver, and . . . pushed on ten miles further and camped for the night opposite Boulder City, a log hamlet of some thirty habitations, covering the entrance to Boulder Diggings, twelve miles westward in the mountains. . . .
>
> We camped all for the night beside a small brook, the rippling of whose waters over its pebbly bed fell soothingly on the drowsy ear. . . .The night was cool and breezy. . . .

Eldorado Springs

South Boulder Creek emerges from the mountains about four miles to the southwest of **Milepost 40** at Eldorado Springs. Now a modest spa and a bedroom suburb of Boulder, Eldorado Springs was once touted as the "Coney Island of Colorado."

A thermal spring at the mouth of the canyon produced what one geologist proclaimed as the finest water on the North American continent. His analysis showed that it contained only 2.68 grains of solid per gallon. In light of that, a group of developers started a resort company that featured bathing pools, a hotel, gourmet restaurant, and other posh appointments. A special railway spur brought tourists from Denver. Later a metropolitan tramway replaced the train service.

Financial problems threatened foreclosure in the wake of the Panic of 1907, and the resort company foundered. In 1918, however, one of the original partners, Frank Fowler, reclaimed the springs. His spa in time lured such notables as author Damon Runyon, boxer Jack Dempsey, comedian Jimmy Durante, and actors Douglas Fairbanks and Mary Pickford. Later-to-be-president Dwight D. Eisenhower and his wife Mamie had their honeymoon at Eldorado Springs on the eve of America's entry into World War I.

Fowler managed to fend off a threat to build a dam and reservoir at the mouth of the canyon to warehouse water that Denver would get from the aqueduct through the Moffat Tunnel (see *U.S. 40* itinerary). That water was eventually diverted to three other reservoirs in the vicinity, Gross, Ralston, and Diversion.

A 1929 Christmas-week fire, "whipped into raging fury by a cannon of wind," destroyed the spa. Reconstruction was underwritten by Frederick Bonfils, the publisher of the Denver *Post*. Less than ten years later a devastating flood built up in the narrow canyon to destroy the resort again. Frank Fowler rebuilt again on a more modest scale.

In 1978 the canyon upstream from the springs became Eldorado State Park. Today the sheer, fractured walls of Eldorado Canyon have become the mecca of rockclimbers from around the world seeking to sharpen their skills. Their forerunner, however, was a five-foot-three highwire acrobat named Ivy Baldwin, who entertained guests at the resort from 1906 to 1948 by crossing a 672-foot cable strung nearly 700 feet above the creek. He gave eighty-nine performances over his career, the last when he was eighty-two.

Baseline Road

Baseline Road, at **Milepost 37**, is laid upon the fortieth parallel of latitude, an important baseline (hence the name) in the topographical surveys by which the West was platted in the 1879s. The surveys were an essential step in opening the West to homesteading under terms of the Homestead Act of 1862.

The person responsible for the survey set along the fortieth parallel was Clarence King, a twenty-four-year old Yale graduate in 1866 when he persuaded Congress to under-write the project. Using the baseline, King and his col-leagues generated the data needed to map a one-hundred-mile swath from about I-25 westward to California (see *U.S. 40* itinerary).

University of Colorado

The University of Colorado, west of the intersection of Colorado Avenue and 28th Street (*U.S. 36*), traces its origins back to Colorado's beginning as a legal entity.

Colorado's first territorial governor, William Gilpin, ap-pointed by Abraham Lincoln on March 22, 1861, asked the General Assembly of the Territory, elected on August 19 and convened on September 10, 1861, to authorize a semi-nary fund for a public university to be located at Boulder. At the time of his appointment Gilpin was well acquainted with the West. He had been on John C. Fremont's third expedi-tion (see *I-25N*, *U.S. 40*, and *U.S. 285N* itineraries) and had undertaken a mission into the San Juan region of southwest-ern Colorado while serving with Gen. Stephen Watts Kear-ny's Army of the West during the 1846-48 Mexican War.

Boulder Creek

Following the important gold strikes at Central City and Idaho Springs (see *I-70W* itinerary), "shot gold" was disco-vered in early 1860 in Boulder Creek, which crosses *U.S. 36* between Colorado and Arapahoe avenues. In June 1860, a vein of gold-bearing quartz called the Horsfal lode was discovered at Gold Hill, twelve miles northwest of the inter-section of Mapleton Avenue and 28th Street along a spec-tacularly beautiful drive through Sunshine Canyon.

The Boulder City Town Company decided that a two-mile stretch of Boulder Creek would make an ideal location for a community that could support the mining operations higher up in the mountains. They laid out 4,044 lots and set the rather exorbitant price of $1,000 for each. They sold

An exceptional photo of a gold mine, the ironically named Small Hopes tunnel of the Consolidated Gold Mine near Boulder. *Boulder Historical Society.*

slowly. Things picked up in 1869, however, when an important silver strike occurred at Caribou on a tributary of Boulder Creek twenty miles up in the mountains. Then in 1872 gold-bearing telluride deposits were unearthed at Gold Hill. The next year two railroads found their way to Boulder, the Colorado Central from Golden and the Denver & Boulder Valley. Eventually, the bounty of the location was manifested even in oil—in January 1902, Boulder's oil wells were producing seventy barrels a day.

Josephine Roche and the Rocky Mountain Fuel Company

A guard with a machine gun was perched on the walkway of a water tower on November 21, 1927. The water tower, located about twelve miles east of the intersection of *U.S. 36* and Valmont Road, **Milepost 35.5**, overlooked a coal mine—the Columbine—owned by the Rocky Mountain Fuel Company. Startled by the boldness of striking miners below him, the guard opened up. Seven miners were killed, twenty-three wounded. It was a reenactment of the bloody Ludlow strike of April 1914 (see I-25S itinerary), except that its consequences were markedly different.

On the board of directors of the Rocky Mountain Fuel Company at the time was a remarkable woman, Josephine Roche, who at forty-one held a graduate degree in social work from Columbia University. While still in her twenties, she had served as Colorado's first policewoman. She had inherited her interest in the coal company from her lately deceased father, John Roche, president of the company from 1914 to 1927. The outspoken Josephine Roche condemned mine operators—and her father was no exception to the practice—who "break labor through force" and try "to terrify them into submission, then . . . call out the state militia."

Josephine Roche charted a startling new path in management-labor relations that eventually won her an executive post with the United Mine Workers. *Colorado Historical Society.*

She gained control of the RMF Co. in her own right in 1928 and was elected president—the nation's first woman mine operator. She signed a new contract with the miners, thus becoming the first Colorado mine operator to recognize the fledgling United Mine Workers.

The contract aimed "to establish industrial justice, substitute reason for violence, integrity and good faith for dishonest practices, and a union of effort for the chaos of present economic warfare. . . ." The RMF Co. committed itself to pay what was the highest wage scale in the state. In turn, it found that the UMW actively promoted the company's sales of coal and that miner productivity climbed. The RMF Co. became second in sales, among Colorado coal producers, only to the giant Colorado Fuel & Iron Company, then directed by John D. Rockefeller, Jr.

The 1929 stock market crash and the onset of the Great Depression, however, undermined Roche's experiment. CF&I cut wages in order to reduce prices, prompting an angry Roche to fire off a telegram to Rockefeller: "Anti-social methods of the past are again being employed by your company. . . .The chaos of the coal industry cannot be corrected by forcing labor to take lower and lower wages."

Rockefeller paid her little attention, but newly elected President Franklin D. Roosevelt took notice. Roche was named assistant secretary of the Treasury, responsible for the Public Health Service. In 1936 she took over the National Youth Administration. In 1937, however, the RMF Co. began to fail, and Roche had to return to Colorado. The company was bolstered briefly by huge loans from the UMW, but started to founder again because of the growing use of natural gas in Colorado until, in June 1939, UMW President John L. Lewis forced Roche to relinquish control of the company to a professional management team. In 1944 the RMF Co. filed for bankruptcy.

Although still RMF president, in 1947 Roche became a special assistant to Lewis in the UMW and a year later was named administrator of the union's pension fund. She resigned the coal company's presidency in 1950, due to the press of union work. She died in Washington, D.C., in 1976 at the age of ninety.

Left Hand Creek

Left Hand Creek, **Milepost 28,** has its headwaters near Ward at the top of Left Hand Canyon. The name commemorates a celebrated Arapahoe chieftain who figured prominently in the affairs of this region from 1858, when the first prospectors arrived, until the Sand Creek massacre in 1864 (see *U.S. 50* itinerary). A transcription of his name in his native language is Niwot, now the name of a town where Left Hand Creek crosses *Colorado 119*, seven miles east of this point.

Chief Left Hand's celebrity derived in large measure from his mastery of English. He was regularly sought out by visitors, such as Horace Greeley, and settlers because he was the rare Arapahoe with whom they could easily communicate.

George Andrew Jackson, the Missouri-born Forty-Niner who made one of the initial strikes in Colorado (see I-70 itinerary), noted in his diary in March 4, 1859: "Niwot came into lodge while was getting supper; going to Auraria for medicine for his sick squaw. His camp is on [South Boulder Creek]. Staid all night with me. I gave him a bottle of Perry Davis 'Pain Killer' and a chunk of rhubarb root for his squaw and he left this morning for his village."

Three months later, Greeley reported his conversation with Left Hand:

> And I yesterday tried my powers of persuasion on Left Hand—the only Arapaho chief who talks English—in favor of an Arapaho tribal farm, say of two hundred acres for a beginning, to be broken and fenced by the common efforts of the tribe, and a patch therein allotted to each head of family who would agree to plant and till it—I apprehend to very little purpose. For Left Hand, though shrewd in his way, is an Indian, and every whit as conservative as Boston's Beacon Street or our Fifth Avenue. He knows that there is a certain way in which his people have lived from time immemorial, and in which they are content still to live, knowing and seeking no better.

An advocate of manifest destiny and as earnest as Rudyard Kipling would later be to hoist the "white man's burden," Greeley concluded that "the Indians are children . . . utterly incompetent to cope in any way with the European or Caucasion race. . . ."

If the Indian problem was not to be solved by making farmers of them, the "final solution" seems to have been tried by Col. John M. Chivington and the "One Hundred Days" regiment, called up by Governor John Evans in the wake of increasing Indian attacks on white settlers (see I-25M and *U.S. 50* itineraries). This was the November 29, 1864, attack on the Arapahoe and Cheyenne village that had settled into winter quarters on the edge of their reservation on Big Sandy Creek in eastern Colorado.

In August 1864, Chief Left Hand had visited a white settler in this vicinity, Robert Hauck, to report his intention to arbitrate between whites and Indians. Coincidentally, or perhaps in consequence of Left Hand's mediation, a group of Cheyenne and Arapahoe chiefs rode into Denver some weeks later to sue for peace with Governor Evans. Due to the settlers' anxiety, Evans felt obliged to equivocate, so the Indians took their followers south to Fort Lyon in the Arkansas valley. Meanwhile, Evans continued with his mobilization of the militia.

A messenger from the governor came to Robert Hauck to try to enlist him in the One Hundred Days regiment, officially the 3rd Colorado Regiment of Volunteers. Balking, Hauck later told his family that the messenger had intimated that "they are going to kill Indians without recourse or arbitration." He was obliged, however, to supply six horses for the regiment's use.

A Hauck neighbor who had participated in the battle of Sand Creek returned to report that Chief Left Hand had been killed in the fray. This was an error; although wounded, Left Hand has escaped.

Hygiene

The Church of the Brethren, also known as German Baptists or Dunkards (for their rite of total immersion) organized their first Colorado congregation two miles east of **Milepost 23** on Hygiene Road. A Virginia-born trader in buffalo robes, Jacob S. Flory, moved here from Greeley in

1877 to buy a ranch and serve as minister to a group of seventeen Dunkards. A stone church was erected in the community in 1880, and the Dunkards held services until 1907. In 1882, in an attempt to capitalize on the Front Range's reputation as a .climate beneficial to consumptives, Flory built a sanatarium, Hygiene Home, which inspired the name for the community. The sanatarium did not prosper, however, and after being transformed into a simple hotel, the building itself was razed in 1926.

Lyons

The town of Lyons, **Milepost 20**, was established shortly after Hygiene to serve as a waystation for tourists en route to Estes Park and as a source of prime building sandstone cut from quarries in the vicinity. The Lyons Depot, in the heart of town, is listed in the National Register of Historic Places as a notable example of 1885 architecture embodying indigenous sandstone blocks.

Lyons to Estes Park

The route from Lyons to Estes Park took several paths before becoming today's *U.S. 36*, which, in fact, closely follows Joel Estes's crudely constructed wagon path of the 1860s (see *U.S. 34* itinerary). In 1873 a territorial charter was issued to establish a toll road. A stage line began to operate five years later, requiring a full day's journey from Longmont to Estes Park.

In 1903, Massachusetts industrialist F. O. Stanley, co-inventor of the famous Stanley Steamer automobile, was sent west for his health. He decided when he arrived that he would drive his vehicle up to Estes Park. Having missed connections with a guide, Stanley drove on alone from Denver. After getting lost north of Boulder, he asked directions of a local resident and steaming up North St. Vrain Valley, west of **Milepost 17**, he finally reached Welch's stage station, midway between Estes Park and Lyons, as night fell. Although warned the next morning not to attempt to complete the trip, Stanley went on anyway and, to the surprise of stationkeeper Welch, he telephoned a mere hour and a half later to report his arrival.

Six years later, Stanley instituted a Lyons-to-Estes Park jitney service, using his Steamers to bring guests to the newly built Stanley Hotel.

Rocky Mountain Jim

In the glade a mile or so south of **Milepost 6** was the cabin of James "Rocky Mountain Jim" Nugent, an alcoholic, expatriate Canadian who had lost an eye to an angry grizzly bear (see *U.S. 34* itinerary). An elegant English writer of travelogues, Isabella L. Bird, came upon the place in 1873:

> With smoke coming out of the roof and window it looked like the den of a wild beast. . . . [The] owner [was] a broad, thick-set man about middle height, with an old cap on his head . . . a knife in his belt and . . . a revolver sticking out of the breast pocket of his coat. . . .
>
> He is a man about forty-five and must have been strikingly handsome. He has large gray-blue eyes, deeply set, a handsome aquiline nose, a very handsome mouth. . . . One eye was entirely gone, and the loss made one side of the face repulsive, while the other might have been modled in marble. "Desperado" was written in large letters all over him.

Needless to say, Miss Bird was smitten. As a result, she saw quite a lot of Rocky Mountain Jim during her stay in Estes Park. "Of his genius and chivalry to women there does not appear to be any doubt; but he is . . . subject to 'ugly fits,' when people think it best to avoid him. It is here regarded as an evil that he has located himself at the mouth of the only entrance to the park, for he is dangerous with his pistols. . . ."

A few months after Miss Bird left, Nugent's fits and his guns combined in an altercation with another resident, Griff Evans, a partisan of Thomas Wyndham-Quinn, the fourth Earl of Dunraven. Lord Dunraven was seeking to develop the park as a tourist attraction. Evans shot Nugent, who succumbed some weeks later in a Fort Collins hospital.

Noted the British aristocrat in his memoirs, ". . . Mountain Jim . . . [was] an extraordinary character, civil enough when sober, but, when drunk, which was as often as he could manage, violent and abusive, and given to declamation in Greek and Latin." Nugent lingered on after being shot, according to Dunraven, because "it is hard to die in the wonderful air of that great altitude. . . ."

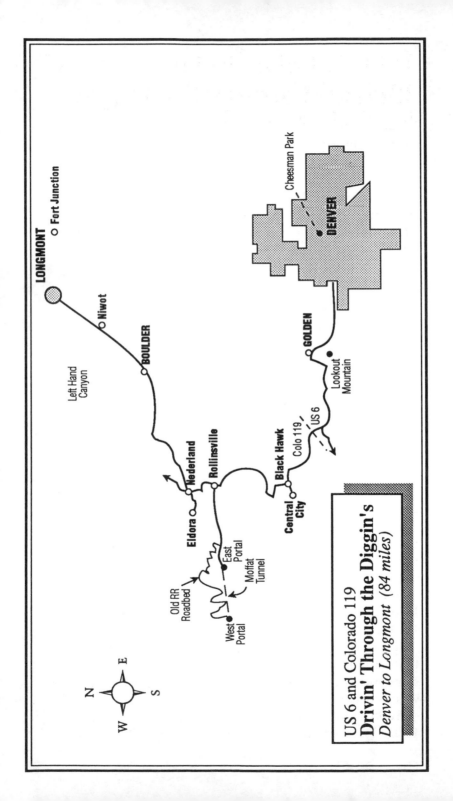

US 6 and Colorado 119
Drivin' Through the Diggin's
Denver to Longmont (84 miles)

US 6 & Colorado 119
Drivin' Through the Diggin's
Denver to Longmont

Cheesman Park

"It takes a peculiar kind of a man to attain success in such a country," a twenty-three-year-old man from Long Island, New York, wrote to his family after arriving in Denver in 1861, "—particularly if without capital."

Even "without capital," as it turned out, Walter Scott Cheesman was that "peculiar kind of a man." Two and three-quarter miles east of the junction of U.S. 6, **Milepost 285,** with I-25 there is a Denver city park named for him. Twenty-three miles upstream on the South Platte River there is a large reservoir as well as a nearby mountain peak named for him. After all, Cheesman was a man of many parts.

When he arrived, he took over a failing Denver drug store from his two older brothers, who returned to their home in New York. Before ten years passed he had become a railroad magnate, mining promoter, bank official, and a director of the Denver City Water Company.

In 1870 the first train of the Denver Pacific to reach Denver from the Union Pacific's transcontinental line in Cheyenne was pulled by the locomotive "Walter S. Cheesman" (see I-25N itinerary). Cheesman was thirty-one at the time.

He bought the famous Eagle Mine among other claims on Gilman's Battle Mountain in 1883, developed them, and held them for the rest of his life (see U.S. 24W itinerary). He had mining interests in Creede and Aspen as well.

It was his position with the water company, however, that brought Cheesman unusual power and influence. In a semi-arid region that had special reverence for water he was to become Denver's Water Czar.

Amid a plethora of companies that were organized in the 1880s to bring water to booming but parched Denver,

Cheesman hit upon the idea of seeking water up in the mountains rather than drawing it from depleting groundwater wells and small suburban reservoirs. He organized the Mountain Works Construction Company in 1889 and in 1893 built the nation's first mechanical filtration plant at the mouth of Platte Canyon, eighteen miles south of Denver.

A year later he managed to outmaneuver other urban water companies to form the Denver Union Water Company, which, with Cheesman as its president, dominated the city's water supply until 1914 when the city bought the company.

Golden

The city of Golden, west of **Milepost 274**, was established as a camp in late 1858 by three prospectors—Thomas L. Golden, James Saunders, and George Andrew Jackson. Jackson was the man who a few months later would make one of the first big gold strikes in the Rockies (see *I-70W* itinerary). The town itself takes its name from Jackson's confidant, Golden, who was the only other person to know initially of Jackson's strike.

Golden in the late 1860s was also the home of William Austin Hamilton Loveland, the founder of the Colorado Central & Pacific Railroad, an enterprise that never got beyond the Continental Divide but won its founder memorials in a city (see *U.S. 34* and *I-25N* itineraries) and a mountain pass (see below). Loveland's railroad did make it, however, to two important mining camps at Georgetown and Central City.

Lookout Mountain Road

Denver had been dubbed the "Queen City of the Plains," but city fathers from the beginning have sought to emphasize the city's kinship with the nearby mountains. Before World War I a plan was developed for a chain of mountain parks to benefit Denver's citizens. The first link in that

chain lay on Lookout Mountain at *Milepost 272* just west
of Golden.

The city hired Frederick Law Olmsted, Jr., a renowned
landscape artist who had designed the spectacular Capitol
Mall in Washington, D.C., to lay out a road up Lookout
Mountain. The result was the breathtaking, twisting, turning, and aptly named Lariat Loop Road.

Completed in 1914, Lariat Loop Road rose more than
one thousand feet in elevation over an as-the-crow-flies
distance of about one mile. In the 1970s hang-gliders would
soar from the summit of Lookout Mountain over gawking
motorists on Lariat Loop Road to land on a tiny triangle of
land where *U.S. 6* merges with *Colorado 58*. Concern for
the safety of both flyers and motorists forced a ban of the
sport.

Notable historic features of the road are its rustic-style
stone guardrails and shelters. At the summit in the same
style is the museum marking the grave of William F. "Buffalo Bill" Cody (see *I-70W* itinerary).

Central City

After founding Auraria at the mouth of Cherry Creek,
thirteen prospectors from Georgia lingered on in the region
after most their colleagues, having despaired of finding anything more than trace gold in the streams of the foothills,
had returned home. One of those who remained, John H.
Gregory, was the first to find a productive vein of gold-bearing quartz at Central City, a mile west of **Milepost 76** of
Colorado 119.

The Georgia company, eager to promote immigration to
the region, invited visiting New York publisher Horace
Greeley to the site a few months later in an effort to revive
the rush to the gold region. A cynical Yankee immigrant,
Libeus Barney, wrote: "With all his sagacity, the
philosopher, it is currently reported, was shamefully imposed upon in relation to the yield of the mines. It was
well known at the 'diggins' when Mr. Greeley would pay
them a visit, and they were, consequently, prepared for

him. More than three times as much gold was worked out in his presence as had been gathered before or since in a single day. . . ."

Nevertheless, philosopher Greeley duly testified to the discovery, but with this caution: "I adhere to my long-settled conviction that, next to outright and indisputable gambling the hardest (though sometimes the quickest) way to obtain gold is to mine for it; that a good farmer or mechanic will usually make money faster, and of course immeasurably easier, by sticking to his own business than by deserting it for gold-digging; and that the man who, having failed in some other pursuit, calculates on retrieving his fortunes by gold-mining, makes a mistake which he will be likely to rue to the end of his days."

Those who followed Gregory to the site of his claim stayed to organize Mountain City in May 1859, and to associate the community with the new government of what was known as the Territory of Jefferson down in Denver. A few weeks later the peripatetic publisher of the *Rocky Mountain News*, William N. Byers, camped nearby and recommended that the locality be called Central City, because it was midway between two other camps, Blackhawk and Nevadaville.

That month of June 1859, a one-time slave and his wife drove a wagon up to Gregory's Diggings. Twenty-nine-year-old Jeremiah Lee was rumored to have been born a chattel of Robert E. Lee of Virginia.

Not long after Lee staked a claim on nearby Yankee Hill, the black population of Central City reached sixteen. This number included Lee's wife, Emily, who worked as a practical nurse tending ill and injured miners.

Lee's gold mine was productive, although not spectacularly so. In 1864, therefore, he filed on a promising silver claim in the Argentine mining district southwest of Georgetown (see *I-70W* itinerary). The resulting OK Mine, jointly owned with Charles Fish, eventually tapped into the bonanza Argentine Lode. In consequence Lee did quite well.

Another Central citizen of substance was Henry M. Teller, the president of the Colorado Central Railroad, a future U.S. Senator, and eventually President Chester A. Arthur's secretary of the interior. In 1871 Teller provided the seed money for the construction of a fifty-room hotel that opened in May 1872 as the Teller House. A year later President Ulysses S. Grant arrived at the Teller House to find the path from his carriage to the hotel's entrance cobbled with silver bars, thoughfully laid down by local promoters.

Meanwhile, railroad magnate Teller looked on approvingly as the citizens of Gilpin County voted a bond issue to underwrite construction of a Colorado Central right-of-way from the mainline in Clear Creek Canyon to Blackhawk, Central City, and Nevadaville. The spur reached Blackhawk on December 14, 1872.

Lee's savings had accumulated by the mid-1870s to the point where he needed an investor's advice. The assistant cashier of the local Rocky Mountain National Bank urged him to finance the building of a stately home on a pair of lots near the Teller House. Thomas Hale Potter offered to oversee the design, and to ensure Lee a return on the investment, he agreed to lease it at $100 a month for an indefinite period. The elegant home at No. 2 Bankers' Row hosted some of Central City's most posh soirees from 1876 to 1884, while the landlords occupied a modest cottage nearby. In 1884, however, Thomas and Mary Ellen Potter moved to Denver.

Jeremiah and Emily Lee took over the mansion and shortly placed an advertisement in the *Daily Central City Register-Call* offering accommodations in the "No. 2 Bankers Row Boarding House - Lee, Prop." Jeremiah Lee died in Central City in January 1904. Three years later Emily succumbed as well. Shortly before her death, sadly, Lee House was sold for back taxes. The house was abandoned altogether in 1916, for Central City too had fallen on hard times.

Ironically, as the rest of the nation sank into the economic torpor to be known as the Great Depression, the house built by Jeremiah Lee gained new life. Bought in 1931 and restored by architect Carl F. Bieler, the Lee mansion provided accommodations for visiting performers at the correspondingly revitalized Central City Opera House. The latter reopened on July 16, 1932, and featured Lillian Gish in the title role of *Camille*.

The Opera House had been built in 1878, just two years after Lee House. It too had fallen into decay following World War I. So that it might be restored, owner Peter McFarlane donated the building in 1931 to Denver University. The annual, summertime Central City Opera program has in succeeding years won national attention.

Chinese Miners

While immigrant Irish are acknowledged to have contributed much of the sweat and muscle that built the Union Pacific west from Omaha, less recognition seems to have been given the tens of thousands of Chinese immigrants who laid track for the Central Pacific eastward from San Francisco to Promontory Point, Utah, where in 1869 it joined with the Union Pacific.

Chinese immigration to America became especially heavy after the English defeated the Chinese in the mid-nineteenth century Opium Wars. According to a report of one Chinese imperial commission, ". . . They have not gone [to America] as a result of deceit, or by being kidnapped, nor under contract as Coolies, but have flown thither as the wild geese fly."

By the late 1880s there were some 110,000 Chinese immigrants in America, most of them from the region around Canton. One of these was a well-educated Cantonese named Chin Lin Sou, who brought some three hundred of his countrymen from railroad jobs to Central City to work in the gold mines. In 1871 he brought his wife from China to a new home in Blackhawk, *Milepost 7*, where they reared a family of six.

Chin and his family eventually joined the Chinese community in Denver where he became a civic leader. He has been memorialized with a chair at the Central City Opera House and a stained glass window in the state capitol.

Rollinsville

The village of Rollinsville, **Milepost 21**, sat in 1873 astride the Rollinsville & Middle Park Toll Road, whose guiding genius was John Quincy Adams Rollins, a forty-four-year-old New Hampshireman who had arrived in the gold rush. Rollins had invested in the Gold Dirt mine on South Boulder Creek and had built the area's first quartz mill to process ore.

In the 1870s the secret of his success lay in the assiduous purchase of failed mining claims. When the decade ended he had accumulated nearly twenty thousand linear feet of gold-bearing veins, three hundred placer claims, and two thousand acres of farm land, most of it near the town that bears his name.

The toll road climbed to 11,600 feet at Corona to cross the pass that bears his name on the Continental Divide. The roadbed is now used by four-wheel-drive enthusiasts seeking some breathtaking rides and spectacular views.

The area's first quartz mill and the home of its builder, John Quincy Adams Rollins, lies beneath Rollins Pass on the Continental Divide, transit of an early wagon road and later railroad. *Boulder Historical Society.*

Moffat Road

In 1903 David H. Moffat took over the right-of-way of the Rollins toll road as a temporary measure to carry his newly organized railroad line, the Denver, Northwestern & Pacific, known familiarly as the Moffat Road (see *U.S. 40* itinerary). In making the approach to the increasingly steep grade that led to Rollins Pass, the railway had to pass through thirty-three tunnels. The last, the 120-foot Needles Eye, opens onto two final trestles of 125 feet and 237 feet along a mountain slope called the Devil's Slide.

On February 26, 1928, two former governors drove a golden spike to complete the track through the Moffat Tunnel at its East Portal, eight miles west of **Milepost 21**. The completion of the tunnel reduced train travel distance by twenty-three miles. More important, it cut travel time in clearing the Continental Divide from two and one-half hours to a mere twelve minutes.

For half a century motorists used the abandoned railway bed, tunnels, and trestles to go from one side of the pass to the other. In 1979, however, the ceiling of the Needles Eye collapsed. This, compounded by deteriorating wooden trestles, forced the U.S. Forest Service to close down the route. An outcry among area residents spurred public contributions to a fund that enabled Boulder County officials in 1988 to repair and reopen the Needles Eye tunnel. The old wagon road bed was improved to permit four-wheel-drive vehicles to bypass the trestles and once again reach the summit of the pass.

Eldora

Silver fueled the success of the Colorado mining industry until withdrawal of federal price supports caused the Panic of 1893 (see *Colorado 62 & 145* itinerary). Bucking the collapse in the industry, of course, were successful gold mines, which were unaffected by the law. Gold was king at Cripple Creek, the Camp Bird mine near Ouray, and if not king, at least important at Battle Mountain near Gilman. In the spirit of the times, the promise of gold was nearly as attractive as the ore itself.

The promise of a "second Cripple Creek" manifested itself in a beautiful setting not far from today's Indian Peaks Wilderness Area in southwestern Boulder County. Some three miles west of **Milepost 25** lies Happy Valley where in 1895 John H. Kemp discovered and, more important, promoted the Happy Valley placer. Nestled comfortably between Eldorado and Spencer mountains, Eldorado lured hundreds of idle miners and prospectors. In time two square miles of Spencer mountain alone was peppered with more than fifty mining claims. The Mogul Tunnel was dug more than 850 feet into the base of the mountain, intersecting as it went at least three promising veins of gold-bearing telluride ores.

One attractive sample of gold-laced telluride from the Virginia mine on Spencer mountain was even sent to Great Britain's long-reigning Queen Victoria for her prized mineral collection.

At one point, postal confusion with Eldorado, California, caused a miner's payroll to be misdirected. Resourceful town fathers decided to lop the last two letters from Eldorado. As a result, the town is known as Eldora.

The high hopes for the Eldora camp, however, proved to be misdirected as well. By 1917 mining activity had virtually come to a halt. The Colorado & Northwestern Railroad had arrived in 1904 to complete the famous Switzerland Trail. But by 1920 rail service to Eldora was halted.

Today, however, at neighboring Lake Eldora a modern Colorado industry has taken hold in the Eldora Ski Area.

Switzerland Trail

A narrow-gauge railroad ran from downtown Boulder, a block north of **Milepost 42** at Canyon Boulevard and Broadway, to the mining camps high above. Doubling as an excursion train, the route from Boulder to the high country was dubbed "The Switzerland Trail."

Built in 1883 with the hopeful, if not indeed pretentious, name of Denver, Salt Lake & Pacific, the line ran for a mere fifteen miles, from downtown up Boulder Canyon (*Colorado 119*) through Four-Mile Canyon, Salina and Wall Street to Sunset. When an 1894 flood eliminated twelve of the fifteen miles of track, a new line was surveyed in 1897 as a prelude to the organization of the Colorado & Northwestern Railway. Thirteen more miles of trackage in 1896 took the line to the mining camp of Ward. In 1905 the line was extended to Cardinal and Eldora, the latter a modern-day ski area.

The Panic of 1907 sent the railway into receivership until 1909, when it was reorganized as the Denver, Boulder & Western. The train survived for another decade, until it was devastated by the effects of another flood and abandoned.

Chief Lefthand

Midway between Boulder and Longmont, at **Milepost 51**, is the town of Niwot, the Arapahoe name for an Indian chief who figures prominently and sympathetically in the journals of early settlers. His name in translation also graces Lefthand Canyon and Creek, which descend through the mountains due west of the town (see also *U.S. 7* itinerary).

The city of Boulder has placed a statue of Niwot in a Boulder Creek park.

Fort Junction

At the confluence of Boulder Creek and the St. Vrain River, **Milepost 62**, sat Fort Junction. It was built by the Lower Boulder and St. Vrain Valley Home Guards, sixty-two men and officers outfitted by the federal government in early 1864 to guard against Indian depredations in the region.

The Hungate massacre of June 11, 1864 (see *I-27M* itinerary), prompted the construction of the fort, a 130-by-100-foot structure of adobe walls, featuring twenty-five-by-ten-foot bastions of alternate corners to provide for loopholes for a line of fire along each of the four main walls. This was a standard feature of forts in all parts of the West in the pioneer era.

Residents of the region fled to the safety of the fort on one important occasion when Elbridge Gerry signalled the Indians' plan to attack white settlements in the South Platte valley in August 1864 (see above).

2. *The Mountains*

It had happened before.

The rush of gold-seekers to the Colorado Rockies in 1859 had had its precedent in California just ten years earlier. When the misnamed Pike's Peak gold rush began, perhaps it was the feeling of *déjà vu* that inspired a flood of wishful souls to come to the Rockies as much to witness fortune as to gain it. Like the flight to California in 1849, they called themselves, rather grandiloquently to be sure, "argonauts."

But in America there was precedent even for the California gold rush. Little remarked upon in popular histories, the first gold strike set the stage both for California and for Colorado. It was the training ground for many of the successful prospectors of the later strikes. Gold fever had raised temperatures in the Cherokee country of northwestern Georgia and southwestern North Carolina in the 1820s, and the argonauts of a generation later owed much to what had been learned in the Blue Ridge Mountains.

From the early experience, for example, came a device for separating gold from gravel called the Georgia rocker. Among the first parties to scour the tributaries of the South Platte River and the mountain valleys beyond it was a group of Georgians, many of whom had participated in the rush to Sacramento.

William Green Russell of Lumpkin County, Georgia, lent the name of his hometown to Colorado's first important mining camp, Auraria. Russell, with his carefully plaited beard, led the Georgia company of prospectors that in 1858 formed the vanguard of all the rest. Despite legend, early results were poor, however, so much so that many of Russell's party, the Georgians and their affiliated company from the Cherokee Nation, returned to their homes.

"Green Russell remained, and, through his instrumentality, they prospected the balance of the season," said Philander Simmons, a Russell colleague, "and kept up the excitement by reporting great discoveries and big strikes, which were in reality never made. Still, it was the means of starting the great immigration the next year."

One of the Georgia company, John H. Gregory, finally gave substance to the hype. Near today's Central City, initially called Mountain City, Gregory found a lode of gold quartz high up near the headwaters of Clear Creek, one of the tributaries of the South Platte River. Another veteran of the California fields, George Andrew Jackson, a Missourian, may have made the first important strike on another fork of Clear Creek. He wrote in his diary on January 8, 1858: ". . . I've got the diggins at last. . . . Dug and panned today until my belt knife was worn out, so I will have to quit or use my skinning knife. I have about a half ounce of gold; so will quit and try and get back in the Spring."

In a Christmas Day toast made on the banks of the South Platte a couple of weeks before Jackson's gold discovery at Idaho Springs, a prominent Kansas town developer, General William Larimer, declaimed: "I wish the emigrant, who come hither, to test the country fairly and fully. For my part, I am satisfied that, aside from the rich deposits of gold, alum, coal, marl, etc., that have already been discovered, we could live longer and better to settle in this country. But we have mineral treasures, sufficient to justify emigration to its fullest extent. . . . Manifest Destiny has shaped its end, and discovered its long hidden treasures."

So manifest destiny, fueled by gold, brought prospectors and gamblers and tradesmen of various sorts to settle a mountainous strip from the Front Range above Boulder to the volcanic San Juan Mountains in the southwestern corner of the present state of Colorado, and from Cripple Creek to Aspen.

Just as the Georgia gold rush had displaced the Cherokee Indians from their ancestral lands in the name of manifest destiny, so would it happen in Colorado. Like the Georgia rocker and other mining devices, legal tools had already been shaped to deal with Indians in possession of gold-bearing lands. The Supreme Court in 1831 had declared in *Cherokee Nation v. Georgia*: "Though the Indians are acknowledged to have an unquestionable, and heretofore unquestioned, right to the lands they occupy, until that right can be extinguished by a voluntary cession to our government; yet . . . their relation to the United States resembles that of a ward to his guardian."

Colorado's Mountain Utes occupied much of the area that showed most promise to miners. In a series of treaties beginning in 1868, they were first moved west of the Continental Divide, then in 1873 from three and a half million acres in the mineral-rich San Juan Mountains, and finally in 1881 from all but a small strip on the southern border of Colorado.

Lone prospectors like Gregory and Jackson might find the precious metals locked away in their mountain fastnesses but, curiously, seemed to find more satisfaction in locating the ore than in exploiting it. They quickly sold out to more seriously inclined entrepreneurs. Many of these were merchants who supplied the mining camps with the necessities of life and work. They would underwrite, or grubstake, the efforts of a prospector and, if they both were lucky, reap the windfall of success.

In time more serious operators came on the scene. "The ground afterward was mainly gobbled up by large companies from the east, who operated on the California plan, which is to take everything in sight," groused Wolfe Londoner, a mining camp provisioner, "and squeeze the laborer down to starvation rates. . . . "

Finally, even foreign capital gained a dominant role in the exploitation of Colorado's mines. From 1876, the eve of Colorado's silver boom, until the end of World War I, for example, British investors alone controlled sixty-eight mining companies in Colorado.

Ranking with the saga of mining is the story of the roads: much as necessity mothered invention, success sired accessibility. Mountain mining camps lay at the end, usually, of often precipitous trails, blazed through a broken, bouldered pine forest. Determined men filled and leveled narrow roadbeds and charged those who would use them. The most remarkable of the lot were the railroad men, particularly those who pioneered the narrow-gauge lines, accepting the challenge of surmounting unprecedented grades and spanning broad chasms with long, curving trestles.

In time the mines were either exhausted or, in an inflationary economy, debased. The booming towns they had supported lapsed into lethargy, if not extinction. The railroads broadened their gauge to match that of the rest of the country and, despite that, often ended up being sold for scrap iron. Like Ophir, the mines of King Solomon, little more remains of this Colorado epoch than the legend.

US 34
The Child's Trail
Loveland to Granby (92 miles)

Loveland

Located on a railroad mainline at the mouth of the narrow and precipitous Big Thompson river canyon, the townsite that became Loveland had both weather and transportation going for it. The site also sat on the edge of the fertile Colorado piedmont whose soil, according to the 1869 view of a distinguished professor, could "make Colorado the greatest sugar-producing state in the world."

Town fathers were so grateful to William Austin Hamilton Loveland, the man who brought the Colorado Central Railroad's line from Cheyenne through here (**Milepost 92**) to Denver, that they named their community for him. The line is now owned by the Burlington Northern.

By 1925, Colorado was the leading sugar beet producing state in the country. Even in 1901 sugar beets were being grown around Loveland in such quantity that the city became the site for the first sugar mill in eastern Colorado. A now-abandoned sugar mill is at Eleventh and Factory Avenue, just south of *U.S. 34*.

Namaqua, Home of Mariano Medina

The Big Thompson is the middle of three major South Platte tributaries that irrigate much of this region. But in the late 1850s, before the farmers had arrived, it was simply an obstacle to travel along the Front Range.

Consequently, the first man to settle in the valley, a New Mexico native named Mariano Medina, did the obvious thing. To meet the need of persons traveling between Denver and Fort Collins he built a bridge across the Big Thompson a half-mile south of **Milepost 89.5** at Kennedy

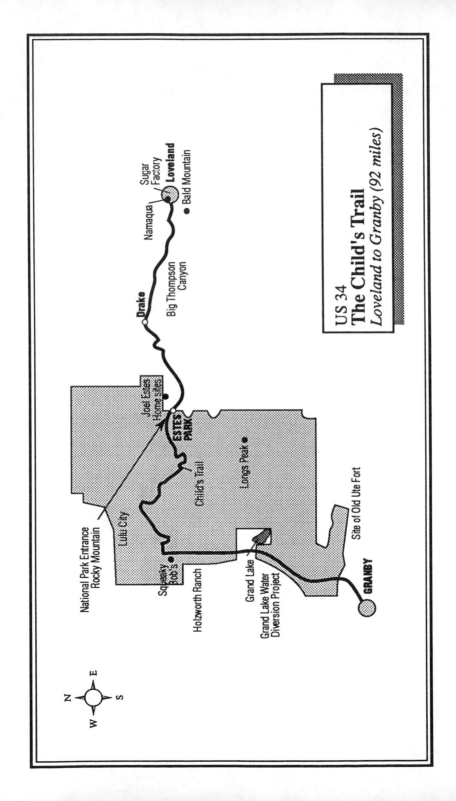

US 34
The Child's Trail
Loveland to Granby (92 miles)

Loveland
Sugar Factory
Namaqua
Bald Mountain
Drake
Big Thompson Canyon
Joel Estes Home Sites
ESTES PARK
Child's Trail
Longs Peak
National Park Entrance Rocky Mountain
Lulu City
Squeaky Bob's
Holzworth Ranch
Grand Lake
Grand Lake Water Diversion Project
Site of Old Ute Fort
GRANBY

N
E
S
W

and charged a toll. To foil those travelers who, objecting to his toll, might try to ford the river, Medina fenced in the surrounding land so as to channel all traffic to his bridge.

Such resourcefulness may have come to Medina by virtue of his thirty-five years as a mountain man. In the mid-1820s, about the time sixteen-year-old Kit Carson fled an apprenticeship to a Missouri saddlemaker to take the trail to Taos, New Mexico, twelve-year-old Medina ran away from his home in Taos. Medina wound up in the Pacific Northwest where, under the tutelage of Louis Papin, a St. Louis fur trader, he acquired the skills of a mountaineer as well as the pregnant wife whom Papin abandoned. Before accompanying Medina into retirement in the Big Thompson valley, Jeanne, a woman of the Flathead Indian tribe, had four children sired by Medina as well as the infant Louis Papin, whom Medina adopted.

Medina and Carson became friends when they were scouts in the 1840s' expeditions of John C. Fremont. A generation later, in 1868, on his way home from Washington, D.C., Carson stopped at the Big Thompson homestead, now dubbed "Namaqua" by Medina in memory of an Indian benefactor. Within weeks, Carson died at Fort Lyon in southern Colorado (see *U.S. 50* itinerary).

On his own death bed, ten years later, the irrepressible Medina asked to be buried in a favorite carriage with two grey horses, a tomahawk, a supply of candles, and a jug of whiskey.

Big Thompson Canyon

Rough passage through the straitened granite walls of the canyon defied construction of a road until the twentieth century. Earlier travelers to Estes Park took a route past Bald Mountain, about five miles south-southwest of **Milepost 83**, and climbed the steep south ridge that parallels the river. Until the introduction of the automobile in 1907, a stage line serviced the route, which one old-timer typed as "cruel to horses" because of its sharp ascent.

An earlier project to construct an electric railroad line on the canyon bottom foundered due to financial problems in the troubled economic period following the Spanish-American War. A single-lane automobile road was eventually built along the right-of-way graded earlier by the railroad developers. The current highway dates from 1937.

Although it took men four decades to build *U.S. 34* to the specifications required of a modern highway, nature managed to destroy it overnight on July 31, 1976.

Weathermen have devised scales for appraising the violence of floods. The top of the scale seems to be a one-hundred-year flood, one that can be expected to occur only once in a century. Ironically, on the eve of Colorado's first century of statehood—August 1, 1976—a flood of almost Biblical proportion ravaged the Big Thompson canyon. At its crest it achieved a volume four times that of any previously recorded flood.

The cause was not the failure of a dam, although Olympus Dam, containing Estes Lake, sat at the head of the canyon, **Milepost 64**. Miraculously, as the surface of the lake reached a level nine inches from the top, the one-hundred-yard earthen dam held.

The flood resulted purely and simply from a deluge of rain that dumped up to eleven and a half inches of water into the canyon and its tributaries within a few hours. The rain fell in such concentration that even when flood stage had been reached halfway down the canyon at Drake, where the North Fork of the Big Thompson meets its parent (**Milepost 75.5**), a drop had not yet fallen at the Canyon's mouth, **Milepost 83**.

It began in the evening when a torrent of water began issuing from the deceptively named Dry Gulch, **Milepost 64**, bypassing Olympus Dam. By midnight 80 percent of Drake was destroyed. Downstream at the Narrows, **Mileposts 83 to 81**, terrified refugees who had managed to climb high enough on the canyon walls to escape harm watched helplessly as camp trailers, houses, cars, exploding propane tanks, and human bodies rushed by in the torrent.

By morning 144 persons were presumed to be dead and $80 million in damage had been sustained in the canyon. Among the dead was State Patrol Sgt. W. Hugh Purdy, who had driven up the canyon from Loveland at the height of the storm to warn civilians to take to high ground. He was within one-half mile of Drake when he was overtaken by the flood waters.

Estes Park

At the head of the Big Thompson's canyon lies Estes Park, one of the earliest and most popular of the nation's Rocky Mountain resort areas. The town's name commemorates Joel Estes, a somewhat restless Kentuckian who in 1860 was the first to settle here. Estes built two cabins in the park, the first on Fish Creek, which empties into Lake Estes opposite **Milepost 64**, and the second at approximately this milepost on the north side of the lake. Lake Estes itself is a modern product of the Colorado-Big Thompson water development project (see below).

Estes was also a pioneer settler of Clinton County, Missouri. Later, with one of his sons, he joined the California gold rush in 1849, struck it relatively rich, sold out, and returned to his Missouri farm. Lured by the Colorado gold rush a decade later, Estes brought his large family of twelve children plus five slaves and his horses and cattle to a plot of land on Cherry Creek, southeast of Denver (see I-25 itinerary.)

After a few months he moved to a place just north of the present town of Golden (see I-70 itinerary), where he established a settlement that he called Golden Gate, probably in tribute to his earlier good fortune in the San Francisco region. Ever restless, he moved again, this time to the already established community of Fort Lupton (see I-25N itinerary).

Here Estes made a notable contribution to the rational colonization of Colorado: he helped to organize a "club" that arbitrated disputes over land. The organization became the first authoritative body in the region to take the trouble to record land titles. In the fall of 1859, scarcely a year into the gold rush, Estes discovered the park now named for him while on a bear hunt up the Big Thompson canyon. He moved his family to the park, raised his cabin, and built a road from Longmont (see *U.S. 36* itinerary) over which he brought the first wheeled vehicle to reach this place.

In 1866, the itch in his feet still not cured, Joel Estes moved his family to New Mexico where, in 1875, he died.

Professor F. V. Hayden, the first chief of the U.S. Geological Survey, had surveyed much of the American West in the years following the Civil War. He said of Estes Park in 1875, "Not only has nature amply supplied this valley with features of rare beauty and surroundings of admirable grandeur, but it has thus distributed them that the eye of an artist may rest with perfect satisfaction on the complete picture presented."

One Colorado pioneer claimed that Long's Peak was unclimbable until one-armed surveyor John Wesley Powell showed him the way. *Colorado Tourism Board.*

German-born artist Albert Bierstadt had already rested his eye on the vistas of Estes Park. Three miles southeast of the Beaver Meadows entrance to Rocky Mountain National

Park, a half-mile north of the park's road to Bear Lake, lies Bierstadt Lake, so named because Albert Bierstadt chose that vantage point for many of his landscape paintings of the region. A notable painting of Long's Peak, five miles due south of Bierstadt Lake, hung for many years in the Capitol Rotunda in Washington, D.C. It now hangs in the Western Room on the fourth floor of the Denver Public Library.

With an eye more covetous than aesthetic, Bierstadt's host and patron, the British Earl of Dunraven, Thomas Wyndham-Quinn, sought to purchase the entire area of Estes Park following a hunting trip here in 1872. Not eligible to file for land under the 1862 Homestead Act because of his British citizenship, Lord Dunraven secretly used local intermediaries to file in his behalf. He eventually accumulated fifteen thousand acres before legal challenges reduced his holdings by about half. Local gossip attributed at least one killing to the British aristocrat's machinations (see U.S. 36 itinerary).

Nonetheless, Dunraven left his mark on the place. His was the first hotel—the Estes Park Hotel—to be built for visitors to the resort. The site along Fish Creek a mile or two south of the original Joel Estes cabin, was selected by Albert Bierstadt. Built in 1878, the hotel was destroyed by fire in 1911. Today the name Dunraven graces a gulch on the upper North Fork of the Big Thompson. At the headwaters of the North Fork, a few miles farther west in Rocky Mountain National Park, there is a Lake Dunraven, and a mile southeast of the lake is Mount Dunraven.

The co-inventor of the Stanley Steamer, F. O. Stanley, and a partner bought up Dunraven's extensive holdings in 1907. Stanley was one of the less known of the nineteenth century's many versatile inventors, although he had an important role not only in the development of the automobile, but also in devising the materials of modern photography.

In Massachussetts, Stanley's doctor had cautioned him in 1903 to take a rest in hopes of postponing his threatened demise by perhaps a year or two. Stanley chose to come to the still scarcely accessible precinct of Estes Park. The summers he eventually spent here added not one but thirty-seven years to his life. He died at the age of ninety-three.

Although his purpose was to obtain rest, Stanley lost no time in becoming involved in the development of Estes Park. He introduced the Stanley Steamer to replace the horsedrawn stagecoaches that had been conveying visitors from Longmont. (see *U.S. 36* itinerary) and Loveland, and he helped build the town's water system and a power and light plant. His most conspicuous achievement is the huge Stanley Hotel, built in 1909, whose white walls still dominate the town.

Another disaster struck along *U.S. 34* on July 15, 1982, leaving at least two dead and $25 million in damage. This time the cause apparently lay in a faulty dam. Eight and a half miles northwest of Estes Park a small earthen dam at Lawn Lake burst, loosing a wall of water down Roaring River to its junction with Fall River. The merchants and purveyors of Estes Park at the height of their brief summer tourist season found themselves engulfed in a sea of mud that filled ground-level shops before rushing on to Lake Estes. Luckily Olympus Dam held once again, sparing the reconstructed settlements in the Big Thompson canyon.

Billing themselves "the gutsiest little town in Colorado," Estes Park's merchants cleaned up their city in time for an annual parade eight days later.

Rocky Mountain National Park

Just west of Estes Park, at **Milepost 58** along the 1982 floodway, is the Fall River entrance to Rocky Mountain National Park. The park was established in 1915 at the urging of resort entrepreneurs Enos A. Mills, F. O. Stanley, and others, aided by the Colorado Congressional delegation. At that time it consisted of only a fraction of its present 412 square miles.

An early park superintendent, L. C. Way, devised a remarkable way to promote the facility in its first year of operation. In collaboration with a Denver newspaper, he hired a comely young lady to stroll about the premises in a leopard-skin costume, snatching fish from streams and picking berries. She was billed in the press as the "Modern Eve," apparently implying that the new park was the modern Garden of Eden—without apple trees.

Rugged as the terrain is, access to the park became a problem in several respects. The state and county governments had collaborated in the construction of a road from Estes Park into Rocky Mountain National Park, whose route to the Fall River entrance was the same as that presently followed by *U.S. 34.** Two miles into the park *U.S. 34* intersects a gravelled road that follows the north bank of Fall River. The Fall River road predates the present *U.S. 34* route by nearly two decades. Built with convict labor, it eventually reached Fall River Pass where in September 1920 it joined another road built north from Grand Lake on the western side of the park.

Controversy erupted in 1919 when an exclusive concession was granted to an Estes Park jitney company to provide motor tours of the park. Resort owners immediately protested that their own touring cars were being denied access to the park. Enos Mills, for one, openly defied his exclusion. The case went to court and the federal government eventually won.

Washington finally took over responsibility for maintenance of park roads from the county and the state. In April 1929, Congress appropriated $450,000 to construct a highway over the 12,000-foot spine of Tombstone Ridge, an engineering phenomenon that would be known as Trail Ridge Road. The highway, topped with bituminous paving, was built from Estes Park all the way to Grand Lake in the summer of 1935.

Three and a half miles from the Fall River entrance, at Deer Ridge Junction, where *U.S. 34* intersects the road to

---

* Because the Park Service has neglected to install mileposts within the park, distances from the Fall River entrance to the Grand Lake entrance will be given in the text as automobile odometer readings, beginning with **Park Mile 0** and ending with **Park Mile 41**. The Park's boundary, forty-three miles from the Fall River entrance, lies at **Milepost 15 on** *U.S. 34*.

park headquarters, the segment over which *U.S. 34* continues westward into the Park was once a rudimentary wagon road that ran to a saw mill at Hidden Valley, **Park Mile 6.** At approximately **Park Mile 14,** the Ute Indian trail known as the Child's Trail crosses *U.S. 34* after rising up the steep slope from the bottom of Windy Gulch, southeast of the highway.

The Utes, whose home was in the mountains, and the Arapahoes and Cheyennes from the plains below used several trails to cross the Continental Divide. The Child's Trail was used by women and children because, despite appearance, it was the easiest of the trails. The Indian warriors preferred a more difficult but more direct route called Big Trail, which departed Estes Park via Bierstadt Lake and crossed the Continental Divide at Flattop Mountain, about five and a half miles south of **Park Mile 14.** The pathway above the highway at **Park Mile 17,** called "Rock Cut" on Park Service maps, coincides with the Child's Trail for a short distance. Here, ruts can still be seen of an old wagon road leading to a quarry that provided material for the construction of Trail Ridge Road.

The overlook at **Park Mile 15** gives an excellent view of the sentinel of the Rockies in northern Colorado, anvil-shaped Long's Peak, rising to 14,151 feet above sea level. Named for Maj. Stephen H. Long, who led a U.S. Army topographical expedition along the Colorado Front Range in 1820, Long's Peak remained unconquered for nearly half a century. In the summer of 1868, Maj. John Wesley Powell, another noted surveyor of the West, decided to make the attempt. The one-armed Powell, with a handful of others, including the founder of Denver's *Rocky Mountain News,* William N. Byers (see I-25 itinerary), elected to tackle the mountain from the west, so far untried by climbers.

Byers had made an unsuccessful attempt on the peak in 1864, after having scaled its neighbor to the east, Mount Meeker. At that time he concluded; "We have been almost all around the Peak and we are quite sure that no living creature, unless it had wings to fly, was ever upon its summit. We believe we run no risk in predicting that no man will ever be, though it is barely possible that the ascent can be made."

With the Powell party, Byers finally gained the summit on August 23, 1868. Three years later, Anna E. Dickinson joined a party organized by Professor Hayden and became the first woman to scale the peak.

Approximately a mile and a half above the switchback curve at **Park Mile 31** lies the ghostly site of Lulu City, a short-lived silver-mining town that was laid out in 1879, boomed in 1880, and died in 1884.

Near the Phantom Valley trailhead at **Park Mile 32**, Squeak Creek passes under U.S. 34. The creek was named for Squeaky Bob Wheeler, the pioneer who arrived here in 1885. Noted for his cooking, Squeaky Bob launched a summer tent resort in 1908, which in time was transformed from Camp Wheeler to the Hotel de Hardscrabble to a more elegant Phantom Valley Ranch. He hosted such dignitaries as Theodore Roosevelt, Supreme Court Justice Charles Evans Hughes, Otis Skinner, and Albert B. Fall, President Harding's secretary of interior who was disgraced in the 1924 Teapot Dome scandal.

Two miles down the road lies another pioneer resort, Never Summer Dude Ranch, which flourished in the 1920s under the direction of two German immigrants. Born in Germany in 1865, John G. Holzwarth came to the United States as a fourteen-year-old to work as a baker in St. Louis, a sheepherder's trail cook in Texas, and eventually a Texas Ranger. He came to Colorado in the 1880s and in 1894 married another immigrant, Sophia Lebfromm, who was working as a maid in Denver. The two operated a Denver boarding house and saloon until the Colorado legislature imposed prohibition on January 1, 1916. They filed for a homestead in 1917 and in 1920 decided to turn their ranch into a resort, in part to satisfy Sophia's ambition to operate a place in the tradition of an Old World mountain inn. The property was transferred to the National Park Service in 1975 to become an on-site museum.

Grand Lake

In past times the Continental Divide, along the crest of the Rocky Mountains, separated not only the waters of the country but hostile tribes of Indians as well. *U.S. 34* now passes from one side to the other at **Park Mile 24**. Clashes between the Plains tribes, Arapahoes and Cheyennes, and the Utes of the mountains were common. One of these battles left a legend with the Utes—the Legend of the Lake.

In a time before the arrival of the white men, a band of Utes had camped on the shores of Grand Lake, perhaps in the vicinity of **Milepost 14**. There they were set upon by a strong war party of Arapahoes and Cheyennes, who had crossed over the Divide in evident search of mischief. As the warriors prepared to confront their attackers, the Utes hastily boarded their women and children onto a huge raft and pushed them out into Grand Lake then, as now, Colorado's largest natural lake. The battle went badly for the Utes; hundreds fell before the Indians of the Plains. Then, a great wind came and capsized the raft in mid-lake, drowning all on board.

In the mystical scales of "good" and "bad" medicine by which the American Indian guided his life, Grand Lake became "bad medicine" in the minds of the Utes, and they scrupulously avoided it thenceforth.

The first white resident at Grand Lake was a Civil War veteran, Joseph L. "Judge" Wescott, who built a cabin on its west shore in 1867. He was soon followed by others, for on July 6, 1869, annals of the area indicate that there was an alarm among Grand Lake residents that an Indian attack seemed imminent.

Indifferent to the scare was James "Rocky Mountain Jim" Nugent, who had come across the mountains from his Estes Park cabin (see *U.S. 36* itinerary) to hunt deer in Middle Park. As he was stalking his prey, armed for some reason with only revolver and knife, Rocky Mountain Jim was surprised to see his panic-stricken dog racing toward him. An angry bear and her cubs were in hot pursuit.

Nugent emptied his revolver into the enraged sow. Undaunted, she knocked him to the ground. As he fought to repel her with his knife, he lost consciousness. Awakening, he found himself in a pool of blood, but the bear lay dead by his side. Nugent himself seemed nearly dead. His left arm was dislocated, his scalp nearly torn off and an eye had been gouged. He managed to mount his faithful white mule and, after falling and remounting several times, he reached Grand Lake, bellowing wildly for aid.

Fearing an Indian ruse, the settlers at first hesitated to go to him. When finally they came out to find Nugent unconscious on the ground once again, one of them observed, "Indians are 'round, for sure. Here is a man scalped."

The Alva B. Adams Water Tunnel

By the turn of the century eastern Colorado's growing population and a burgeoning agricultural industry required more water than nature had elected to send eastward from the Divide. A greater river flow was especially needed to keep irrigation ditches supplied in the expanding fields of sugar beets and other capital crops in the fertile piedmont between the Front Range and the South Platte River.

As early as 1905 someone had suggested diverting water from the Western Slope of the Rockies, where the population and farming were still modest, to the east. Not until the summer of 1933, however, was an organization dedicated to this aim actually set up. Called the Grand Lake Water Committee at the outset, its members, several of them tied to piedmont agricultural interests, lobbied for a tunnel to be dug under the Divide to draw water from Colorado's largest lake into eastern rivers.

Although Colorado officials had been zealous to maintain state control over local waters, the state was ill-prepared at the height of the Great Depression to finance such an enormous undertaking. So the federal Bureau of Reclamation was prevailed upon to fund a survey of the project in 1935. Based on conclusions of the survey, Congress agreed in 1937 to back the project, appropriating funds for construction of what is now the thirteen-mile Alva B. Adams (for a Colorado Senator) tunnel that diverts Grand Lake water to Lake Estes where it is dispatched down the Big Thompson River to irrigation ditches in the valley below Loveland.

Subsequently the Colorado River below Grand Lake was dammed to form the Shadow Mountain and Lake Granby reservoirs, **Milepost 10**, in order to sustain the level of Grand Lake, a demand imposed upon the Bureau of Reclamation by environmental advocates.

Milepost 3.5 marks the approximate location of another Arapahoe-Cheyenne invasion route used in their seemingly ceaseless conflicts with the Mountain Utes in Middle Park. In a skirmish that took place sometime in the early nineteenth century, according to Ute oral history, a war party of Plains Indians appeared here en route to a raid on their enemies, the Utes, as occasion might offer.

As it happened, there was a much smaller Ute hunting party, accompanied by women and children, situated about three miles south of here along the Fraser River. They were busy cleaning hides and jerking meat. A Ute youth, Standing Bear, not yet initiated into the ranks of the warriors, happened to see the invaders approaching this point from the north along Willow Creek.

Standing Bear alerted his comrades, who quickly threw up a three-sided rock and timber barricade backed against a fifty-foot precipice. Besieged by the Arapahoes and Cheyennes who were forced by the dense woods to attack on foot, the Utes managed to hold their own, but they feared time might run out for them. So Standing Bear volunteered to seek help from the main body of their band, in camp at Hot Sulphur Springs about twelve miles west (see *U.S. 40* itinerary).

The Utes lowered Standing Bear over the steep cliff. In the trees below Standing Bear managed to capture a loose pony before being challenged by a Cheyenne warrior. Before he could be recognized as a hostile Ute, Standing Bear killed the Cheyenne. Speeding to the main Ute camp, he rallied a war party to ride to the aid of the hunting party.

Standing Bear joined the pursuit of the routed Plains Indians and in isolated combat with an Arapahoe warrior, he took a second scalp. His remarkable courage merited Standing Bear formal recognition as a warrior of the tribe. In the years to come, he was elected a subchief. Moreover, according to Ute lore, the Battle of the Barricade discouraged depredations against the Utes for years afterward.

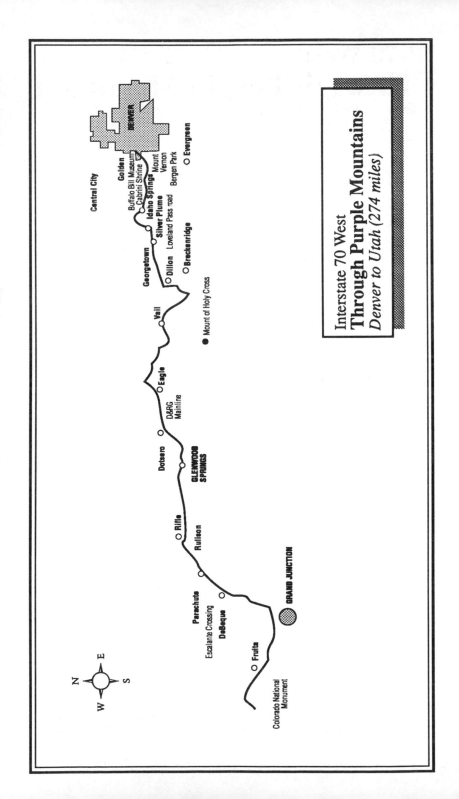

Interstate 70 West
Through Purple Mountains
Denver to Utah (274 miles)

I-70 West
Through Purple Mountains
Denver to Utah (274 miles)

Denver

America's first ice cream soda was created a few miles south of **Exit 274** in the heart of Denver. One morning in 1871 a regular customer entered Otto Baur's restaurant for his usual glass of soda pop on ice. "No ice," said Baur, for the iceman had yet to deliver that day. Rather than disrupt his customer's habits, however, Baur was quick to suggest that the soda be chilled with ice cream. Thus expediency introduced a new American tradition.

The Territory of Jefferson

The Territory of Kansas stretched through much of today's Colorado at the time of the gold rush in 1858 and 1859. In the West the remainder of the modern state came under the jurisdiction of Utah's territorial governor, Brigham Young. With the seat of government at least six hundred miles away from the argonauts, law and order suffered in the stretch.

"Owing to the absolute and pressing necessity for an immediate and adequate government," the immigrants at the mouth of Cherry Creek, two miles south of **Exit 274**, decided to take matters into their own hands.

A congressman from Georgia, Alexander H. Stephens, was prompted to introduce a bill to Congress on January 28, 1859, to establish the Territory of Jefferson. Stephens was persuaded to take this action because an important segment of the early Colorado prospecting fraternity consisted of Georgians, principal among them William Green Russell of

Auraria, Lumpkin County, Georgia (see I-25N itinerary).
Even so, Stephen's bill failed.

Undismayed, the immigrants convened on April 15,
1859, on the south bank of Cherry Creek to arrange for the
creation of their own "State of Jefferson." A three-day session that began on October 10 drew up a constitution, not for
a state but merely for a territory, which was endorsed by
popular vote two weeks later. An Ohioan, Robert W. Steele,
was elected governor.

The conventioneers defined their own boundaries for the
newly created political entity, which coincided with the
present state boundaries on the east and south but extended
north nearly half the distance through present Wyoming to
the latitude at which Nebraska and South Dakota now meet
and fifty miles into today's state of Utah.

In the constitution's preamble is this prayerful supplica-
tion: "We the people of the gold region of the Rocky Mountains, grateful to the Supreme Ruler of the Universe for his
blessings, and feeling our dependence upon Him for a con-
tinuance of the same; do ordain and establish a free and
independent government to continue until such time as the
Congress of the United States shall provide a government
for us; to be known as the Provisional Government of the
Territory of Jefferson."

After Kansas's controversial entry into the Union on
January 29, 1861, Colorado was officially proclaimed a territory by Congress on February 28, 1861. Governor Steele,
a Democrat, unprotestingly relinquished his position to
President Lincoln's appointee, William Gilpin, a Pennsylvania Republican.

Wheat Ridge Sod House

Just south and west of **Exit 267**, off 44th Street in Wheat
Ridge, is a sod house dating from 1886. Located at 4610
Robb Street, the privately owned structure is listed in the
national Register of Historic Places as a "well-preserved and
rare area example of sod construction."

Mount Vernon

Just south and west of **Exit 259** lies the site of the village of Mount Vernon, at the head of Mount Vernon canyon through which I-70 passes on its climb over the Front Range of the Rockies. Mount Vernon came into being at the outset of the gold rush, about the same time as Denver and Auraria. It served as a waystation from the Cherry Creek settlements to the mining camps in the mountains at Idaho Springs and Central City. The governor of the rump government of the Territory of Jefferson, Robert W. Steele, had his residence at Mount Vernon. The house, privately owned, still stands.

Abraham Lincoln named a Pennsylvania attorney, S. Newton Pettis, to be associate justice of the Colorado Supreme Court in the spring of 1861. That summer, looking over his new domain, Pettis stopped in Mount Vernon. He wrote to a friend back East: "This very flourishing little spot presents a fine appearance slumbering in her beautiful valley. . . . Farmers in the neighborhood are in good spirits and prognosticate much fertility for this young territory. . . . The hills and valleys of Mount Vernon's surroundings are fairly carpeted with flowers. . . ."

Cabrini Shrine

Along the frontage road, west a mile and a half from **Exit 259**, lies the entrance to the Cabrini shrine, a site chosen by Mother Francis Xavier Cabrini, founder of the Missionary Sisters of the Sacred Heart, as a place where her nuns could find periodic respite from their labors. Mother Cabrini was the first U.S. citizen to be canonized as a saint by the Roman Catholic Church.

According to legend, Mother Cabrini, when confronted with the realization that the location she had chosen had no water available, tapped her walking stick at a spot on the hillside and instructed workmen to dig at that place. A spring was uncovered which has been flowing year round ever since. Mother Cabrini died in 1917 and was canonized in 1946.

Buffalo Bill's Grave

Five miles northeast of **Exit 254** at the summit of Lookout Mountain, overlooking Golden at its base and Denver in the distance, is the grave site of William Frederick "Buffalo Bill" Cody, attended by an impressive museum featuring artifacts and materials associated with the life of the famous buffalo hunter *cum* showman (see I-76 and I-70E itineraries).

Bergen Park

Southwest of **Exit 252** is a small valley, first known as Elk Park and later as Bergen Park. One-armed John Wesley Powell arrived here from Denver in July 1867 in his initial expedition to survey parts of the Rocky Mountain region (see *U.S. 34* itinerary). As the party prepared to move south toward Pike's Peak, one of Powell's aides, Joseph C. Hartzell, described for the Bloomington (Illinois) *Pantagraph* the toils attending the movement of wagons through these rugged mountains:

> All hands were at work—some ahead clearing the way and acting as pilots, others behind "chocking,"—that is following with large pieces of wood to block the wheels when at rest. Sometimes the mules would gain but a few feet when, with locked and blocked wheels, the wagons were held till a new start could be made. Nothing could exceed the faithfulness of our animals as they toiled up and down mountain steeps. . . . The method of descent would be, perhaps, most novel to an Illinoisian. Locking the wheels so they could not turn . . . the force of half a dozen men holding back with all their power, by a long rope hitched to the axle tree, the driver tugging at the reins, the mules settled back on their haunches, plowing the dirt with their feet, and you have the picture. . . .

As the crow flies, it is sixty miles from Bergen Park to Pikes Peak. For wagon-pulling mules in 1867 the distance was not given.

Gold trapped in quartz form was found nearly simultaneously in two places in the spring of 1859. One was nine miles north of **Exit 244** along *Colorado 119* at a place known as Mountain City (subsequently Central City). The second was ahead at **Exit 240**, Idaho Springs. Both strikes were on branches of Clear Creek, the stream that exits the mountains at Golden and enters the South Platte River north of Denver. Divided by towering peaks, the sites are only about five miles apart.

Idaho Springs

George A. Jackson, a thirty-two-year-old Missourian and veteran of the California gold rush, developed another rich vein of gold-laden quartz near **Exit 240**, where Chicago Creek empties into Clear Creek. His strike, in May 1859, was the culmination of a five-month effort inspired by the following turn of events recorded in his diary:

Jan. 6[1859]. Pleasant day. Built big fire on rim rock to thaw the gravel; kept it up all day. [Wolverine] came into camp while I was at fire. Dogs killed him after I broke his back with belt axe; Hell of a fight.

Jan. 7. Clear day. Removed fire embers, and dug into rim on bed rock; panned out eight treaty cups [about one and one-half pints each] of dirt and found nothing but fine colors; ninth cup I got one nugget of coarse gold. Feel good tonight. Dogs don't. Drum is lame all over; sewed up gash in his leg tonight—[wolverine] no good for dog.

Jan. 8. Pleasant day—well, Tom [Golden], old boy, I've got the diggins at last. . . . Dug and panned today until my belt knife was worn out, so I will have to quit and use my skinning knife. I have about a half ounce of gold; so will quit and try to get back in the Spring.

Others followed Jackson to his diggings to establish the town of Idaho Springs in 1860. The antecedence of the name is uncertain, but, as in the state of Idaho, the word seems to be of Shoshone Indian origin, referring to the columbine, now Colorado's state flower. If so, the name may have originated with the wife of some resident mountain man, many of whom were married to Shoshone women.

Louis Dupuy, Georgetown Hotelier

By the time he arrived in New York in 1866, the Frenchman could boast a catalogue of endeavors that would have filled another person's lifetime, though he was only twenty-two. And he would prove to be not only streetwise but erudite—and a little crooked.

Adolphe François Gérard immigrated to the United States after fleeing a Roman Catholic seminary, serving as a scullery worker and apprentice chef in a Paris restaurant, and working as a sometime journalist and translator for a London publisher. He managed to sell some articles to

The Hotel de Paris on Georgetown's Alpine Street serves now as a museum evoking the memory of a remarkable imposter, Louis Dupuy. *Colorado Tourism Board.*

Frank Leslie's *Illustrated Newspaper* in New York, until someone discovered that his grasp of English was perhaps less than precocious and sued him for plagiarism.

Gérard quickly signed on with the U.S. Army and was conveniently dispatched to the 2nd Cavalry Regiment, then stationed at Fort D. A. Russell near faraway Cheyenne, Wyoming Territory. Seven and a half months into his enlistment, just as spring was coming to the high plains on April 1, 1869, Private Gérard deserted his unit.

When, a short time later, he appeared in Denver, he was Louis Dupuy of unmentioned antecedents, an identity he retained until the day he died. Returning to his haphazard trade as a freelance journalist, Dupuy also worked briefly as a distributor for the *Rocky Mountain News*. Within a short time, however, the lure of the mining camps attracted him.

Eighteen seventy-three was a troubled year in the United States. In Colorado, silver mining was displacing efforts to extract gold from now-depleted deposits when, on February 12, Congress eliminated the highly prized silver dollar as a legal coin. It was the so-called "Crime of '73" Coinage Act. In June a world financial crisis began, culminating in the United States with September's Panic of 1873. And that same year Louis Dupuy was maimed in the belated explosion of some charges he had planted in a mine in Silver Plume, **Exit 226**.

During his convalescence, Dupuy set the course for the remainder of his life. Drawing from a Georgetown fund for injured miners, he bought a bakery and transformed it into a hotel and restaurant. The Hotel de Paris opened in 1875 in Georgetown, a mile or so south of **Exit 228**, with a bill of fare that would have befitted Maxim's of Paris.

The hotel featured things unheard of in the region at that time: hot and cold taps in rooms, baths, ice water piped in from a mountain glacier to refrigerate a cellar ice-box, trout swimming in an Italianate fountain in the restaurant.

Everything here I have got by my own work [Dupuy told a visitor a generation later]. I built this house with my own hands, and everything in it has been earned by my own labor. I have never asked help of any sort from any human being and I never will. And I owe no man anything.

Why, the tax-collector of this town had the nerve to ask me to pay taxes, if you please, as if I owed this godforsaken town anything! And when they proposed to levy on my property, I told them to come on. The first man to step over the doorsill would be shot in his tracks, and I would fire the building and myself with it. They took the hint and I still pay no tax.

Five days short of his sixty-sixth birthday in 1900, Louis Dupuy died, a victim of pneumonia, which seems to have resulted from the daily ice water baths he affected. Only then was his true identity revealed, but his alter ego was so celebrated that no one really cared. Today, the Hotel de Paris, on Georgetown's Alpine Street, is an impressive museum.

The Georgetown Loop

Another Georgetown monument, an extraordinary feat of engineering, was initiated by the notorious Jay Gould, crafty New York financier and Colorado railroad magnate. Already in control of the Kansas Pacific, Gould managed in 1879 to gain control of the Colorado Central & Pacific Railroad from W.A.H. Loveland. At that time the Leadville silver boom (see *U.S. 24W* itinerary) was in full swing and, as yet, no railroad had been built to the mining town on the upper Arkansas River (see *U.S. 50W* itinerary). The sixty-mile wagon route from Georgetown to Leadville was a long day's haul for a four-horse team, so Gould decided to take the Colorado Central due west over the mountains. The result was the famous and indeed awesome Georgetown Loop, which featured a convoluted track doubling back on itself on a ninety-foot-high trestle that came to be called the Devil's Gate Viaduct. Four and a half miles of track were laid to reach Silver Plume, only one and a half miles distant from Georgetown but several hundred feet higher.

A narrow-gauge train passes over the ninety-foot-high Devil's Gate on a famous section of the Georgetown Loop. *Colorado Historical Society.*

Due to some serious errors in construction, the famous trestle had to be dismantled and rebuilt so that in the end the short line from Georgetown to the Silver Plume mining area was not completed until 1884. By that time the Denver & Rio Grande had already reached Leadville from Canon City and Gould's other railroad, the Denver, South Park & Pacific, was on its way over Boreas Pass (see *U.S. 285N* itinerary). So what was nominally the Georgetown, Breckenridge & Leadville Railway never got beyond Graymont, Exit 221. The Loop remained in use until the eve of World War II, when the line was sold to the Silver Plume Mine & Mill Company and the trestles were dismantled for use as mine-shoring timbers.

After operating on an abbreviated run that carried tourists from the Georgetown vicinity to Silver Plume, the Georgetown Loop excursion train began taking passengers over an equally spectacular, rebuilt Devils Gate on August 1, 1984.

Argentine Central Railway

Still another notable but short-lived narrow-gauge had its starting point in Silver Plume. Begun in September 1905, the Argentine Central Railway took its name from the mountain pass southwest of Silver Plume where it was headed.

Begun by E. J. Wilcox to serve the sixty-five mines he owned in the vicinity, the line ran eight miles south to Waldorf where with a transcontinental flourish, it was secured with a gold spike. It proved to be an inauspicious symbol for the silver-mining Wilcox.

A post office was duly established at Waldorf; at 11,666 feet, it claimed to be the highest in the country's postal system. Over virtually unprecedented grades of 6 percent the line was extended another eight miles up the slopes of a nearby mountain where, on August 1, 1906, it halted at 13,423 feet. It became a popular excursion for area tourists.

In 1907 a British syndicate was sufficiently impressed with the sixteen-mile Argentine Central Railway that it offered Wilcox three million dollars for it. Unfortunately, another of the world's cyclical financial crises struck—the Panic of 1907—and the deal fell through. In 1909, Wilcox, who had invested $300,000 in the railroad, was forced to sell out for a mere $44,000. Three years later the line was sold again, this time for only $5,000. Two days before Armistice Day, on November 9, 1918, state officials granted permission to dismantle the Argentine, and the tracks were taken up the following year.

Loveland Pass

A pass across the Great Divide lies five miles south of **Exit 216** at the head of Clear Creek, the once busy railroad canyon that today boasts only the truncated Georgetown excursion line. The pass is named for early railroad developer W.A.H. Loveland.

Breckenridge

Beyond 11,992-foot Loveland Pass, eight miles south of **Exit 203**, on *Colorado* 9, lies Breckenridge, an 1859 mining camp that has lingered into municipality. Founded by Alabaman George E. Spencer and a group of prospectors, the town was named for President Buchanan's vice-president, James C. Breckinridge of Kentucky. When his ticket was defeated by Lincoln in 1860, Breckinridge returned to Congress where his opposition of Lincoln's war measures led to his expulsion from the Senate and his flight to join the Confederacy. He became a Confederate army general and eventually President Jefferson Davis's secretary of war.

Because of Breckinridge's role in the Civil War, the pro-Unionist residents of the Colorado town named for him petitioned Congress to change the name of the town. Washington's legislators obliged by changing the first "i" to an "e"—Breckenridge.

Mount of the Holy Cross

At **Exit 190**, a quarter-mile below the summit of Vail Pass, a dirt road runs across Shrine Pass to an observation point about three and one-half miles from I-70. It is one of the few places from which one can view the celebrated 14,005-foot Mount of the Holy Cross.

An historic photograph of the cross was made in 1873 by the official photographer of the Hayden Survey, William H. Jackson (see *U.S. 160* itinerary). "We have just made a tremendous climb to the top of the grandest peaks in the Rocky Mountains," wrote Hayden's assistant, James Gardiner, to his mother. "We could not get our animals within many miles on account of the fallen timber and the trip had to made on foot packing the great 50-pound theodotite, while three men carried the photographic apparatus. . . ."

Like so many other explorers, they were deceived in their judgment of distances in the pristine air of the high country. Remote objects seemed always to be nearer than they actually were. Expecting a mere day's hike up and back, they did not prepare for what would face them. "We had [little] to eat for two days of tremendous climbing, while at night we lay on the mountain side without shelter or covering. We succeeded in getting splendid observations and photographs. One large photograph, 12x14 inches, shows the peak culminating in a dark precipice 3,000 feet high on which rests the great White Cross, 1,500 long, as perfect in form as you can imagine."

D&RG Goes to Standard Gauge

The Eagle River and what, in 1890, became the mainline of the Denver & Rio Grande Railroad join I-70 at **Exit 171**. In that same year the pioneer narrow-gauge railroad (see *U.S. 50W, U.S. 24W,* and *U.S. 160* itineraries) decided not only to shift its mainline between Salida and Salt Lake City from the Gunnison River valley to the upper Arkansas River valley, but also to switch from its narrow three-foot-wide trackage to standard four-foot-eight-inch tracks, to facilitate linkage with transcontinental rail systems. The track laid through this point, from Redcliff to the Utah state line, was set on standard-gauge ties. Narrow-gauge rails were put down initially as far as **Milepost 105** in anticipation of the changeover to standard-gauge. Narrow-gauge roadbeds from Denver to Pueblo, Salida, and Leadville were converted to standard widths. In 1890, the D&RG had seventeen hundred miles of narrow-gauge right-of-way. Much of the remainder of the system continued as three-foot trackage, however, for the same reason that it was used in the first place—because of the difficult terrain to be crossed.

Dotsero

The Eagle River empties into the Colorado River at Dotsero, **Exit 133**. Another, later railroad, the Denver & Salt Lake, came down the Colorado River to join the D&RG right-of-way in 1934, when the Dotsero Cutoff was completed. The D&SL, also known as the Moffat Road, originated in Denver and reached this point by way of the remarkable 6.2-mile Moffat Tunnel under James Peak on the Continental Divide (see *U.S. 40* itinerary). The road and tunnel were the projects of David H. Moffat, at one time a president of the D&RG. The D&SL was absorbed by the Denver & Rio Grande in 1947.

The town of Dotsero was founded in 1880 and is reported to have gained its name because it was the base point in a topographical survey of the region—"Dot Zero." A mile north of **Milepost 131** lies the 1,700-foot crater of an extinct volcano, which has provided the material for a pumice quarry.

Glenwood Springs

Glenwood Springs, originally a Ute spa, (see also *U.S. 160 and U.S. 40* itineraries), became a town in 1882 on the heels of the Ute evacuation to Utah (see *U.S. 50-550* and *Colorado 13* itineraries). Well-to-do residents of the mid-1880s' mining town of Aspen enjoyed the comforts of Glenwood Springs by riding the forty-two mile railway that served the mines to its junction with the D&RG mainline.

In 1887 a consumptive dentist, John Henry Holliday, died in Glenwood Springs, having sought in vain the restoration of his health. More celebrated as gambler and gunman "Doc" Holliday, he was at the time of his death still resisting extradition to Arizona to stand trial for some killings related to the famous shoot-out at the OK Corral in Tombstone (see I 25S itinerary)

New Castle

New Castle, **Exit 105**, like its English namesake, is a coal-mining town. Two railroads, the Colorado Midland and the Denver & Rio Grande, passed through here on their way from Leadville to Grand Junction. The coal-fired locomotives stopped to take on fuel from New Castle's mines.

As with many coal mining regions, New Castle has its endlessly burning mine. Situated in Burning Mountain west of town, coal in the depths of the Vulcan mine have been burning since 1896 when an explosion killed forty-nine miners.

Following his inauguration in April 1905, President Theodore Roosevelt returned to Colorado (see also *U.S. 40* itinerary) and established the temporary White House at the Hotel Colorado in Glenwood Springs.

Armed this time with a .30-40 Springfield, Roosevelt came for bear. Once again he was accompanied by Philip B. Stewart of Colorado Springs and guide John Goff, assisted this time by Jake Borah, a relative of another Roosevelt comrade, William E. Borah, a Republican who in 1906 would be named U.S. Senator by the Idaho legislature.

The 1905 hunt took place on West Divide Creek and Clear Creek at the base of Uncle Bob Mountain about twelve miles south of **Milepost 99**. Roosevelt bagged only a yearling bear. His friend Stewart chided, "That skin is not big enough to use for anything but a doily."

Teddy Roosevelt obliged the press by making jokes about his "doily bear." A game joke, however, soon inspired toymakers to create a product that would bring comfort to four generations of American infants—the "Teddy bear."

Anvil Points

North of **Milepost 83.5** lies Anvil Points, site of a federal oil shale research center (see *Colorado 13* itinerary) and locus of a 1,300-acre reserve of oil shale deposits, set aside for contingent development by the U.S. Navy.

At Rulison, **Exit 81**, the frontage road doubles back to the Anvil Points installation. Another crosses a bridge over the Colorado River. Six miles south of that bridge, 8,442 feet underground, a tremendous explosion took place on September 9, 1969. "The crumbling slate bluffs along 10,000-foot Battlement Mesa sent up plumes of dust as the shaking earth set off small rock slides," reported the New York *Times*.

The event marked the climax of Project Rulison, which featured the detonation of a forty-kiloton nuclear device. The aim was to release natural gas that was locked in the limestone shale at that depth. The Atomic Energy Commission, which oversaw the experiment, said there was no mishap and predicted that the test would prove to be a success.

A sequel to the Rulison blast, one with many reverberations (see *Colorado 139-64* itinerary), took place twenty-five miles northwest of **Exit 81** in 1973.

Parachute

The town of Parachute, at **Exit 75**, takes its name from the creek that empties into the Colorado River at this point. The headwaters of the creek, consist of three symmetrically spread forks, resembling, on a map at least, a parachute. For much of its existence the town had been known as Grand Valley, earning its appellation not for its proximity to a mere creek but for being on the banks of the mighty Grand River, the original name of the Colorado River until its legislated change in 1921.

The creek above the town flows through deposits of kerogen-laden shale, a circumstance that prompted a forward-thinking group of graduate students at Cornell University in Ithaca, New York, to advance a plan in 1958. "One new development being considered which might revolutionize the shale oil industry is the use of nuclear explosions underground to recover kerogen from the shale. The large quantities of energy released in the form of blast and heat would be used to break up the ore and retort the kerogen in place . . . [at] relatively small cost. . . . The idea is a very new one and has yet to be tested and proven on a large scale."

One hundred and eighty-two years earlier, another group of travelers descended the Grand Mesa south of **Milepost 70**, crossed the river, and sized up the same location. Fray Silvestre Vélez de Escalante, of the Franciscan mission of Santa Fe in New Mexico, recognized the river neither as the Grand nor as the Colorado on September 5, 1776. He chose instead, to call it El Rio de San Rafael. While he and his colleague, Fray Francisco Atanasio Dominguez, and their expedition of Indian and New Mexican explorers were camped for the night in the meadow near **Milepost 70**,

Escalante noted in his journal that here "there are no prospects for a settlement."

De Beque

A Canadian-born physician with three medical degrees and a pronounced case of wanderlust made this notation in his diary on November 15, 1888: "Today we moved into our new home in the town of De Beque—the first family in town and the only one at this date." Dr. Wallace A. E. de Beque had lived earlier in Fairplay (see *U.S. 285N* itinerary) and Grand Junction before moving, in 1883, to a ranch called Ravensbeque, three and one-half miles south of here, where he was joined on an adjacent spread by his brother, Col. Robert de Beque. The doctor remained in De Beque, **Exit 62**, until his death in 1930.

Dr. de Beque was one of seven partners in an 1884 enterprise known as the Grand River Toll Road Company, which constructed the road preceding the existing one between Grand Junction, **Exit 31**, and Glenwood Springs, **Exit 116**. The toll road opened for traffic on December 5, 1885.

Five years later, two railroads forswore the rivalry that had characterized the industry in the previous half-century. Although they were competitors, the Colorado Midland and the inevitable Denver & Rio Grande decided, for the first time, to embark on a joint venture. They collaborated in building a single right-of-way through this stretch of Grand Valley. Their joint venture ran from Rifle, **Milepost 90**, to Grand Junction. The Colorado Midland (see *Colorado 82* itinerary) was the first to reach this point, building from Rifle. The D&RG, however, was the one to survive.

Grand Junction

Almost two years after the tragic Meeker massacre (see *Colorado 13* itinerary), in September 1881, the Colorado Utes were removed to Utah, resignedly in the case of some, reluctantly in the case of others, inevitably for all. With their departure under terms of the 1880 treaty, the remarkably fertile river bottom lands of the Western Slope were made available to the white farmer.

Scarcely had the dust settled behind the Utes when, on September 26, 1881, George A. Crawford, in the name of the Town Company, claimed a section of land at the junction of the Gunnison and Colorado rivers, **Exit 31.** Other would-be homesteaders squatted on plots up and down the two rivers, so Crawford took the precaution of hiring two men to build a cabin on the Town Company's section in order to hold off claim jumpers. A town was laid out, lots defined, and by January 1882, 150 men and two women had immigrated to the site, most of them from Gunnison, 125 miles upstream.

To diversify gender in this male outpost, an enterprising pair of immigrant lawyers made the offer of "a choice town lot to the first lady that gets married in our town, a free ceremony in the bargain, and will tie the knot either hard or soft, tight or loose." The first wedding in the new town of Grand Junction took place on August 10, 1882. Unrecorded, however, was the degree of tension applied to the knot.

Many of the settlers in Grand Junction discovered a perplexing ambiguity in the legal aspects of land tenure. These newcomers to the evacuated Indian reservation had assumed—incorrectly, as it turned out—that western Colorado had become public land subject to the generous terms of the Homestead Act. The 1880 congressional act disposing of the reservation land had, on the other hand, conceded title, if not possession, to the Utes "in severalty." Finally, on July 28, 1882, Congress made plain its intention by declaring that, for the land they elected to occupy, settlers must pay the Indians the "price fixed by law."

Whatever the cost, there were those who found it worth every penny. D. S. Grimes of Denver organized a company that planted 100,000 fruit trees along the river. Grimes unhesitatingly proclaimed the soil to be "the best fruit growing portion of the country lying between Salt Lake, on the west, and the eastern part of Kansas."

In June 1882, the first irrigation ditch—that inevitable

amenity of Colorado life—brought water to the streets of Grand Junction, sparing use of the town's solitary well.

As the Denver & Rio Grande Railroad (see *U.S. 50-550* itinerary) emerged from the Gunnison River valley, the town looked so promising that the railroad company bought a half-interest in the Town Company. Throwing a bridge over the mainstream of the Colorado River, the D&RG sent its first train across the waters into Grand Junction on November 21, 1882.

With trees and trains and townspeople, the year 1883 spelled boom for Grand Junction. In less than a generation another important agricultural industry arrived: the Colorado Sugar Manufacturing Company erected the state's first sugar mill in 1899.

Colorado National Monument

The Colorado National Monument reflects the effects of a

The twelve-million-year-old Coke Ovens in the Colorado National Monument excite the imagination of our modern industrial age. *Colorado Tourism Board.*

billion years of erosion—sloshing tidal seas, windswept fresh water lakes, swamps, blowing sand, and rushing torrents. Around 1900, John Otto moved into Monument Canyon and, fearing that the venerable area might finally have met its match with the arrival of man, petitioned Washington to do something to preserve the place. Congress eventually conceded his point and in 1911 President Taft signed the proclamation that made the thirty-two-mile plot, just south of **Exit 19** at Fruita, a national monument.

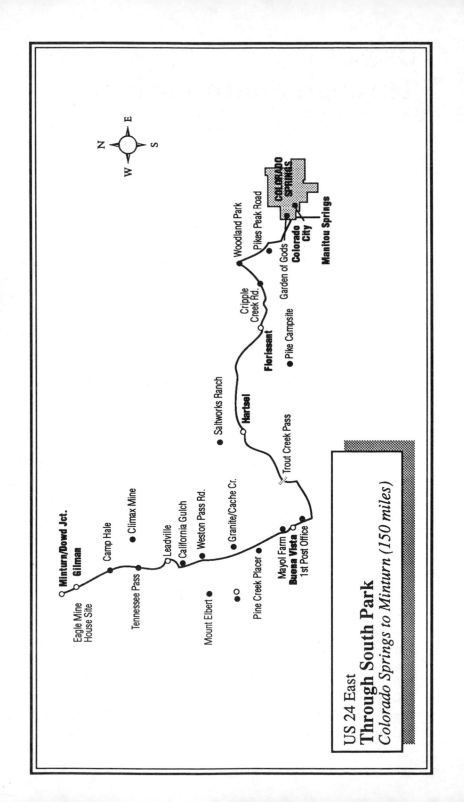

US 24 East
Through South Park
Colorado Springs to Minturn (150 miles)

US 24 East
Through South Park
Colorado Springs to Buena Vista (86 miles)

Colorado Springs

Colorado Springs is the product of an aspiring railroad magnate's strategem. In 1871, Colorado City, at **Milepost 301**, was a municipality already in its twelfth year; it had even been the first capital of Colorado Territory. But its promise was shattered when Colorado Springs was organized that year by the romantic (see *U.S. 50* itinerary) but ruthless (see *I-25* itinerary) **Gen. William Jackson Palmer**, founder and guiding light of the Denver & Rio Grande Railroad.

In laying out the first stretch of the D&RG from Denver, Palmer deliberately avoided bringing the line into Colorado City. The railhead was sited a few miles east on a completely new townsite platted by the Colorado Springs Company, a real estate subsidiary of the D&RG. So successful was Palmer's ploy that Colorado Springs eventually supplanted Colorado City as the seat of El Paso County, whose 2,157-square miles were delineated by the territorial legislature in 1861 as one of the seventeen original counties.

Ute Pass

The county's Spanish name alludes to the Ute trail that winds down from South Park through the break between Pike's Peak and the Rampart Range to the north. The route was acknowledged by the territorial legislature when, on August 8, 1862, the Ute Pass Wagon Road company was commissioned to build a toll road from Colorado City to the South Fork of the South Platte River in South Park. Travelers were already making their way along this trail to the diggings at Tarryall (see *U.S. 285* itinerary). By 1871 traffic had become so heavy over the Ute Pass roadway that its maintenance as a highway rated the first bond issue ever voted on for a Colorado county road.

Garden of the Gods

The dramatic sandstone formations north of **Milepost 299** were dubbed Garden of the Gods in 1859 by Rufus Cable, one of the charter residents of Colorado City. Cable was the attorney of Col. Melancthon F. Beach, the founder of Colorado City. They both were members of the El Paso Claim Club, an early cooperative association that, in the absence of organized government, sought to ratify property claims.

In one of his long-distance efforts to woo Queen Mellon from the comforts of the eastern seaboard to the lot of a pioneer wife, General Palmer wrote in 1870 of the Garden of the Gods: ". . . I thought, 'Could one live in constant view of these grand mountains without being elevated by them into a lofty plane of thought and purpose?, . . . and I felt so happy that I would have such a wife, who was . . . wise and good and pure enough that a wild home amidst such scenery was preferable to a brown stone palace in a fashionable city."

The Garden of the Gods, west of Colorado Springs, is the setting where narrow-gauge railroad pioneer William J. Palmer wanted to build a home for his fiancee, an eastern society belle. *Colorado Tourism Board.*

Miss Mellon's reply is not on record, but she did exchange marriage vows with the passionate Palmer later that very year.

Pike's Peak

Edwin James, geologist, botanist, and surgeon for the 1820 expedition into the Rocky Mountains headed by Maj. Stephen H. Long of "Great American Desert" fame (see the High Plains section), was the most celebrated of the three men who first ascended Pike's Peak. Had history taken Major Long's suggestion the peak would now be called James's Peak, for the man who climbed it, rather than Pike's for the man who tried and failed.

In his published account of Long's expedition James observed: "The guide, who had conducted us to the foot of the Peak; and left us with the assurance, that the whole of the mountain to its summit was covered with loose sand and gravel, so that though many attempts had been made by the Indians and by hunters to ascend it, none had ever proved

Pikes Peak looms above the heights of the Rampart Range. Named for Captain Zebulon Pike who tried but failed to reach the summit in 1806, the peak was first climbed in 1820 by Edwin James, chronicler of the Stephen H. Long expedition. *Colorado Tourism Board.*

successful. We passed several of these tracks, not without some apprehension for our lives, as there was danger when the foothold was once lost of sliding down, and being thrown over precipices."

James and his companions tackled the peak from the site of Manitou Springs, **Milepost 298**. The ascent took almost a day and a half. They departed on foot from the springs just after lunch on July 13, 1820, and, after establishing a small base camp halfway up the mountain, they struggled from daybreak until 4:00 p.m. before reaching the summit.

"There is an area of ten or fifteen acres," continued James, "forming the summit, which is nearly level, and on this part scarce a lichen is to be seen. It is covered to a great depth with large splintery fragments of a rock, entirely similar to that found at the base of the Peak, except, perhaps, a little more compact in its structure. . . . They were found to rest upon a bed of ice, which is of great thickness, and may, perhaps, be as permanent and as old as the rocks, with which it occurs."

Thirty-eight years after James viewed the world from the summit of Pike's Peak, Mrs. J. H. Holmes arrived here in the first wave of the so-called Pike's Peak gold rush. After two days of climbing, she reported in the following letter datelined Pike's Peak, August 5, 1858: "Nearly every one tried to discourage me from attempting it, but I believed that I should succeed, and now, here I am. . . . In all probability, I am the first woman who has stood upon the summit of this mountain, and gazed upon this wondrous scene. . . ."

In 1874, the U.S. Army established a weather station near the summit of Pike's Peak and manned it with personnel of the Signal Corps. What would have been a tedious and even forlorn job, however, became quite the opposite when Sgt. John T. O'Keefe arrived in January 1876 to earn notoriety for himself as the "Pike's Peak Prevaricator."

Nine months after O'Keefe's arrival a news story appeared in the Pueblo *Chieftain* recounting an attack of "mountain rats" upon O'Keefe and his wife and child at their alpine outpost. The tale might rival Daphne DuMaurier's story "The Birds": Beleaguered by rats, O'Keefe hastily contrived a cylinder of metal roof sheeting in which he encased his wife. Then, having thrust his own legs into stove pipes, he battled the horde that had invaded his cabin. He somehow overlooked his alleged two-month-old daughter, Erin, who was supposedly devoured by the rodents. To this point, however, she had never been seen by O'Keefe's acquaintances.

The story caused a national sensation, dramatizing the perils of life in the wilds of Colorado's mountains.

By the fall of 1880, O'Keefe had really hit his stride. The Colorado Springs *Gazette* carried an O'Keefe-inspired account of the volcanic eruption of the heretofore solidly granite Pike's Peak. "Sergeant O'Keefe . . . portrays the majesty of the scene as the grandest that he has ever witnessed, not excepting that of Vesuvius seen by him in 1822 when he was a lad and before he left his native Italy for America. . . . The eruption has but just begun and should it continue any length of time, there is no doubt that Colorado Springs will meet the same fate as that which destroyed the flourishing cities of Pompeii and Herculaneum!"

The Denver press growled that O'Keefe had come to America not in 1822 but in 1862 and not from Italy but from Ireland. They failed to note, however, that he had left Ireland by way of Blarney.

Cripple Creek

The town of Divide, at **Milepost 278**, lies at the entrance of another Colorado road to riches—the Cripple Creek gold mining district, fifteen miles south. The Cripple Creek gold rush began in July 1891, when a canny Colorado Springs carpenter, Winfield Scott Stratton, made some important calculations based on his appraisal of the volcanized geology of the Cripple Creek area. On the basis of these, he staked a couple of claims, which became the Washington and Independence mines. They were so successful that the Independence alone was sold in 1899 for $10 million, the biggest mining transaction on record at the time.

As elsewhere in Colorado, along with prospectors and merchants, the railroads rushed into this remote region on the backside of Pike's Peak. David Moffat, later to be the inspiration behind the remarkable Moffat Tunnel (see *U.S. 40* itinerary), built a narrow-gauge line from Florence (see *U.S. 50* itinerary) north to Cripple Creek in 1849. The same year the Midland Terminal Railroad built south from Divide to Victor, Cripple Creek's companion mining town. In 1901 the Colorado Springs and Cripple Creek District Railroad arrived from the east. Well known to "Monopoly" game players as the Short Line, the CS&CCD brought the combined total of trackage in the Cripple Creek district to 235 miles, involving a capital investment, exclusive of rolling stock, of $10 million for all three railroads.

Julian Street, a writer for a national magazine, passed through Cripple Creek in 1914. The town was in the doldrums following the decline in gold mining. The writer paused only long enough to speak to one or two persons on Myers Avenue, which, he said, consisted of "false-front saloons and Parlor Houses." One of them was Madam Leo, who urged him to send her "some nice boys."

When Street's magazine article appeared, Cripple Creek residents were outraged. In revenge they renamed Myers Avenue, the heart of the redlight district, "Julian Street."

Victor

Victor, the home and professional training ground of world-traveling journalist Lowell Thomas, won celebrity in its own right. Less than two miles south of Stratton's Independence mine, Victor was promoted as a townsite by the Woods Investment Company, a partnership of three brothers. To illustrate the Midas touch enjoyed by the trio, simple foundation excavations for the Woods-backed Victor Hotel uncovered a gold lode that became the Gold Coin mine, a source of $5.5 million of the precious metal over a period of five years.

In addition to the Gold Coin, the Woods also owned the Pikes Peak Power Company, the First National Bank, and the Short Line Railroad. Success in those days was tenuous, however. Bankruptcy overtook the brothers in 1910.

As a candidate for the U.S. vice-presidency, Theodore Roosevelt campaigned in the mining camp of Victor in September 1900. It was a typically audacious move by the Republican Party candidate. The town's economy was severely depressed by what its citizens perceived to be the economic policies of the incumbent Republicans. The mining industry in Colorado had been hit especially hard by the government's refusal to support the price of silver. Ever prepared to beard the lion in his den, however, Roosevelt put himself promptly on record in a Denver speech in which he declared: "I am for a Progressive Tariff, for the gold standard, expansion and the honor of the flag."

Travelling on the old Colorado Midland line from Colorado Springs to Cripple Creek and Victor by way of Divide, the Roosevelt campaign train failed to arrive on time. The delay gave opposition leaders in Victor an opportunity to work a political dirty trick. Through a ruse they emptied the lecture hall of Roosevelt supporters and replaced them with their own followers.

Sniffed the pro-Roosevelt Denver *Times* afterward, ". . . The toughs had done their work well. There was room for only a few of the decent class."

Recognizing the trick, Roosevelt and his party, including a bodyguard of former Rough Riders, left the hall. But in the street he was jostled and someone jabbed him sharply in the chest with a broken banner pole. As his railroad car pulled out of the station, it was stoned.

A year later Roosevelt's running mate, President William McKinley was assassinated by an anarchist in Buffalo, New York.

A great tragedy struck Victor in 1904 when antagonism between striking members of the Western Federation of Miners and the mine operators reached its climax. The WFM had claimed its first success in an 1894 Cripple Creek strike in which it won important concessions from operators. In 1904, however, unionists made an ill-advised decision to enlist the services of Harry Orchard, a professional agitator. Orchard secretly planted a bomb in a local railroad station. The detonation caused thirteen deaths and untold wounded among a party of strikebreakers who had crowded the station on their way to the mines. Goons hired by the operators, in turn, wrecked the offices of a local newspaper supporting the miners, seized seventy-three miners at gunpoint, and abandoned them on the prairies near the Kansas border.

Florissant

The wagon road to Cripple Creek originally ran from Florissant, **Milepost 270**. Florissant was named by its founder, Judge James Castillo, who, when his business interests failed at Florissant, Missouri, emigrated west to establish a trading post for Indians and a store for Ute Pass travelers.

In 1871 David P. Long, a Civil War veteran and disenchanted fundamentalist minister, arrived here. He and his family settled on the remarkable land of the petrified forest just south of here, although they lacked legal claim to a homestead because this part of the territory had yet to be surveyed. Undismayed by lack of title, absence of neighbors and annoying, if amiable, intrusions of curious Indians, the Longs enjoyed their new home. Their main diversion was a visit to Castillo's little store over the hill.

Long took more than casual note of the impressive petrified redwood stumps in the vicinity and even uncovered the skeletal remains of a massive mastodon, a discovery that brought visits from professors at Colorado Springs to consult with him.

The family's livelihood was gained in cutting live timber, which was dragged from the forest by a couple of oxen. One day the enterprise ended abruptly when lightning killed one of the animals. Ex-minister Long forsook the fossils of Florissant, enlisted in the ranks of the Latter Day Saints, and in 1873 moved his family to Utah.

Florissant Fossil Beds National Monument

A mile and a half south of Florissant lies the six-thousand-acre monument comprising the Florissant Fossil Beds. Although the magnificently preserved fossils and the splendid petrified redwood trees are ancient in the extreme, the history of this national monument is a relatively recent one. The nearly ten square miles containing the fossils had been privately occupied and owned for more than a century.

When conservationist pressure to have the area set aside under official protection reached its peak in the 1960s, there were two tourist enterprises here that invited visitors, for a fee, to enter the beds and take what they could find of fossils and petrified wood. Even more threatening was the prospect that the site would be subdivided into residential lots, a fate that had already befallen land on three sides of the present monument.

A private group sought to have the land condemned and turned over to federal jurisdiction. Their cause was pressed in the courts and before a subcommittee of the U.S. Senate by a future governor of Colorado, Richard Lamm, then a Boulder attorney. In the end this group prevailed and, in 1969, a presidential proclamation declared the fossil beds a national monument, under administration of the Interior Department's National Park Service.

Eleven-Mile Reservoir

Five miles south of **Milepost 250**, the meandering South Platte River now pauses to fill Eleven-mile Reservoir. There, on December 13, 1806, Capt. Zebulon Montgomery Pike made a historic observation in his journal: "Found a river 40 yards wide, frozen over which after some investigation I found run northeast. . . . Must it not be the head waters of the river Platte? If so, the Missouri must run much more west than it is generally represented."

Hartsel

The town of Hartsel at **Milepost 239** takes its name from

Samuel Hartsel, a Fifty-Niner from Pennsylvania who found gold in the lush grasses of South Park. Hartsel turned cattleman shortly after arriving in the region in 1860. He began his South Park herd by purchasing footsore oxen brought by gold-seeking immigrants. Eventually he introduced shorthorn Durhams to South Park. Early on the scene, Hartsel acquired extensive land holdings in the region around this 1866 townsite, which stands near the center of his ranch site.

Like so many high country-pioneers, Hartsel became on one occasion a reluctant participant in the incessant and inevitably gory clashes of the Plains and Mountain Indians. An appreciation of the persistent hostilities among the Indians themselves has been a frequent oversight of American historians, preoccupied with battles between red and white men.

Hartsel was on good terms with resident Ute bands who hunted in South Park and eventually lent their name to the route that *U.S. 24* follows from the park down to Colorado Springs. He was captured by a Cheyenne war party that had entered South Park to strike a blow against their enemies, the Utes. Forced to serve as a guide, Hartsel witnessed the destruction of a village of his friends, the Utes. Then seeking to flee to the safety of their own territory on the plains, the Cheyennes obliged Hartsel to guide them through Ute Pass, where they freed him.

Broadway's Tony Awards

A Broadway dynasty of sorts is associated with the Salt Works Ranch, two miles north of **Milepost 227**. The daughter of a Colorado pioneer who had made a mining fortune, Mildred Hall was a Broadway actress who, with her husband, toured theaters in the West at the turn of the twentieth century.

In 1910, as a widow, she married a South Park cattleman, Thomas McQuaid, and took up life as a housewife at the Salt Works Ranch. She passed on her love of the theater, however, to her niece, Antoinette Perry.

Miss Perry made her acting debut in Chicago on June 26, 1905, and later that year on Broadway. She gave up a stage career in 1909 when she married the president of the Denver Gas & Electric Company, Frank Wheatcroft Frueauff. Frueauff left Denver to reside with his wife in New York, where their two surviving daughters, Margaret and Elaine, also turned to acting.

After Frueauff died in 1922, Antoinette Perry returned to the stage. In 1928 she became a director, the profession in which she made her most profound mark on Broadway. She directed thirty Broadway plays in eighteen years, including *Harvey* by Denver playwright Mary Chase.

During World War II, Miss Perry was an executive of the Apprentice Theater and the Experimental Theater and helped to establish the American Theater Wing which provided USO entertainment to U.S. troops at camps and in hospitals.

After Antoinette Perry died at 58 in New York of heart problems complicated by overwork, the American Theater Wing, in her memory, instituted the annual Tony awards for outstanding Broadway actors, writers, directors, composers, and set designers.

Antoinette's daughter Elaine Perry, in turn, became a Broadway producer whose productions included *Anastasia*, which in 1956 became a high-powered Hollywood movie starring Ingrid Bergman and Yul Brynner.

Miss Perry herself moved to the Salt Works Ranch a few years before she died in 1986 at the age of sixty-five.

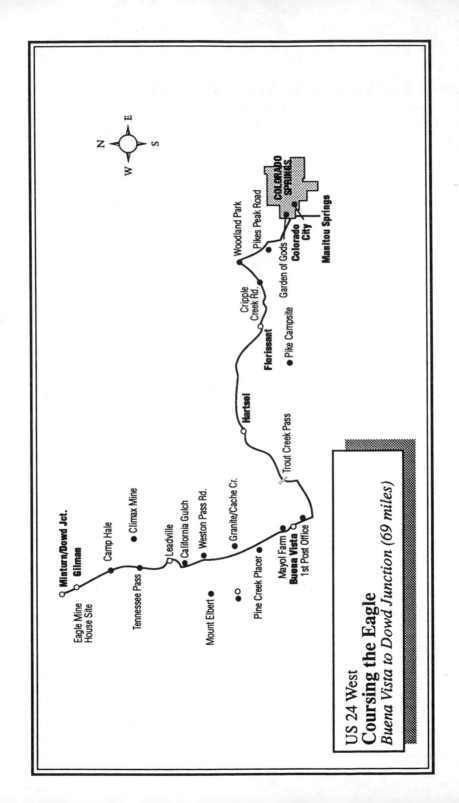

US 24 West
Coursing the Eagle
Buena Vista to Dowd Junction (69 miles)

US 24 West
Coursing the Eagle
Buena Vista to Dowd Junction (69 miles)

Buena Vista

The Arkansas valley's first post office was established in 1865 near **Milepost 212**, the present site of the Colorado State Reformatory. Because federal postal authorities required a name for each of their facilities and because the upper Arkansas valley was devoid of towns at that early date, the postmaster, rancher John McPherson, chose to honor his wife. He dubbed the postal facility that operated from his ranch "Helena."

The town of Buena Vista, at **Milepost 210**, did not come into existence until 1879. The town, "Good View" in Spanish, merits its designation for the panorama that the location commands of the Collegiate Range to the west.

The identity of the person who named the town (pronounced locally as "Bee-oona Vista") seems to have been lost in the mists of more than a century. It was not, however, that tireless dispenser of Spanish names, Alexander Cameron Hunt, former governor and official of the Denver & Rio Grande Railroad who named Alamosa, Durango, and Salida, each as the D&RG arrived to establish its depot. Buena Vista was founded a year before Salida was laid out by the D&RG. Not until June 5, 1880, did the narrow-gauge railroad reach Buena Vista on its dash to Leadville following the Royal Gorge War (see *U.S. 50W*).

Riverside and Pine Creek

The ubiquitous argonauts were the first persons on record to commit more than a transient presence to the upper Arkansas valley. As early as 1863 Frank Mayol planted what was probably the first cash crop in the region. He grew potatoes at Riverside, **Milepost 203**, to sell to the mining camps that had developed along the Continental Divide and the streams that drained from it.

The first recorded placer gold camp was located around **Milepost 198** near the mouth of Pine Creek, at whose headwaters today is the Silver King mine.

Cache Creek

Among the early gold prospectors in the area were two who would do well in the California Gulch discoveries near today's Leadville—H. A. W. Tabor and S. B. Kellogg. Both tried in 1860 to develop placers along Cache Creek, **Milepost 194**. Tabor went on to fame, fortune, and folly as a silver magnate, and Kellogg grubstaked Charlie Baker, who made the early gold discoveries in the San Juan Mountains of southwestern Colorado (see *U.S. 50-550* itinerary).

Granite

Granite, the town that grew at the mouth of Cache Creek, provided the scene for the climactic episode of the Lake County War. There, on July 3, 1875, vigilantes assassinated Judge Elias F. Dyer in his own courtroom.

The so-called war was actually a feud whose first fatal incident had occurred nearly a year prior to Judge Dyer's murder, when George Harrington was gunned down near Salida, then merely a stage stop called Bale's Station. Harrington's neighbor, Elijah Gibbs, was known to have quarreled with Harrington over their respective rights to water. Consequently, he was arrested, along with his hired hand, and both were bound over for trial in the Granite court. Mounting antagonisms between friends of the murdered Harrington and those of Gibbs prompted a venue change so that the trial could take place in supposedly neutral Denver.

The Denver jury's verdict of acquittal, however, did nothing to ease Lake County rancor. After Gibbs had returned to his farm, twenty miles south of Granite, vigilantes appeared one night in January 1875 to serve a new warrant for

Gibbs's arrest. With Gibbs in his cabin were his pregnant wife, a child, and a visiting neighbor woman. Nevertheless, he chose to resist. The ensuing fusillade killed three of the vigilantes. An inquest ruled that Gibbs had acted in self-defense, but, still fearful for his life, he fled to Denver.

Persons identified with the absent Gibbs, among them Judge Dyer, received threats from vigilantes. Antagonisms began to congeal at this point around individuals with common political party affiliations. Republicans, such as Judge Dyer, held control of county offices, so the Democrats organized a Committee of Safety, embodying a "people's court" and a panel of twelve jurors. Democratic and Republican newspapers around the state took up the quarrel among themselves.

On April Fools' Day, 1875, another murder occurred at Bale's Stage Station. The victim was a Gibbs supporter.

Judge Dyer launched his own investigation of the extralegal Committee of Safety and, as he prepared to question witnesses, was shot and killed in the Granite courthouse. With that, somehow, tensions lessened. John McPherson, pioneer postmaster, succeeded Dyer as probate judge. Gibbs apparently never returned to his Centreville home. Lake County eventually (in 1879) seceded from the troubled southern portion, which, from Granite to Salida, became Chaffee County.

Mount Elbert

Colorado's highest mountain at 14,443 feet, Mount Elbert, seven miles west of **Milepost 188**, was named after the son-in-law of territorial governor John Evans. Samuel Hitt Elbert had been named territorial secretary by President Lincoln at the time his father-in-law received designation as governor. When John Evans stepped down in anticipation of being named a U.S. Senator for the territory in 1865, a New York newspaperman, Alexander Cummings, was named governor by Lincoln's successor, Democrat Andrew Johnson. Elbert stayed on amid Cummings's charges that he was trying to undermine the new governor's administration of the territory. Cummings, a man who was both impulsive and choleric, seized Elbert's implement of office, the state seal, and refused to turn it back to the territorial secretary. Finally, in January 1866, Elbert resigned in apparent despair and returned to the east.

In 1873, President Ulysses S. Grant, a Republican, sent Elbert back to Colorado to serve as territorial governor, succeeding Edward Moody McCook (see *U.S. 40* itinerary). Elbert was in office only a year when McCook was restored to the governorship. Elbert stayed this time and eventually was named to the Colorado Supreme Court.

Colorado's highest peak at 14,431 feet, Mount Elbert commemorates a Colorado secretary of state who was ousted by his governor. *Colorado Tourism Board.*

Weston Pass

The stage and wagon road that served the early town of Oro City (later Leadville) joined today's highway near **Milepost 184**. Freight wagons and Spotswood & McClellan stagecoaches made the run from South Park over 11,921-foot Weston Pass on their way from the Denver, South Park & Western's end-of-track, wherever it was on a given day, to this point en route to the diggings in California Gulch (see *U.S. 285N* itinerary). Beyond Weston Pass, of course, other roads led down the Ute trail to Colorado City (see *U.S. 24E* itinerary).

Oro City–Leadville

A frustrated California prospector from Virginia, Abe Lee, made the first big gold strike on the upper Arkansas just above **Milepost 180** in California Gulch. Lee himself named the site when he announced to his buddies, "I've got the whole state of California in this goddam pan!" That was in May 1860.

H.A.W. Tabor, meanwhile, had abandoned his placer diggings downstream at Cache Creek and was driving his wagon north with his wife and child when he heard about Lee's strike. The Virginian Lee welcomed Maine Yankee Tabor and helped him select a site for a claim. It paid off. Tabor, down to his last few dollars, soon amassed more value in gold than he had ever possessed in anything. The rich location was dubbed Oro City.

Tabor's wife Augusta gained celebrity for being the first woman in the region and reverence for her pluck and sagacity. The all-male community pitched in to build a cabin for Tabor's family—the first in California Gulch—and in time came to rely on Mrs. Tabor as the repository and custodian of their gold dust. As such, she was the first banker on the upper Arkansas.

In the early gold rush period the attitude of prospectors toward women was a singular one. "[Canon City] was an exact counterpart of every such camp in a mining district," observed one old prospector. "There were perhaps five women [there]. They were treated with the greatest respect and as though they were creatures from another world."

Over the next decade the gold fever subsided, ebbing with the supply of gold. In 1874 two partners in a gold placer claim, W. H. "Billy" Stevens and A. B. Wood, became curious about some black igneous lumps that had fouled their sluice box. They sent a sample off to Edwin Harrison's smelter in St. Louis, Missouri, where most of Oro City's gold ore was processed. The assay report showed it to be lead carbonate, rich in silver. Another rush began that would make Oro City into Leadville and, for a time, second only to Denver in size and importance.

Horace Tabor turned to storekeeping and obtained a commission as postmaster. He eventually went on to become county treasurer, Leadville's mayor, Colorado's lieutenant governor, and finally, interim U.S. Senator. He had acquired shares in some valuable Leadville silver mines, notably the Matchless, and had shed his long-suffering pioneer wife, Augusta, for the affections of the comely Baby Doe. But in 1893, when Congress repealed the Sherman Silver Purchase Act, he became nearly destitute.

After his death Baby Doe camped out for years near the entrance to the Matchless mine, heeding Tabor's dying words; "Whatever happens, hold on to the Matchless." In February 1935, Baby Doe, then a wizened eccentric, was found in her shack on the mine property, frozen to death, with the Tabor fortunes yet unreclaimed.

A veteran Leadville prospector held two claims in 1877 near the bonanza silver mine in California Gulch, the Little Pittsburg. His name was A. Y. Corman and his mines were the A.Y. and the Minnie. As with so many of his kind, his pleasure lay in the search; as soon as his claims showed promise, Corman sold them. The mines were bought by a handful of adventurers from Philadelphia who had left staid lives to try their luck in the Leadville mining boom.

Underfinanced, however, they ran into trouble. One of the partners, a former Philadelphia grocer, Charles H. Graham, brought in a fellow Philadelphian who had remained behind to prosper in the new technology of machine-made lace. Meyer Guggenheim bought a half-interest in a mining operation that promised two hundred tons of lead carbonate ore per month.

The distance between promise and reality, however, threatened to be the same as that between Philadelphia and

Leadville. The mines became flooded and came to a standstill. Guggenheim decided to visit Leadville before investing any more in the mines. He arrived in July 1880, looked over his acquisition, carefully sized up the risks and decided to finance the purchase of pumps to clear the mines. It was a wise move, for by fall of that year the A.Y. mine alone was producing $200-$400 a day in silver, plus lead, a tidy sum for the time. The diggings eventually intersected the lode that had made the Little Pittsburg rich.

The enterprise made Guggenheim richer and launched one of the world's dominant mining and refining companies, whose modern descendant continues to operate all over the world as well as in Leadville where it began. Today's ASARCO Corporation is a fashionable acronym for the old American Smelting & Refining Company (see I-25S itinerary).

Leadville Silver Boom

When Stevens and Wood made the original lead carbonate discovery in 1874, ore from the region was shipped all the way to St. Louis for assay by Edwin Harrison. Their find brought Mohammed to the mountain: Harrison left St. Louis to establish a reduction works in Leadville to do the preliminary processing of ore being excavated from the hills around California Gulch. Harrison's role in the mining camp gained such prominence that a faction sought to have the community, still known as Oro City, renamed Harrison. Obviously they failed, but Leadville's main street today bears the name of Harrison Avenue.

By 1878 Harrison's reduction works was shipping nearly twenty thousand tons of ore per year by wagon to Colorado Springs and Canon City. Freighters were earning as much as eighteen dollars per ton. Harrison wanted dearly to see the railroad arrive, for he expected to increase the yearly volume of ore leaving Leadville to twenty-four thousand. What he wanted from the speedier and more efficient railroad was a freight contract for just ten dollars a ton.

The D&RG, victor in 1880 over the Santa Fe in the bloodless Royal Gorge War, reached Leadville on July 20, 1880. What finally brought it was silver ore. A decade earlier when he was promoting the idea of his railroad with prospective London investors D&RG president William Jackson Palmer had declared, "A population engaged in mining is by far the most profitable of any to a railway. A hundred miners, from their wandering habits and many wants, are better customers than four times that number otherwise employed."

Ice Palace

The 1890s were to the nineteenth century what the 1920s or perhaps the 1960s have been to the twentieth. In the minds of some, an extravagance is only as grand as it is ephemeral. Among the extravagances of the 1890s were the ice palaces. St. Paul, Minnesota, had its ice palace in 1894. Montreal, Canada, would have its ice palace. Each was designed and realized by Charles E. Joy, who also did the job for Leadville in 1896.

The imposing 1896 Leadville Ice Palace, at an altitude of more than ten thousand feet, survived from January until July. *Colorado Historical Society.*

The site was the block between Sixth and Eighth streets of Capitol Hill in the western section of Leadville. Two hundred sixty workmen began on November 1, 1895, to fashion twenty-by-thirty-inch blocks of ice into an elaborate castle of Norman style. The ice was taken from the numerous nearby lakes, which had inspired Lake County's name. Even early in the winter season the mountain lakes offered ice that was already twenty inches thick. Ice of more specialized quality was brought in over the Denver & Rio Grande Railroad from Palmer Lake, on the divide between Denver and Pueblo (see I-25M itinerary).

Contractor Joy originally had hired some stone cutters to trim the ice blocks that would form the building, but they proved to be too slow. He then hired some Canadian lumberjacks who, with their double bit axes, did an exemplary job. In two months an ice edifice covering five acres was completed, featuring ninety-foot Norman towers on the front and sixty-foot towers at the rear. Huge interior halls were appointed with ice pillars, which were imbedded with electric incandescent lamps, at that time little more than a decade beyond their invention. Snow statues were fashioned depicting prospectors and miners and the others who had given Leadville its character and acclaim. The ice palace opened on January 1, 1896. With ten thousand yards of canvas shading its south wall from the sun, it survived until July 1, 1806, at Leadville's cool and rarified ten-thousand-foot altitude.

The 1878 Healy House and adjacent Dexter Cabin, at 912 Harrison Avenue in Leadville, are fine museums depicting the period of the silver mining boom. Both are carried on the National Register of Historic Places.

Eleven miles northeast of **Milepost 175**, on *Colorado 91* near Fremont Pass, is the Climax Mine, the world's largest molybdenum mine.

Railroad Expansion

Competition was fierce between the railroad lines in search of the mining dollar. For example, the D&RG built a spur from Leadville over Fremont Pass to the mines in the Kokomo region, a distance of a mere sixteen miles. The spur was completed six months after the D&RG had reached

Leadville, in December 1880. Undaunted, the Denver, South Park & Pacific built a line from Como in South Park (see *U.S. 285N* itinerary) over tortuous, precipitous Boreas Pass four years later, arriving at Leadville also by way of Kokomo. The South Park line went down the valley of the Blue River through Breckenridge (see I-70W itinerary) to Dillon and south again along Tenmile Creek to Fremont Pass.

Mountain railway travel was perilous and often hindered by the weather. In the winter of 1898-99, the Denver, South Park & Pacific was paralyzed for seventy-three days following a ferocious blizzard on Ground Hog Day. As a result the citizens of Dillon were on the verge of famine.

In the paroxysm of expansion that afflicted the D&RG after the nearly two-year stalemate of the Royal Gorge War in the late 1870s, Palmer's road built not only over Fremont Pass but also over Tennessee Pass, **Milepost 166**, and into the valley of the Eagle River, where once again silver had beckoned. Prospectors had found more deposits of lead carbonate near Redcliff, **Milepost 154**. Today some of the state's most extensive deposits of zinc are also found there.

In 1890 the Denver & Rio Grand Railroad had seventeen hundred miles of narrow-gauge track running through three states—Colorado, New Mexico, and Utah. The D&RG's mainline from Denver to Salt Lake City ran south to Pueblo, then west up the Arkansas valley to Salida, over Marshall Pass to Gunnison, and along today's *U.S. 50* to Grand Junction and the Utah border (see *U.S. 50W* itinerary).

The man who introduced the narrow-gauge to America's western mountains, Gen. William Jackson Palmer, was no longer in control of the D&RG, and railroad technology had made strides in the generation since he began the line at Denver (see I-25M itinerary). The new management decided to refit much of the entire D&RG system in 1890. They also decided to reroute their mainline traffic over a standard-gauge roadbed from Denver to Pueblo to Salida, then north past Leadville over Tennessee Pass, **Milepost 166**, down the Eagle River to the Colorado (then called the

Grand River—see *U.S. 40* itinerary), down the Grand valley to Grand Junction, and on to Utah. Despite the seeming magnitude of the job, it was done in a matter of months (when they extended the line into the Eagle River valley, for example, they attached narrow-gauge trackage to standard-gauge ties).

Camp Hale

North of Tennessee Pass at **Milepost 160** lies Camp Hale, on the east side of *U.S. 24*, a vast potter's field filled with the concrete skeletons of dismantled buildings. The camp was established during World War II to accommodate ski troops of the U.S. Army, the 10th Mountain Division. Because the location of the installation was remote, a camp for German prisoners of war also occupied the site.

It was here that a Nazi sympathizer and Harvard honors graduate, Dale Maple, embarked on an odyssey in early 1944 that earned him conviction and a death sentence for treason, a penalty later commuted to life imprisonment and later, when the war had ended, to ten years incarceration.

Maple was a member of the 620th General Engineering Corps, a two-hundred-man unit stationed at Camp Hale. His enthusiasm for the Nazi cause prompted him, during an ostensible leave of absence from his army unit, to smuggle himself into the POW camp and pose for several days as a member of the defeated Afrika Corps. During his sojourn with the prisoners, Maple worked out plans for two German prisoners to escape. Returning to his unit and his true identity, Maple arranged to buy a used car in Salida. He feigned illness to explain an absence from his duty post and drove his German comrades south toward the Mexican border.

Unfortunately the car broke down. On foot, Maple and the two Germans were arrested by Mexican immigration officers just inside the borders of Mexico and returned to the United States, where Maple was tried.

Organized in 1942 around a nucleus of skiing enthusiasts from the East, the 10th Mountain Division, thirteen thousand strong, eventually fought in the Italian campaign of World War II.

"All that running up and down the mountains in Colorado served us well," said one 10th Division veteran after the war. "We were in great condition."

In 114 days of combat north of Rome and Florence, the division incurred 992 combat deaths and some four thousand wounded, among them future Senator from Kansas and presidential candidate Robert Dole.

Deactivated in 1958, the 10th was reactivated in 1985 at Fort Drum in the Adirondack mountains of New York. "No single group played a prouder role in the long campaign . . . to set Italy free," Senator Dole told listeners at the 10th's reactivation ceremony.

Many of the veterans of the mountain division helped to develop the U.S. ski industry after the war. The National Association of the 10th Mountain Division was organized in 1971. It now has three thousand members. Ironically, the association is now affiliated with the International Federation of Mountain Soldiers, which came into being in 1985, uniting ski troops from the U.S. and France in camaraderie with some of their erstwhile adversaries in Germany, Austria, and Italy.

The Eagle Mine

On the banks of the Eagle River at Gilman, just west of **Milepost 151**, lies the Eagle mine, first developed in 1879. The Eagle was operated by the New Jersey Zinc Company from 1915 to the late 1970s, when it was shut down because of a depressed metals market. A notable feature of the Eagle is its seven-million-ton tailings pile, much of which lies terraced on the 125-acre property resting on the bluffs of the Eagle River.

The mine was shut down and its milling machinery transferred to another company mine in the east at a time when gold was selling on the world market for around $800 an ounce. According to an estimate by state mining officials, the Eagle mine's tailings alone contain 105,000 troy ounces of gold (not to mention more than five million ounces of silver and thousands of tons each of many other minerals). Its value at one point amounted to roughly $84 million. It is testimony perhaps to the imponderable economic mysteries inherent in mining that its extraction was not worth the cost.

William H. Jackson made this spectacular photograph of the Mount of the Holy Cross (southwest of Redcliff) in 1873 after a torturous climb to this exalted viewpoint (See p. 139) *Colorado Historical Society.*

Minturn and Dowd's Junction

Minturn, **Milepost 146**, and Dowd's Junction, where *U.S. 24* joins I-70, are communities named by the powers-that-were of the railroad. The first was Thomas Minturn, a D&RG employee at the time (1885) the town was established. The second was Jim Dowd, whose sawmill, a short way up Gore Creek to the east, supplied ties for the construction of the D&RG through the valley of the Eagle River.

Colorado 82
Over the Fourth of July
Twin Lakes to Glenwood Springs (84 miles)

Twin Lakes

The Twin Lakes, **Milepost 79**, are gigantic potholes resulting from the scouring done ten million years ago by the Lake Creek glacier, whose bed is followed by Colorado 82. The glacier gave its name to Lake County, one of the state's original seventeen counties (see *U.S. 24W* itinerary).

Independence Pass

Gold inspired the construction of the tortuous roadbed that follows Lake Creek to the beginning of its north fork at the base of a toweringly steep cirque gouged by the ancient glacier. The discovery took place a few miles beyond the pass on the Fourth of July, 1879, prompting both the camp and the pass to be named Independence. Cresting at 12,095 feet, Independence Pass, **Milepost 61** remains one of the highest passes in the country. Even today it is closed due to snow most of the year.

Construction of a toll road was begun at Twin Lakes in 1880, and, by fall, it had breasted the pass to reach the gold camp, an overland distance of more than twenty miles. In another year's time the road was extended a cliff-hanging stretch of nearly twenty miles to reach yet another new mining camp. This one would be known as Aspen.

Prospectors Bill Hopkins, Philip Pratt, and Smith Steele came first upon the site at the base of Aspen Mountain in the early summer of 1879. They staked claims and, in recognition of their intrusion onto the Ute Reservation, called their camp Ute City. By fall when a Kansas bookkeeper, Henry Bramblet Gillespie, arrived to buy up the Pratt and Steele claims, there were thirty-five prospectors in residence. On October 4, 1879, however, a courier sent by Governor

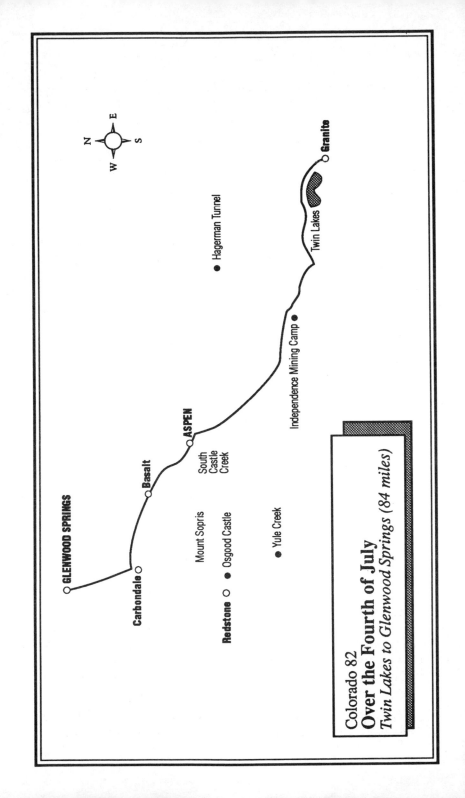

N W E S

GLENWOOD SPRINGS ○

Carbondale ○

Mount Sopris

Redstone ○ ● Osgood Castle

● Yule Creek

Basalt ○

ASPEN ○

South
Castle
Creek

Independence Mining Camp ●

● Hagerman Tunnel

Twin Lakes

Granite ○

Colorado 82
Over the Fourth of July
Twin Lakes to Glenwood Springs (84 miles)

Frederick Pitkin hurried up the Roaring Fork valley to warn them that, a few days earlier, angry Utes had massacred Indian Agent Nathan C. Meeker and others at White River, ninety miles to the northwest. Fortunately Ute Chief Ouray interceded to dampen hostilities (see *Colorado 13* itinerary). Renamed and slightly relocated by town builder B. Clark Wheeler, Aspen eventually transcended its silver camp origins to become today's international skiers' mecca.

One early arrival, William M. Dinkel, recalled the difficulties of a wintertime journey to the west side of the Sawatch Range, the highest mountain range in Colorado, with fifteen of Colorado's thirty-five peaks higher than fourteen thousand feet, including the state's highest, Mount Elbert, at 14,431 feet. In the winter of 1880 Dinkel and a colleague heard of a shortage of flour in Aspen. They bought eight hundred pounds of flour in Buena Vista, packed it on mules, and started over the Continental Divide. Plodding through deep snow, negotiating narrow ledges, overlooking hair-raising dropoffs, and finally being forced to shoulder some of the load carried by their exhausted animals, the determined entrepreneurs reached Aspen and sold, for twelve and one-half times its cost, the flour they had bought only fifty miles away.

Hagerman Pass

Despite the soaring height of the Continental Divide along the Sawatch Range, the Colorado Midland Railway Company undertook the first successful attempt to run standard-gauge trackage through the daunting terrain. Starting from Colorado Springs, where they had run lumber trains up Ute Pass to Woodland Park (see *U.S. 24E* itinerary) for three years, the Colorado Midland's owners started in the spring of 1886 to build westward through South Park. A year later the line's railhead had reached Buena Vista. From there it went north to Leadville, skirted Turquoise Lake and headed for the Divide. On June 14, 1887, Denver's *Rocky Mountain News* disclosed, "The great Hagerman Tunnel, the largest on the Midland road, was completed tonight.

The Hagerman, which pierces the mountain at an elevation of 11,500 feet, is 2100 feet long and is drilled through solid rock."

Named for a Milwaukee businessman who became Colorado Midland Railroad president, Hagerman Peak looms above Snowmass Creek. *Colorado Tourism Board.*

Named for Milwaukee businessman James J. Hagerman, president of the Midland, the tunnel was bored under Hagerman Pass, eleven miles north of **Milepost 62**, where it brought the right-of-way from one side of the Continental Divide, the headwaters of Busk Creek, to the headwaters of Ivanhoe Creek, a tributary of the Fryingpan River, on the Pacific side.

The ghost of Independence mining camp lies about **Milepost 57**, where even today derelict log cabins and mining structures still dot the banks of the Roaring Fork River.

Aspen

Prussian-born Henry P. Cowenhoven had prospered as a merchant in Black Hawk, near the site of one of the original Colorado gold diggings at Central City. He had arrived in that region, in fact, just about the time John Gregory's discovery was confirmed to the world by the manifestly reliable witness of Horace Greeley (see I-70W itinerary).

For some reason, shortly after his sixty-sixth birthday in the spring of 1880, Cowenhoven decided to move on and start over again. He loaded family and goods into two mule-drawn wagons to take the same route that Dinkel would follow in the winter. They crossed Cottonwood Pass west of Buena Vista and passed through Taylor Park northwestward to Taylor Pass in the volcanic crests of the Elk Mountains. The descent into the Roaring Fork watershed at South Castle Creek, **Milepost 39**, was so steep that frequently the two wagons had to be unloaded, "rough-lock" chains threaded through the spokes of the wheels, and the wagons tethered to windlasses improvised on tree trunks in order to get them down to the next safe level. Cowenhoven and his family made it to Aspen in late July.

Purchasing a city lot for seventy-five dollars, Cowenhoven built his store and went into business. A veteran not only of the Colorado gold rush but also the 1849 California strike, he knew how to deal with miners. Cowenhoven sold what he could, extended magnanimous credits frequently, and grubstaked a few. Faith in the ability and willingness of his customers to repay their debts paid off quickly as the Roaring Fork valley revealed its riches. In four years when he reached seventy, Cowenhoven had made his second fortune, so he retired.

The catalyst of Cowenhoven's fortune was the arrival in the spring of 1883 of the wealthy junior partner of Macy's department store in New York. Jerome Byron Wheeler had married into the Macy family and had acquired a forty-five percent interest in the firm following a series of untimely deaths in the Macy family. Although a successful businessman in his own right, Wheeler was denied an active role in the management of Macy's. Eager to get involved in some other endeavor, Wheeler was persuaded to invest in some Aspen mining claims by a young friend, Harvey Young, an artist who dabbled in prospecting.

When Wheeler arrived to survey his acquisitions, he immediately realized that Aspen needed a smelter to upgrade the camp's silver mining operations. He bought out the interest of a group of Texans whose plans to build a smelter had foundered due to a lack of capital. When Wheeler stepped in to save the day, the Aspen *Times* thundered: "The Most Important Sale Ever Transacted for the Material Interests of Pitkin Co." An editorial added, "All thanks to J.B. Wheeler."

Wheeler's smelter and the later arrival of the railroad made Aspen a mining community second in importance only to Leadville.

Basalt

The town of Basalt, **Milepost 23**, at the mouth of the Fryingpan River was a company town. It prevails, however, while the company failed. The company in this case was the Colorado Midland Railway, which expired in 1918 to the dismay of many. One of them, Sam Phillips, recalled that the railroad catered to local fishermen, dropping them off along the several streams on the right-of-way when a favorite fishing spot had been reached. On the return run later in the day, the Midland engineers would pull their train to a halt when the fishermen, ready to go home, would flag them. Congenial as it surely was to operate a full-scale railroad with the folksiness of a trolley car, it clearly did not pay.

Aspen to Glenwood Springs

The Midland reached Aspen by way of Basalt in February 1888. It was competing for the business of the affluent Aspen mining community with the Denver & Rio Grande Railroad, which had already built its own right-of-way along the south bank of the Roaring Fork. The success of the Midland's standard-gauge trains in making their way through the high Rockies evidently obliged the narrow-gauge pioneer, the D&RG, to change its mainline trackage to standard gauge in 1890. The D&RG had had the foresight to install standard-gauge ties in building its roadbed north of Leadville, down the Eagle River to the Colorado, where the Midland would meet it at Glenwood Springs.

When the D&RG's new four-foot-eight-inch tracks were laid from Glenwood Springs westward down the Colorado River valley to Rifle, the Midland's owners opted to share the line, under lease, with the D&RG. Then, in an uncharacteristic joint venture, the two lines built a common right-of-way from Rifle to Grand Junction.

Meanwhile, until the train arrived, two stage lines, the Kit Carson and the Western Stage Company, were busy vying for the traffic between Aspen and Glenwood Springs, where moneyed citizens of the Roaring Fork mining community had taken to basking in the warm waters of the spa.

Carbondale

There was a single stage stop on the forty-mile run from Aspen and that was at Carbondale, **Milepost 12.** Operating the stage stop and an adjacent store was the indomitable flour purveyor William M. Dinkel. The region around Carbondale had been settled to the extent that potatoes and onions were being grown as cash crops by local farmers. And about the time the Midland arrived coal was discovered in the vicinity.

Mount Sopris

Nine miles south of Carbondale the double peaks of Mount Sopris dominate the skyline, with both peaks reaching precisely the same height—12,953 feet. The mountain is named for Indiana-born Capt. Richard Sopris, another argonaut who arrived in Auraria in 1859. He quickly penetrated beyond the gold camps of the Front Range and in July

1860, with a group of companions, discovered Glenwood's hot springs. Sopris was later elected to the legislature of Kansas Territory, which at that time, before February 28, 1861, comprised much of Colorado. From 1878 to 1881, just as Aspen and the Roaring Fork communities were coming into their own, Sopris was mayor of Denver.

Redstone

Beyond Mount Sopris, eighteen miles south of Carbondale near the village of Redstone, is Cleveholm "Castle," at **Milepost 51** on *Colorado 133*. Now on the Register of National Historic Places, the mansion was the home of John C. Osgood, a Colorado mine operator and financier who pre-

This view of an old mill on the Crystal River is a modern photograph that has won such favor it promises to be a classic. *Colorado Tourism Board.*

sided over the amalgamation of the Colorado Fuel & Iron Company (see I-25S itinerary). Brooklyn-born Osgood fused his own Colorado Fuel Company with the Colorado Coal & Iron Company, founded by the D&RG's William J. Palmer, shortly after Osgood arrived in Colorado in 1882.

In a gesture rivaling a later mine operator, Josephine Roche (see *U.S. 36* itinerary), Osgood established Redstone to accommodate the men who worked his nearby mines and coke ovens, most of them immigrants. He had an architect design cottages for each family, each dwelling in some way unique. He built the imposing Redstone Inn, which featured the amenities of a posh private club, including a theater, for the use of his workers. This paternalistic experiment was begun in 1903. Osgood died in 1926, for some reason an infrequent visitor to his idyllic workingmen's community.

Yule Creek Marble Quarries

Thirteen miles southeast of Redstone near the town of Marble, on the county road that departs *Colorado 133* at Milepost 46, are the quarries of Yule Creek. These provided the marble for the Lincoln Memorial and the Tomb of the Unknown Soldier in Washington, D.C. The quarries were closed in 1940 due to persistent landslides in the vicinity.

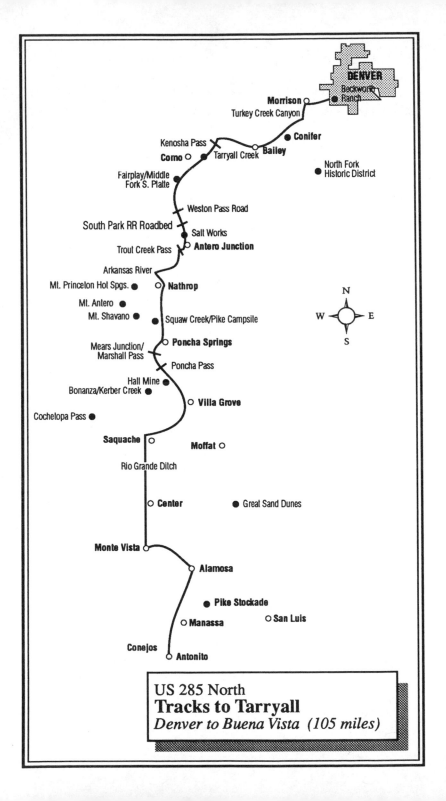

DENVER
Beckworth Ranch

Morrison
Turkey Creek Canyon
Conifer

Kenosha Pass
Como ○ Tarryall Creek Bailey
North Fork
Historic District
Fairplay/Middle
Fork S. Platte

Weston Pass Road
South Park RR Roadbed
Salt Works
Trout Creek Pass ○ **Antero Junction**

Arkansas River
Mt. Princeton Hot Spgs. ● ○ **Nathrop**
Mt. Antero ●
Mt. Shavano ● Squaw Creek/Pike Campsite
○ **Poncha Springs**
Mears Junction/
Marshall Pass
Poncha Pass

Hall Mine ●
Bonanza/Kerber Creek ●
Cochetopa Pass ● ○ **Villa Grove**

Saquache ○
Moffat ○
Rio Grande Ditch

○ **Center** ● Great Sand Dunes

Monte Vista ○
○ **Alamosa**

● **Pike Stockade**
○ **Manassa** ○ **San Luis**

Conejos ○ **Antonito**

N
W—E
S

US 285 North
Tracks to Tarryall
Denver to Buena Vista (105 miles)

US 285 North
Tracks to Tarryall
Denver to Buena Vista (105 miles)

James Beckwourth, Indian Friend

A mulatto ex-slave, James W. Beckwourth, left behind one of the most bizarre life stories of the many that chronicle Colorado history. He was at various times a mountain man, a Denver storekeeper, and a Crow Indian chief. In the seven years he lived in the Denver area, Beckwourth resided in several homes and had at least two young wives.

At the time of his ritual assassination, he occupied a cabin on a piece of land abutting property of William N. Byers, the founder of the *Rocky Mountain News*. Beckwourth's property lay on the east bank of the South Platte River three and one-half miles north of **Milepost 259** on *U.S. 285*.

In his lifetime Beckwourth was nearly as celebrated as Kit Carson (see I-25, *U.S. 50* and *U.S. 160* itineraries) and for much the same reason. A romanticized biography appeared in 1865, when Beckwourth was not yet sixty, recounting his exploits in the fur trade and his adoption into the Crow Indian tribe where he had risen to become a much-honored chief.

He was living in Beckwourth Valley, California, at the time gold was discovered in Colorado. In the summer of 1859 he left his Pacific valley to take a job with Louis Vasquez, who a generation earlier had established Fort Vasquez on the South Platte (see I-25N itinerary), and Louis's nephew A. Pike Vasquez, son of Zebulon Pike's guide (see *U.S. 50* itinerary).

Beckwourth brought a wagon train of merchandise to the newly created town of Auraria from Westport, Missouri, to stock a Vasquez store on what is now Eleventh Street in downtown Denver. His stint as a storekeeper continued with one notable hiatus in late 1864, when he served as a guide for Col. John M. Chivington's expedition to eastern Colorado's Big Sandy Creek, where the infamous Sand Creek massacre was to occur (see *U.S. 50* itinerary).

The Sand Creek role was an incongruous one for Beckwourth, who had been an outspoken defender of the Indians' lot and, as such, much favored with the presence of numerous tipis around his Denver cabin. In 1866, in fact, the Crows sent a delegation from their homelands at the headwaters of the Missouri, in Montana, to urge that the sixty-nine-year-old black come visit them.

As William N. Byers described it later:

> They entertained him with all the honors an Indian can bestow . . . [and] used every means and argument to

James Beckwourth, fabled black mountain man and honorary Crow Indian chief, was reluctantly killed by his Indian followers when he refused to rejoin the tribe. *Colorado Historical Society.*

persuade him to again become their chief. Upon his final refusal and his preparation to return to his home [in Denver], the Indians honored him with a great farewell dog feast. The meat that was served him was poisoned and he died on the spot. The Crows freely acknowledged the crime, saying: "He has been our good medicine. We have been more successful under him than under any chief." Their excuse was that if they could not have him living it would be good medicine to them to have him dead.

Turkey Creek Canyon—Denver to South Park

Rich gold placers were discovered in the summer of 1859 in South Park along Tarryall Creek and across the Continental Divide near today's Breckenridge, just months after important discoveries had been made in the mountains west of Denver (see I-70 itinerary). From Denver the most likely route to the new South Park diggings, for both merchants and miners, was along another old trail followed by the Mountain Utes (see *U.S. 34* and *U.S. 24* itineraries). It ran a few miles south of the present *U.S. 285*, across a spine of hills that divides the waters draining into Turkey Creek from those emptying into the South Platte's North Fork. The route was too rugged for wagons, so goods had to be packed to the diggings on horses. By 1867, however, a road was built through Turkey Creek canyon beginning at **Milepost 248**, south of Morrison, which was the precursor of *U.S. 285*.

From Bailey, **Milepost 222**, the two routes followed the North Fork of the South Platte River to the mouth of Kenosha Gulch, **Milepost 207.5**, where they turned to surmount Kenosha Pass and then descend into the vast and splendid meadows of South Park.

The Turkey Creek canyon route facilitated the introduction of a stage line, which was immediately established by Robert J. Spotswood. Spotswood was a veteran superintendent of the Julesburg-Denver-Laramie division of the Overland Stage Company in its heyday before the completion of the transcontinental Union Pacific Railroad. In 1873 he began a profitable but necessarily temporary collaboration with an enterprising local railroad man, former territorial governor John Evans, whose Denver Pacific line from Cheyenne had put the Overland Stage out of business. After resigning as president of the Denver Pacific Railroad (see I-25N itinerary), Evans shook off the effects of the Panic of 1873 and organized the Denver, South Park & Pacific Railroad. Initially the South Park line ran only from its Denver terminal at Sixth and Larimer streets to Morrison, where Spotswood & McClellan's stages and freight wagons carted passengers and goods the rest of the way to South Park and eventually to Leadville. Evans's original ambition was to build a line from Denver across the Rockies to the Pacific.

Evans began work in 1877 on the right-of-way for the railroad's mainline, which left the Morrison spur at the mouth of Bear Creek (**Milepost 259**) and followed the north bank of the South Platte to Kassler, then known as Platte Canyon.

Five miles east of Pine Junction, **Milepost 229**, on *Colorado 126* lies the officially designated North Fork Historic District, incorporating the villages of Pine and Buffalo Creek, among others, each of which lay along the route of the Denver, South Park & Pacific Railroad. Many of the buildings in the district date from the late nineteenth century and are preserved in their original design and construction. The DSP&P reached Buffalo Creek in the fall of 1878.

In May 1879 the line left the North Fork of the South Platte to top Kenosha Hill, **Milepost 203**, and reach Tarryall Creek, **Milepost 194**, in South Park. At this point the notorious Jay Gould, only a decade after his abortive attempt to corner the country's gold market, sought to buy the Denver, South Park & Pacific from the Evans consortium. Although already in control of the Denver Pacific, Kansas Pacific, and Missouri Pacific, Gould was rebuffed by Evans.

Spotswood, meanwhile, continued to pick up passengers and freight at the railroad's end-of-line, wherever on a given day that happened to be. From Tarryall Creek, for example, the Spotswood & McClellan stages left what is now *U.S. 285* at **Milepost 178**, south of Fairplay, to negotiate precipitous Weston Pass in order to reach booming Leadville (see *U.S. 24* itinerary).

Tarryall and Hamilton

About six miles west, up Tarryall Creek, are the sites of the original diggings that spawned the towns of Tarryall and, across the creek, Hamilton. The discovery came as a rather roundabout consequence of a tragedy.

On June 26, 1859, three prospectors, the first to try their luck in South Park, were attacked by Indians. Two of them died. On July 13 fourteen prospectors from the Gregory diggings (see I-70 itinerary) near what is now Central City decided to go to South Park to avenge their comrades. They were camped on Tarryall Creek when, frustrated in their efforts to track down the Indians who had attacked the earlier party, they considered returning to the Central City region. An exploratory hole dug along the creek bank, however, produced what one prospector classified as "good pay." Another reported that the placer gave forth gold "in scales nearly as large as watermelon seeds, smooth, and very bright yellow. . . . " As a consequence, "the company made preparations to tarry-all."

The enterprising and seemingly ubiquitous William N. Byers, having already launched the *Rocky Mountain News* in Denver-Auraria, decided that the South Park diggings showed promise that merited the presence of a newspaper. The *Miner's Record* published its first edition on July 4, 1861. Such was the fate of the Tarryall Creek placers, however, that Byers's final edition went to press just ten weeks later. By 1867 the two towns had been nearly emptied, and, finally, in 1873 even the buildings that remained were moved to the vicinity of the newly completed railroad station at Como, **Milepost 192**.

Como

Extensive coal deposits were discovered in the 1870s at Como, a town established and named by Italian miners supposedly nostalgic for the Lake Como region of northern Italy. One early traveler to the region noted, however, that the mines were worked in the 1880s less by Italians than by Chinese immigrants—an estimated 350 Chinese in 1880.

The dauntless Jay Gould, meanwhile, returned in 1884 to satisfy an earlier ambition. Then in control of the Union Pacific, Gould used the resources of the transcontinental railroad company to absorb the Denver, South Park & Pacific. One of his first moves, following its acquisition, was to build what proved to be a profitable shortcut to Leadville from Como up Tarryall Creek, over Boreas Pass (11,481 feet) to the silver-mining town on a route that passed through Breckenridge, Dillon and Kokomo.

Fairplay

Before the Tarryall diggings had expired, a group of prospectors, feeling themselves victimized by some of their more unscrupulous and acquisitive comrades, decided to pull out of the community and set up another. They picked a site on the Middle Fork of the South Platte River, at **Milepost 183**, and in testimony of their desire for justice and equity called it Fairplay. By April 1860, they had instituted a semblance of government to meet their needs. The town remains the county seat of one of the original seventeen Colorado counties.

The roughshod norms of civic decorum, incidentally, were not peculiar to South Park at the time. Eight lawyers in Denver put this advertisement in the *Rocky Mountain News* on July 5, 1861:

NOTICE. We the undersigned Attorneys and Counsellors at Law, convinced from long experience here, that without organized Courts, either of Kansas Territory or some other Government,—which certainly do not exist—the practice is worse than useless both for ourselves and the public; announce by this notice, our determination to close our Law Offices after the 31st day of the present month; and thereafter our professional business ceases, until such time as regular and constitutional tribunals of Justice are established in our midst. . . .

The Fremont Expedition

Long before "civilization" had planted its dubious mark in the region, the celebrated army explorer John Charles Fremont, with Kit Carson as his guide, crossed into South Park over Hoosier Pass and followed the Middle Fork of the South Platte to the vicinity of today's Fairplay. The time was late June 1844, and it was the season for one of those perennial battles between the Plains Arapahoes and the Mountain Utes. The Fremont party encountered Ute women and children fleeing the battle scene. The explorers carefully skirted the skirmishing Indians and made their way down Fountain Creek to the little settlement of Fort Pueblo (see I-25S itinerary) on the Arkansas River.

Another incident of the savage rivalry that had from time immemorial engaged the Indians of the plains against those of the mountains was witnessed in July 1861 by an Easterner recently arrived to take up an appointment as justice on the Territorial Supreme Court:

A war party of Arapahoes arrived in the city about noon today from South Park [noted S. Newton Pettis in a letter to a friend].   [They brought] with them eight Ute prisoners and a half dozen scalps. . . . The capture consisted of live squaws and three infant children. One of the squaws was the wife of a Ute chief, who was killed in the conflict. Her features were more than interesting [:] she was pretty. . . . She was made to dance around the scalp of her husband and companion. Two other squaws were in great agony in consequence of the murdering of their infant children in coldness and barbarity. . . .

Fremont's 1843-44 expedition, which had taken him over the mountains to the Pacific coast and back by yet another route, was counted in Washington as the most significant survey of the American west since Lewis and Clark's famous trip at the beginning of the century.

Fremont's exploits have been well remembered in Colorado. A South Park hill to the west of **Milepost 197** is known as Fremont's Knoll. To the south of the park lies fifteen-hundred-square-mile Fremont County, one of the original seventeen territorial counties created in 1861. Near Climax on *Colorado 90* is Fremont Pass, a crossing of the Continental Divide that Fremont apparently never negotiated.

South into South Park

The Denver, South Park & Pacific continued southward some miles east of *U.S. 285*, crossing the Middle Fork of the South Platte at Garo, on *Colorado 9*. The railroad right-of-way rejoined the current highway briefly at **Milepost 165**. Near this point the line served another early-day industry, the Salt Works. Salt Spring lies just east of **Milepost 164**, its tall brick chimney still rising against the backdrop of Antero Reservoir in the opening between two buttes.

The *Rocky Mountain News* carried this advertisement in its April 26, 1862, edition: "Pike's Peak Salt.—We are in receipt of a six-pound bag of fine table salt from the Salt Works of Messrs. C.M. Smith & Co., Laurette, Buckskin Joe. The Buffalo Salt Works are situated in South Park." The enterprise was probably named for Buffalo Creek, issuing from Buffalo Mountain to the west and crossing *U.S. 285* near **Milepost 166** to empty into nearby Antero Reservoir.

The reservoir, Antero Junction where *U.S. 285* and *U.S. 24* join, and Antero Peak, southwest of Poncha Springs, are named for a Ute chieftain who signed the 1873 Brunot Treaty ceding much of the mineral-rich San Juan Mountains of southwestern Colorado to the U.S. government.

Trout Creek Pass at **Milepost 161** (marked **226** due to *U.S. 24's* conjunction with *U.S. 285*) has been the historic passage from South Park into the upper Arkansas valley since Zebulon Pike came over it in 1806. The South Park railroad also followed this route to the Arkansas River before bridging it to continue on through Chalk Creek Gulch to the south. In July 1887, a standard-gauge railroad, the Colorado Midland, arrived at this point from Colorado Springs and turned north to Leadville and eventually Aspen. It was the first full-width line to cross the Continental Divide in Colorado (see *Colorado 82* itinerary).

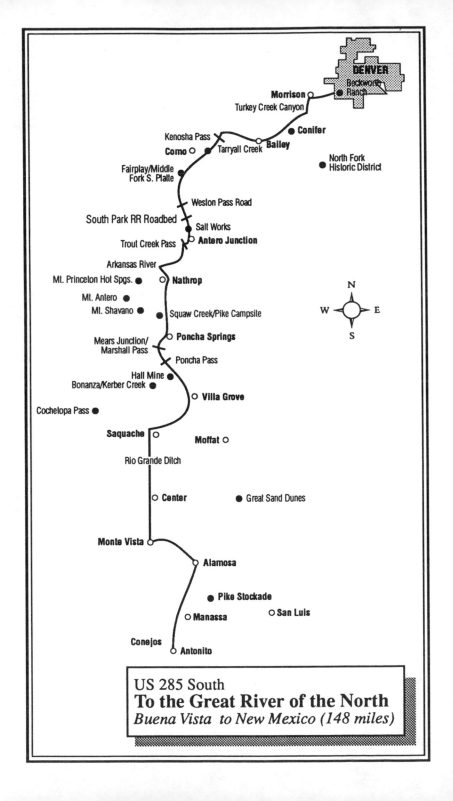

US 285 South
To the Great River of the North
Buena Vista to New Mexico (148 miles)

US 285 South
To the Great River of the North
Buena Vista to New Mexico (148 miles)

Nathrop

Captain Zebulon Pike came down Trout Creek Pass, **Milepost 226** on *U.S. 24*, from South Park and encountered the Arkansas River just east of **Milepost 148** of *U.S. 285*. The date was December 8, 1806, and he noted, "Some of our lads supposed [this] to be . . . Red River which here was about 25 yards wide, ran with great rapidity and was full of rocks. Determined to remain a day or two in order to examine the river's source. Snowing."

Pike and his men turned upriver to explore the region that little more than half a century later would become first Oro City and then, when the gold ran out, Leadville (see *U.S. 24W* itinerary). These later years would find disappointed prospectors drifting south from Oro City to homestead in this lush valley of the upper Arkansas River. One of the early homesteaders in 1868 built a grist mill at about **Milepost 142** along the river. The name of Charles Nachtrieb was early corrupted to a more manageable Nathrop, the name by which the community is still known.

Chalk Creek Gulch

In Chalk Creek Gulch, four miles east of **Milepost 142** on *Colorado 162*, there is a series of hot springs that attracted visitors as early as the 1860s. It became a waystation on the stagecoach line that ran from Nathrop over the Continental Divide to Tin Cup. At the head of the gulch near Romley, in 1875, two miners, John Royal and S. A. Wright, developed the Mary Murphy mine, which at its high point turned out seventy-five to 100 tons of gold and silver-laden ore each day.

The Mary Murphy mine did so well that its profits were used to bankroll the Mount Princeton Hot Springs & Improvement Company, which set out in the early 1880s to develop a spa around the hot springs lying to the southeast of Mount Princeton. By 1884 the Mt. Princeton Hot Springs Hotel had been built. By that time, fifty mines were being worked in Chalk Creek Gulch.

In 1880, former governor John Evans's Denver, South Park & Pacific Railroad had emerged from South Park along the same Trout Creek route as Pike, bridged the Arkansas, and turned north to the new town of Buena Vista. Evans saw fit to run a line south to Chalk Creek Gulch, as well, and within a year the DSP&P had reached St. Elmo. Plans were made to rival the Denver & Rio Grande Railroad in providing the best and fastest route to Gunnison, across the Continental Divide.

A derelict flume mocks the Yellow Brick Road as it leads not to Oz but the old Chalk Creek Canyon mining town of St. Elmo.

The climb over the Divide was too demanding this time, even for the plucky narrow-gauge trains, so the DSP&P dug a tunnel beneath Alpine Pass. The tunnel, more than a third of a mile long, was braced with durable California redwood timbers to withstand the effects of freezing seepage. The biggest problem for the DSP&P in keeping the tunnel open, however, lay outside. One hundred and ten men were kept busy during the winter shoveling snow from the tunnel's portals.

The DSP&P folded in 1889, and the Chalk Creek line and tunnel were taken over by the Denver, Leadville & Gunnison, which operated for another decade. Finally, in 1910, the Colorado, Southern & Pacific abandoned the right-of-way.

Meanwhile, the Mt. Princeton Hot Springs Hotel, itself possessed of a private railroad siding, was reaching the end of years of litigation that had kept the hostelry from operating. In 1915, the hotel spa began operations with a panache that by the mid-1920s rivaled some of Germany's Black Forest inns. With the Great Depression and World War II, however, the splendid health resort went into decline until it was razed in 1950. The lumber was used for a housing development in Abilene, Texas.

Mount Antero

South of Mount Princeton and forming the other side of Chalk Creek Gulch, west of **Milepost 138**, is Mount Antero, named for the same Ute chief whose name graces the reservoir in South Park (see *U.S. 285N* itinerary). Immediately south of Antero Peak is Mount Shavano, named for another Ute chief who was tragically murdered by an irate tribesman after the Utes were forced to abandon Colorado for resettlement in Utah. Mount Shavano, west of **Milepost 134**, holds the headwaters of Squaw Creek, which *U.S. 285* crosses near **Milepost 131**. Near the mouth of Squaw Creek, in 1806, Zebulon Pike and his men spent Christmas. "Here, 800 miles from the frontiers of our country," he reported, "in the most inclement season of the year, not one person clothed for the winter, many without blankets, having been obliged to cut them up for socks, and now laying down at night on the snow and wet ground: this was in part the situation of the party whilst some were endeavoring to make a miserable substitute of raw buffalo hide for shoes."

At this point the Arkansas River turns eastward on its way to Pueblo and the prairie. *U.S. 285*, however, continues south to intersect with *U.S. 50* and, a half-mile beyond at **Milepost 126**, the south Arkansas River. This is the site of another hot spring, Poncha Springs, a community whose first building, a log cabin, was erected in 1865 by Nat Rich and Bob Hendricks.

This location was so remote in 1865 that Rich at one point had seen no one in three months. Desperate for company, he built a huge fire to attract attention. Ute Indians, mistaking the fire for a signal that their Plains Indian enemies, the Cheyennes, were invading , descended upon Rick's homestead by the score, ready to do battle. The gregarious Rich, nonetheless, was popular with the Utes who roamed the region. One pioneer recalled that, when his parents had bought Rich's cabin, a party of Utes showed up to warn them that they had three days to clear out and restore their friend Rich to residence.

Poncha Pass

Ascending Poncha Creek from its mouth on the south Arkansas River, one follows a trace that has existed since the days of the Spaniards in the eighteenth century. Fur trappers later used it. It was the usual route for those who would pass from the upper Arkansas valley to the San Luis valley and, beyond it, to Taos and Santa Fe. Capt. John W. Gunnison and his railroad survey expedition detoured in their journey across the San Luis valley to Cochetopa Pass in 1853 to examine Poncha Pass.

Following Gunnison's death in an Indian ambush, his second-in-command, Lt. E. G. Beckwith, reported to the U.S. Senate, "As a testimonial of respect to the memory of the officer [Gunnison] who explored it, I have given his name to the pass." Today, Gunnison is memorialized in a Western Slope town and river, but the pass continues to be known as Poncha.

At **Milepost 119** Poncha Pass crests the Sangre de Cristo range at just over nine thousand feet and in its time was so rugged that use of it was limited to pack trains. In 1867, a remarkable twenty-seven-year-old orphan from Russia found a mother in necessity. Since being mustered out of the Union army, Otto Mears had been growing wheat and operating a store in Saguache, **Milepost 86**, in the heart of the upper San Luis valley. With the mining boom in Oro City, he found that he had a great many potential customers for his wheat and flour. The rugged trail over Poncha Pass played havoc with his wagons however, so he resolved to build a better road at his own expense.

As he was doing so, former territorial governor William Gilpin chanced by. He offered Mears two suggestions: first, apply to the territorial legislature for a charter to operate a toll road in order to recoup his expenses, and second, make the toll road's incline gradual so that it might accommodate a railroad. Mears's wagon road dates from 1868, but it was not until the Denver & Rio Grande had settled its Royal Gorge War with the Atchison, Topeka & Santa Fe Railroad (see *U.S. 50W* itinerary) that a train climbed through Poncha Pass to enter the San Luis valley. The D&RG management in 1880 decided to become the railroad of the Rockies. Pushing on from Canon City through the Royal Gorge to Salida, the D&RG went north to Leadville, south over Poncha Pass to mines in the upper San Luis valley, and west over Marshall Pass to Gunnison on a route that, for a time, would be the D&RG's mainline extending all the way to Ogden, Utah, by 1883.

The Marshall Pass route, discovered by a topographer with a toothache in 1873 (see *U.S. 50W* itinerary), had been another of Otto Mears's toll roads, built in 1875 and sold later to the D&RG. At **Milepost 121**, Mears Junction, the Poncha Pass and Marshall Pass routes part. In 1890 the Poncha Pass narrow-gauge was extended from Villa Grove,

Milepost 104, almost due south to Alamosa to carry the traffic related to yet another belated silver strike at Creede (see *Colorado 149* itinerary).

Five miles west of **Milepost 107** lies an old mine that was originally worked for its copper ore. In time, someone discovered that the mine's discarded tailings contained good quality turquoise gem stone, long favored and quarried by the Pueblo Indian tribes farther south for jewelry. The Hall mine became the first turquoise deposit to be discovered and developed by white settlers in Colorado.

Bonanza

Also in the recesses of the Cochetopa Hills, fifteen miles west of **Milepost 105** at Villa Grove, important silver-bearing lead outcroppings were discovered along Kerber Creek. The discovery was made by James Kenny, an Irish-born veteran of General Custer's 7th Cavalry who narrowly missed the fatal Battle of the Little Big Horn. Four years after the Custer massacre, on May 21, 1880, Kenny, joined by James Downman and William Applebee, laid claim to the Rawley lode, which they worked profitably for more than a generation before selling it to a New York-based mining corporation. Their find and others related to it led to the founding of the mining town of Bonanza.

Corporate interests continued to invest in the Bonanza mining district well into the twentieth century. A Denver-based firm, for example, bought into the enterprise in 1923, built a three-hundred-ton concentrating mill, installed electrified equipment, including a railway and aerial tramway, and erected accommodations for three hundred workers. The ubiquitous American Smelting & Refining Company had to take over the Denver firm, however, when the latter found itself financially overextended. Under the new ownership the diggings at one point were producing twenty-five hundred tons of silver and copper-bearing ore per month.

Disaster struck the community on June 24, 1937, however, when fire destroyed most of the Bonanza business district.

Saguache

Saguache, **Milepost 86**, (pronounced "S'watch") is a site that has figured in the comings and goings of San Luis valley residents into the indefinite past. The name itself is a rather arbitrary rendering of a Ute word that refers to a spring in blue earth. The region is made lush each spring by the flooding Saguache Creek when the snows melt on the Continental Divide in the heights of La Garita wilderness. The Saguache vicinity enjoys an abundance of forceful artesian springs as well. Otto Mears helped to found the community in 1866, when he arrived to plant crops of wheat.

A member of a congressionally authorized transcontinental railroad survey team, visiting Fort Massachusetts in 1853, suggested that the U.S. military post ought to be moved to the valley of Saguache Creek, "so rich in pasturage, so well adapted to tillage, and so abundantly watered and timbered. . . ."

The town of Saguache maintains a notable regional museum housed in a decommissioned county jail, part of which dates from the 1870s. In 1874 a notorious if transient prisoner was Alfred Packer, a protagonist in a grisly case of cannibalism (see *Colorado 149* itinerary). Packer managed to escape his incarceration in Saguache but is featured in one of the museum's exhibits.

Cochetopa Pass

Roadbuilder Mears built a route from Saguache up the Saguache Creek valley over Cochetopa Pass to the Ute Indian Agency at Los Pinos, seventeen miles beyond the Divide. The agency was provisioned from Mears's store in Saguache. The present highway, *Colorado 114*, crosses North Cochetopa Pass, a few miles above the original, which is still served by a graveled road. The Ute name Cochetopa signifies a passage for buffalo herds, whose comings and goings to the high parks had left heavily rutted traces throughout the mountains. John C. Fremont, reporting on his second expedition in the mid-1840s, remarked on the "great highways, continuous for hundreds of miles, always several inches, and sometimes several feet in depth, which the buffalo have made in crossing from one river to another, or in traversing the mountain ranges."

The ruts and even the familiar contours of the terrain through which the Cochetopa trail ran were obliterated in the winter of 1857 when U.S. Army Capt. Randolph B. Marcy sought to lead a desperate contingent of soldiers down from the high country. Their plight resulted from Col. Albert Sidney Johnston's cumbersome expedition over the Oregon Trail to subdue the recalcitrant territorial government of Mormon leader Brigham Young in Salt Lake City. Mormon guerrillas had harried Johnston's columns of soldiers until they had lost most of their horses and provisions just as the climate was forcing them into winter quarters on the Green River in what is now the southwestern corner of Wyoming.

Marcy's mission was to make the hazardous trek across the crest of the Colorado Rockies to obtain supplemental supplies from the nearest army depot, which at the time was in New Mexico. His sixty-five men were on the verge of exhaustion when finally Marcy confronted the last obstacle—the twelve-thousand-foot Cochetopa Hills. Soldiers took turns crawling through the heavy snow in order to break trails for the rest. Their thirty-day supply of rations was used up long before they reached the place where they supposed the pass to be. "There was not the slightest sign of a road, trail, or foot mark to guide us," recounted Marcy. "All was one vast, illimitable expanse of snow as far as the eye could penetrate; and the mountains rose before us, peak upon peak, until they were lost in the clouds."

At last one of Marcy's horse wranglers, Mariano Medina, ventured a guess as to the location of Cochetopa Pass. Medina, a native of Taos, had served on the expeditions of Fremont as a scout with Kit Carson (see I-25N itinerary).

"I asked the Mexican if he was willing to act as guide," said Marcy, "Telling him I would, in addition to his regular pay, make him a handsome present for his services . . . ; but I also informed him that if at any time I discovered he was leading us in a wrong direction, I should hang him from the first tree."

Piqued at his commander's attitude, an apparent legacy of Marcy's participation in the 1846 Mexican War, Medina replied, "I will risk my neck on it, captain."

Medina was right, and when the troop was safely across the Divide he rode ahead with another mountain man to fetch emergency rations from the military outpost of Fort Massachusetts across the San Luis valley (see *U.S. 160* itinerary). Remarkably, not a single man was lost in the grueling, fifty-one day journey.

Rio Grande Irrigation Canal

Rio Grande irrigation canal passes under the highway near **Milepost 80**. Water for the canal is taken from the Rio Grande del Norte at the outskirts of the city of Del Norte (see *U.S. 160* itinerary). With its lateral lines that cross the valley to the east, the canal has watered several hundred thousand acres for more than a century.

Moffat

The town of Moffat, thirteen miles east of **Milepost 80**, commemorates David H. Moffat, a pioneer railroad magnate, and remains the only vestige of the D&RG line that in the 1890s ran from Poncha Pass to Alamosa.

Despite its early prominence in the San Luis valley, the railroad did not contribute appreciably to the development of the valley's now important agricultural industry, whose fortunes instead seem to have ebbed and flowed with the nation's foreign policy. The valley's first important cash crop, potatoes, did not win favor with farmers until the late 1890s, due to low potato prices and high freight rates. But in 1898, U.S. hostilities with Spain caused freight rates to be lowered and the demand for potatoes to rise. To take advantage of the opportunity, growing and marketing specialists from the state agricultural college were dispatched on a whistlestop tour of the valley. Two thousand farmers heard lectures on the latest farming techniques, and the farmers themselves organized a Potato Growers Association to aid one another. By 1917, when the United States entered World War I, potato prices had increased fivefold. Unfortunately in just six years the post-war farm depression sent potato prices down to a mere 10 percent of their wartime high.

Even so the 1920s marked a burgeoning of San Luis agriculture. Packers promoted the growing of head lettuce, and area farmers increased their acreage in that crop from 138 in 1922 to 4,127 in 1925. Farmers in Conejos County on the New Mexican border tried growing thirteen acres of peas in 1922. By 1929 the valley had 5,450 acres in peas plus a pea cannery at Monte Vista, **Milepost 51**. Cauliflower was first planted in 1924 and by 1930 was a major valley crop.

As the new crops were introduced into the valley, state agricultural official W. H. Odin admonished farmers, "We must gain and hold our reputation for the best quality lettuce to be found. . . . We have the soil, the altitude, the climate and the irrigation that insures quality in our mountain truck crops and vegetables."

Great Sand Dunes National Monument

Center, at **Milepost 63**, marks the heart of the valley's agricultural industry. Thirty miles east lies the Great Sand Dunes National Monument, the antithesis of a verdant and fruitful land. The desert is a product of millennia of ceaseless winds blowing southwest to northeast across the arid valley. The dunes were the first thing encountered in the San Luis valley by Pike and his men in their 1806-07 trek. After leaving Squaw Creek, Pike had led his men down the Arkansas until they came upon an earlier campsite and he realized that they had traveled in a circle. Striking out southward into the Wet Mountain valley, they crossed over the impos-

ing Sangre de Cristo range at Medano Pass still seeking the
Red River boundary of the Louisiana Purchase. In his journal, Pike noted: "Jan. 28 [1807]—We discovered . . . sandy
hills . . . Their appearance was exactly that of the sea in a
storm except as to color, not the least sign of vegetation
existing thereon."

A mile north of **Milepost 219** on the shores of Homelake is
the Colorado State Veterans Center. The facility was established in 1891 as the State Soldiers and Sailors Home to
accommodate mainly veterans of the Civil War.

Alamosa

Alamosa, **Milepost 34**, became the railroad center of the
San Luis valley. The first track reached here in July 1878
from La Veta Pass, then the highest railroad right-of-way in
the world (see *U.S. 160* itinerary). The line turned southwest toward Antonito, then climbed westward over the
Continental Divide at Cumbres Pass enroute to Durango,
which was reached in July 1881. The same year the line was
extended from Alamosa along the Rio Grande to Del Norte.
Eventually the Poncha Pass-Alamosa line was built, making
Alamosa, a town laid out and named by D&RG executive A.
C. Hunt, the hub of narrow-gauge rail traffic running to the
four points of the compass.

Pike's Stockade

Meanwhile, back at the beginning of the nineteenth century, Zebulon Pike and his men had negotiated the sand
dunes to arrive at the banks of the Rio Grande, as confused
as ever regarding their actual location. "Jan. 30 [1807]—We
marched hard and arrived in the evening on the banks of the
Red River. . . . Jan. 31— . . . We descended 18 miles when
we met a large west branch [the Conejos River] emptying
into the main stream, up which about five miles we took up
our station."

There ten miles east and north of La Jara, **Milepost 20**, is a
replica of the stockade Pike built in early 1807 to "defend

against the insolence, cupidity and barbarity of the savages. . . ."

On February 26, however, Pike and his men were visited by a detachment of Spanish dragoons. "'What?' said I. 'Is this not the Red River?' I immediately ordered my flag to be taken down and rolled up, feeling how sensibly I had committed myself in entering their territory, and was conscious that they must have positive orders to take me in."

Pike neglects to explain why, if indeed it were the Red River and the limit of American territory, he chose to build a fort five miles beyond it. He was arrested and delivered to Santa Fe and then to Chihuahua, in Old Mexico, before he and his comrades were repatriated, by way of the real Red River in Texas to Nachitoches, Louisiana Territory.

Spain was in turmoil in 1807 due to Napoleon's machinations. The Spanish king was forced to abdicate to be replaced by Napoleon's brother, Joseph. There was much agitation in Spain's American colonies, New Spain (Mexico) included, against the regime in Madrid. In the United States such would-be empire builders as former vice-president Aaron Burr, fresh from having fatally wounded Alexander Hamilton in their famous duel, had been plotting to invade Mexico and overturn the government in Mexico City. In the midst of such international intrugues, Pike was fortunate to be treated as well as he was by the Spanish.

San Luis

The little town for which the entire valley was named, San Luis, lies thirty-five miles east of Romeo, **Milepost 13**. Founded by emigrants from Taos and other New Mexican towns, San Luis in 1851 became the first recognizable town in what is now Colorado. The settlers of that time were progenitors of families that today abound in Colorado— Medina, Pacheco, Rivera, Jacquez, Vigil, Gallegos, Martinez, and Valdez. Within a span of two years and a radius of five miles the villages of San Pablo and San Acacio also sprang up. By 1852 the settlers had dug the most enduring irrigation canal in the state. Still in use, the San Luis ditch holds the first priority of any waters in the state under Colorado's archaic and now unique water law, by which entitlement to water is bought and sold like mineral rights.

Manassa

A generation or so later another group of immigrants whose progeny remain as apparent as those of the San Luis pioneers came to this part of the valley. These were the Mormons, brought to the Conejos River valley, **Milepost 7.5**, by Elder John Morgan in the late 1870s. The colonists were southern converts to the Church of the Latter-Day Saints who came by train from Scottsboro, Alabama, to Pueblo in response to an admonition from Brigham Young, who wrote to Morgan in June 1877: "As Zion is constantly growing, so must we extend our settlements. . . . It would be well . . . to locate in some favorable spot in the western portion of Texas or in New Mexico . . . near the homes of some of the tribes of Lamanites [Indians] over whom our brethren and sisters could yield an influence for good...."

Jack Dempsey, the Manassa Mauler and former world heavyweight boxing champion, lived in this now refurbished cabin on Manassa's main thoroughfare.

Aided by the urgings of A. C. Hunt, Morgan elected to settle his people along the D&RG's southward line. The Mormons purchased 1,280 acres around the present site of Manassa, a town they founded three miles east of **Milepost 13**. Fifty charter families were joined in late 1879 by four hundred more persons. The next year a company of eighty converts came from Virginia, among them the John Dempseys who, sixteen years later, had a son they named William Harrison Dempsey. He was to become the heavyweight boxing champion of the world, known as Jack Dempsey, the Manassa Mauler. The Dempsey cabin is on Manassa's main street.

In the past century, the Mormon colony has grown to thirty-five hundred members in the San Luis valley.

First Roman Catholic Church, Conejos

Another religious group that left their mark on this part of Colorado were the Roman Catholics of Spanish ancestry. The first Roman Catholic church in what was to become the state of Colorado was Our Lady of Guadalupe in Conejos, **Milepost 7**. It was established on June 10, 1857.

In December 1871, the parish came under the administration of priests of the Society of Jesus—the Jesuits. The first Jesuit pastor was a thirty-eight-year-old Italian, Fr. Salvatore Persone, who, with his colleagues of the Jesuit Province of Naples, had been expelled from Italy by the triumphant followers of Garibaldi, the revolutionary who founded the modern Italian Republic. Father Persone was to become the first president of Denver's Regis College in 1888.

In an August 1874 progress report to his provincial superior, the Italian priest remarked upon the high degree of devotion among his New Mexican communicants. In particular he described the self-inflicted ordeals of a lay brotherhood called the *Penitentes*, a semi-secret society that practiced a rigorous form of self-flagellation. "The Mexicans believe in the rule of this congregation," reported Father Persone, "as if it were a fifth Gospel, so to speak."

Nominal head of the society was the parish priest, but the actual leader was called the *Hermano Mayor*—for which "Big Brother" is a tempting translation. Each village had a chapter that met only sporadically during the year, except for Lent, in an isolated hall known as *la morada*, which, in conventional Spanish, means simply "the dwelling." There were two categories of initiates, the brothers of light and the brothers of the mask. Meetings were normally held at night, perhaps for no more sinister reason than that the day had to be dedicated to work. During Lent, however, meetings took place each Friday night.

The most conspicuous activity of the *Penitentes*, according to Father Persone, was the ritual mortification of the flesh that was practiced in religious processions. In funeral vigils and processions, for example, these religious zealots, stripped to the waist, would flail themselves about the shoulders until they bled.

"The next day," wrote Persone, "you might see all the walls spattered with blood." The mourners prayed and sang throughout the night as they guarded the corpse "with a perseverance equal to a desert monk."

During Lent the various *moradas* would conduct midnight processions to a distant cross, in emulation of Calvary. On Good Friday, in addition to carrying crosses and scourging themselves, some *Penitentes* would have themselves tied and raised upon a cross. "This year [1874]," observed the Italian Jesuit, "one of these crucified brethren died, I was told, from sheer pain."

"Some of them count on buying heaven with such indiscretions," he concluded, "and maybe they do, because they do it in good faith."

Somewhat like their Mormon neighbors, according to anthropologist Frances Leon Swadesh, the *Penitentes* may have come to the San Luis valley to escape the reproach of more mainstream Catholics in New Mexico. "Through prayer services to the saints and wakes for the dead, Brothers brought to sufferers and their loved ones the consolations of their religion. They also provided material aid by

digging graves, helping bereaved families with their plough-
ing and heavy tasks, and by organizing food sharing during
Lent and Holy Week. These activities were vital to community unity. . . ."

Antonito

The fabled Denver & Rio Grande Railroad has its current
railhead at Antonito, **Milepost 6**. From Antonito an excursion train, the Cumbres & Toltec Scenic Railroad, runs over
the narrow-gauge track abandoned by the D&RG in a twisting, thirty-mile climb over Cumbres Pass on the Continental Divide to Chama, New Mexico, a right-of-way that once
formed a key link in the D&RG's service to Durango and the
important mining districts of the San Juan mountains (see
U.S. 160 itinerary).

Colorado 149
Going for Goulash
Blue Mesa to South Fork (119 miles)

On April 1, 1882, the Denver & Rio Grande Railroad had its railhead approximately at the intersection of *Colorado 149* and *U.S. 50*. The D&RG was on its way from Gunnison to Grand Junction and its own junction with the Denver & Rio Grande Western, which was building from Ogden, Utah, toward the Colorado border.

A toll road already existed between Gunnison and Cebolla, ten miles to the west, on the south bank of the Gunnison where, in 1882, some important iron mines were in operation. The toll road had been built by Sylvester Richardson, the founder of Gunnison, who in turn sold it to the already famous toll road builder and operator, Otto Mears. Mears had intended to build the road himself and, in 1879, had even included it in his plans for the Saguache & San Juan Toll Road Company, which he had organized that year.

The 1873 Brunot Treaty

But Mears became involved in the federal government's negotiations with the Ute tribes, whose reservations covered most of western Colorado. In the aftermath of the massacre of Indian Agent Nathan C. Meeker and his colleagues at the Ute agency on White River in September 1879 (see *Colorado 13* itinerary), Mears had little time for roadbuilding.

The eastern boundary of the Confederated Ute Reservation was set in 1868 at the 107th meridian, four miles east of **Milepost 112**. In the 1868 treaty the Utes forfeited claim to the San Luis valley. In exchange for the territory vacated, the Utes received annual supplies from the federal government and the services of a resident Indian agent.

The first agent was 2nd Lt. Calvin T. Speer of the 11th

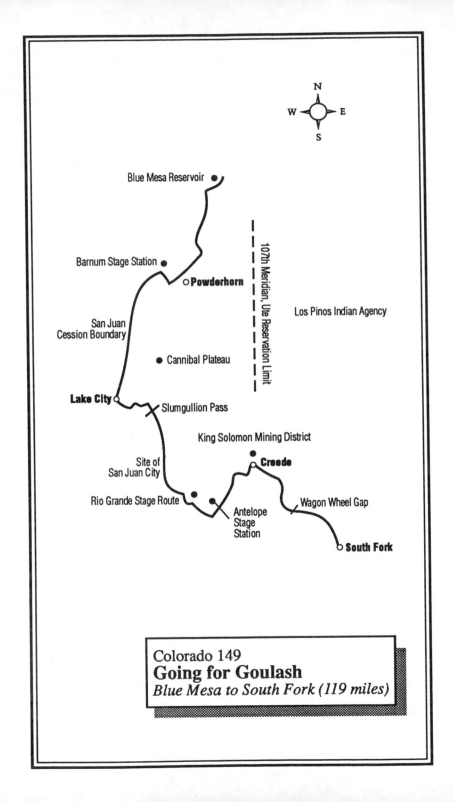

N
W E
S

Blue Mesa Reservoir ●

Barnum Stage Station ●

○ **Powderhorn**

107th Meridian, Ute Reservation Limit

Los Pinos Indian Agency

San Juan
Cession Boundary

● Cannibal Plateau

Lake City ○

Slumgullion Pass

King Solomon Mining District

Site of
San Juan City

● **Creede**

Rio Grande Stage Route

Wagon Wheel Gap

Antelope
Stage
Station

○ **South Fork**

Colorado 149
Going for Goulash
Blue Mesa to South Fork (119 miles)

U.S. Infantry Regiment, who helped set up the agency headquarters on a site chosen by the Indians, Los Pinos Creek, twelve miles west of the place where Cochetopa Pass traversed the Continental Divide.

The Indians, unfamiliar with the science of cartography, assumed that the eastern boundary of the reservation followed the crest of the Divide. Ute chief Ouray had declared at one point that "the rivers that run to the east from the mountain range are off the Reservation; and the rivers that run to the west are on it." Los Pinos Creek, of course, ran to the west.

The improbable Otto Mears, born in Russia of Jewish parents, had become a close friend of Chief Ouray. At the end of the Civil War, in 1865, Mears was mustered out of the Union army in New Mexico to become a merchant and supplier to the Indians. He was operating from the town of Saguache (see *U.S. 285S* itinerary), when the agency was established at Los Pinos. Mears had built a toll road over Cochetopa Pass to the agency to get his wares to customers.

Meanwhile a somewhat eccentric agent showed up in 1870 to replace Lieutenant Speer. A Unitarian minister and recent graduate of Harvard University, Jazeb N. Trask quickly developed some misgivings about the highly regarded, English-speaking Chief Ouray. Ouray had been on the government payroll since 1856 as an interpreter, receiving an annual salary of $500.

"He is of little account as an interpreter," claimed Trask, "for he has but limited use of English and Mexican. He speaks [nevertheless] with remarkable facility. I think he has been over-estimated."

Trask was replaced in June 1827 by another foreign-born immigrant, Charles Adams (see I-25M and *Colorado 13* itineraries), who was also a friend of Mears.

Mears and Adams became involved in negotiations with the Utes to move the agency and the Utes to the other side of the 107th meridian, where it seemed they belonged, and, because some important gold and silver deposits had been discovered in the San Juan Mountains, to persuade the Utes to forfeit ownership of that important range. As territorial governor Edward McCook had complained in 1870 to officials in Washington, "One-third of the territory of Colorado is turned over to the Utes who will not work and will not let others work." Thus began negotiations that would lead to the Brunot Treaty of 1873.

Named for Felix R. Brunot, president of the federal Board of Indian Commissioners, the parley with the Utes began in the summer of 1872, but due to the obduracy of the Indians the talks had to be adjourned and resumed again in the summer of 1873. Spurring resumption, Washington policymakers invoked the work-ethic-according-to-Governor-McCook and instructed Brunot: "The people of Colorado desire to have that portion of the Reserve not needed for Indian purposes thrown open to entry and settlement as public land in order that the agricultural and mineral resources may be developed—especially that portion lying between the southern boundary and the 38th degree of north latitude [**Milepost 72**]."

What was troubling bureaucrats was the fact that as many as three hundred prospectors had already invaded the San Juan Mountains in response to important gold and silver discoveries. The undermanned frontier army was powerless to halt this influx and reluctant to remove those who were already there. And not for the first time, to prevent flouting of the law, the law was changed.

Launched in that atmosphere, the negotiations abounded in ironies. In the first place, the Ute tribe destined to be evicted from the San Juans—the Weminuche—was not represented at the talks. An altogether unlikely participant, however, was the commercial representative of a British investment company who at one point offered to buy the reservation on behalf of his well-heeled overseas clients.

Even more bizarre, perhaps, was the realization that the success of the negotiations would turn on the recovery of Ouray's lost son, Cotoon. At the age of five the boy had been seized, in the early 1860s, by a band of Sioux in an encounter with the Utes near the South Platte River. At Ouray's insistence Brunot promised to deploy the resources of the U.S. government to find the boy.

As the negotiations continued, however, the search showed little evidence of success. When the time came, on September 13, 1873, to sign the treaty ceding the San Juans to white settlement, the boy had yet to be produced.

Mears proposed a more immediate inducement to get the influential Ouray to endorse the treaty: Offer him $1,000 a year for life, as long as the Utes do not go to war with the whites.

"Bribery," was Brunot's purported appraisal of the suggestion.

"A just salary," returned Mears.

Indifferent to its implications, the Utes signed on schedule to open up the San Juans. Meanwhile, a youth, supposedly a Ute who fit Cotoon's description, was discovered in Indian Territory, today's Oklahoma, where he was the adopted son of a Northern Arapahoe chieftain named Friday, himself a waif adopted at one time by the celebrated frontiersman Thomas "Broken Hand" Fitzpatrick. Ouray confronted his lost son in an 1874 visit to Washington, D.C., where initially he was rebuffed by the boy. A year later, the youth changed his mind but in a final quirk of fate died suddenly en route to rejoin his father in Colorado.

Los Pinos Indian Agency

Colorado's only convicted cannibal, Alfred Packer (see below), appeared in late April 1874 at Los Pinos Agency. The agency employee who greeted him later observed: "He didn't seem different from any other man who had been exposed to winter weather. His hair and beard were long and matted; but he showed little sign of having suffered from severe winter weather, lost in a wild uninhabited country with the thermometer showing 30 and 50 degrees below zero many mornings. Naturally, one would expect that no man could stand the exposure this man had been through and live; but here was the man alive and seemingly none the worse for his experiences."

Powderhorn

The town of Powderhorn, one and one-half miles southwest of **Milepost 102,**dates from 1876. It arose at the site of
the Cebolla Creek hot springs, a popular spa in the region.

Barnum

Gateway, at **Milepost 95,** is near the site of an early stage
station called Barnum, named not for the circus impresario
but for an obscure but revered stage line employee, Lewis
Barnum. The Barlow & Sanderson Stage Company ran from
Canon City, then the Denver & Rio Grande's railhead, up to
Bales Station, today's Salida, over Poncha Pass to Saguache.
From Saguache the line crossed Cochetopa Pass on the road
pioneered by Otto Mears, past the old Los Pinos Agency,
which had been vacated finally in November 1875, and came
up through White Earth and Powderhorn to this point.
From Barnum the route went southward to Lake City, a
jumping off point for the San Juan mining districts. Between
Barnum and Lake City the route followed was approximately that of today's highway.

Later in the 1870s Barnum was a stop on the Mears toll
road that ran to Cimarron (see *U.S. 50W* itinerary) and
southward along Cimarron Creek to a pass that led to the
new Ute agency on the Uncompaghre River. In busy seasons the coaches driven over this route were the twenty-two
passenger Concords drawn by fast six-horse teams.

With the removal of the Utes ordered by Congress in
1880, immigrants to the new communities on Colorado's
Western Slope passed through Barnum over these same toll
roads and some new ones. A Grand Junction pioneer reported to the Gunnison *Daily Review* in January 1882:

> [On] every trip made from Gunnison with two horses
> and a wagon, via Barnum, from $10 to $15 is yanked out of
> the freighter by the toll road company. This is extremely
> hard on the freighters, particularly when they have to
> drag through snow banks and over steep mountain roads

made dangerous to travel by ice and snow. . . . And it does not appear that the owners of the roads are doing anything to make them better. . . .
Your County Board should at once prepare the direct road down the Gunnison[River]. It is 30 miles shorter and should be free of that nuisance of Colorado, "toll, toll, toll" over roads, ferries and bridges. Let us have free roads and free bridges.

In time this came to pass, and the *Daily Review*'s opinionated correspondent, R. D. Motley, became Grand Junction's first mayor.

Cannibal Peak

Four miles east of **Milepost 82** Cannibal Peak rises to 12,600 feet, a landmark on Cannibal Plateau, where Alfred Packer, as a modern Colorado politician has put it, "served his fellow man" in the winter of 1873-74.

Lake City

The Gunnison-Hinsdale county line, **Milepost 83**, marks the southern limit of the Ute reservation created in the Brunot Treaty of 1873 and the northern boundary of the San Juan cession. Hinsdale County was created in February 1874 in rather bald anticipation of formal Senate ratification of the treaty, which eventually took place on April 29. Thanks in part, perhaps, to Alfred Packer, the county has been the most sparsely populated of all Colorado's counties. Lake City remains the only town within its borders.

Despite its modest size, Lake City, **Milepost 74**, was an important crossroads for stage lines and freight companies serving the San Juan mining communities and the Ute Indian Agency after it was moved to the Uncompaghre River (see *U.S. 50-550* itinerary). The town was founded by the tireless Otto Mears, who not only saw Lake City as a transportation center but also managed to discover gold on the banks of nearby Lake San Cristobal.

Lake City was a stopping place for wagon road traffic coming from Saguache by way of Barnum, as we have seen. It also accommodated stagecoaches transporting mail and passengers from the Denver & Rio Grande's railhead, first at La Veta, then Fort Garland, and finally Alamosa (see *U.S. 160* itinerary). In 1877 the big Concord coaches took thirty-one hours to go from La Veta to Lake City by way of Del Norte, Wagon Wheel Gap, and Slumgullion Pass. The cost was just twenty-seven dollars. By 1879, when the railhead had moved to Alamosa, the stagecoach driving time over the 115-mile course to Lake City was reduced to twenty hours.

The Sanderson stage line continued to carry Western Slope travelers, such as those headed for Ouray on rich Red Mountain's north side (see *U.S. 50-550* itinerary), by way of Barnum and Cimarron Creek and the Uncompaghre River agency. A rival stage line went to Ouray by way of the Henson Creek toll road which ran due west from Lake City.

The trial of Alfred Packer (who signed his name "Alferd") took place in Lake City nine years after the crime for which he was to be convicted. Pennsylvania-born Packer was thirty-one when he appeared at the Los Pinos Agency to confess to cannibalizing several of his six companions and killing one:

Old Man [Israel] Swan died first and was eaten by the other five persons about ten days out of camp. Four or five days afterwards Humphreys [James Humphrey] died and was also eaten; he had about one hundred and thirty dollars ($133). I found the pocketbook and took the money. Some time afterwards while I was carrying wood, the butcher [Frank "Butcher" Miller] was killed—as the others told me, accidentally—and he was also eaten. [Shannon Wilson] Bell shot "California" [George Noon] with Swan's gun and I killed Bell. Shot him. I covered up the remains and took a large piece along. Then traveled fourteen days into the Agency.

On the strength of his confession, signed, dated (May 4, 1874), and witnessed by Los Pinos Indian agent Charles A.

A rare photograph of confessed cannibal Alfred "Alferd" Packer, pardoned after serving fifteen years of a forty-year sentence. *Colorado Historical Society.*

Adams, Packer was turned over to the nearest sheriff, Amos Wall in Saguache. There he was held in a makeshift jail on Wall's ranch until August 22, 1874, when he escaped.

Coincidentally, but probably unknown to Packer, one and possibly two persons had stumbled across the mutilated corpses of Packer's apparent victims. One of these was *Harper's Weekly Magazine* artist John A. Randolph (or Reynolds), who was on assignment for his employer. The other might have been a Capt. C. H. Graham of Del Norte, according to a *Rocky Mountain News* story of the time. It was enough, in any case, to prompt Packer's arraignment for murder.

The order was issued by a judge in Hinsdale County's only community at the time, not Lake City, which did not yet exist in 1874, but San Juan, at the mouth of Clear Creek, **Milepost 39**, a town that not only no longer exists but whose site is no longer in Hinsdale County.

Packer revealed himself, for some reason, to an old acquaintance in January 1883 at Fort Fetterman in Wyoming Territory, where he was living under the alias John Schwartze. Amidst much prejudging in the press and among the public, he was returned for trial at Lake City, convicted on Friday the 13th of April 1883, and sentenced to be hanged. His May 19 execution was stayed by the state Supreme Court, however, on a technicality. He was ordered to be tried not for murder but for the lesser charge of manslaughter. The second trial, held in Gunnison in 1886, found Packer again to be guilty. He was sentenced this time to forty years in the state penitentiary in Canon City. He was pardoned on January 10, 1901, in Charles S. Thomas's last official act as governor, and he died in 1907.

Lake City to Creede

Some traveler, apparently as famished but more discriminating in his tastes than the omnivorous Packer, proclaimed the name of the pass he had crossed at **Milepost 65** Slumgullion Pass.

An early and difficult but more direct route to the mines in the heart of the San Juan Mountains followed the Rio Grande River from **Milepost 41** to its upper reaches in Lost Trail Creek, whose name suggests some of the uncertainties of early day travel. Two miles beyond, at **Milepost 39**, lies the abandoned site of San Juan, the juridical seat of Hinsdale County at the time Packer was first jailed.

Antelope Springs, **Milepost 35**, was also a popular stage line stop.

Creede

In the summer of 1889 two prospectors from Salida (see *U.S. 50W* itinerary) were exploring the heights above **Milepost 21** along Willow Creek. One of them, Nicholas C. Creede, had had some success in the Monarch Pass mining district of the upper South Arkansas River. Here on Willow Creek, he hit a bonanza.

Creede and partner George L. Smith uncovered a vein of silver so rich that they were able to sell the mine within months of its discovery to railroad magnate and financier David H. Moffat for the grand sum of $75,000. Moffat's unhesitating investment launched yet another frantic boom. Even Creede was prompted to return to the now aptly named King Solomon mining district, where he uncovered two more mines, the Ethyl and the Amethyst. The latter produced $2 million in one year.

"Capitalists came every day, and were carried off up the mountains to look at a hole in the ground, and down again to see the assay tests of the ore taken from it," wrote Richard Harding Davis to his New York newspaper when he visited in 1892.

One of Colorado's most resourceful and unscrupulous con men, Jefferson Randolph "Soapy" Smith was eventually barred from most of the state's important towns and mining camps in the 1890s. *Colorado Historical Society.*

"Prospectors scoured the sides of the mountains from sundawn to sunset, and at night their fires lit up the range, and their little heaps of stone and their single stick, with their name scrawled on it in pencil, made the mountains look like great burying grounds. All of the land within two miles of Creede was claimed by these simple proofs of ownership—simple, yet as effectual as a parchment sealed and signed."

Inevitably, the fraternity of thieves descended upon the booming camp. In 1892, chief among them was a masterful bunco artist, Jefferson Randolph Smith, otherwise known as "Soapy." He earned his nickname early in his career in Denver when, outside Union Station, he ran his soap scam.

"Cleanliness is next to godliness, but crisp greenbacks in the pocket is paradise itself," he chanted. "For $5 you get a bar of soap and maybe $100." Bystanders were invited to select a sample from a bucket of wrapped soap bars. Some of the bars were wrapped in bills of various denominations and then rewrapped in blue covers. The people in the crowd who exclaimed over their good fortune were Soapy's shills who were passed greenback-loaded bars of soap by prearrangement.

Success in Denver led him to try his luck in the mining camp of Creede, where he opened the Orleans Club, a saloon and gambling hall that specialized in shaking down prosperous prospectors. Smith even contrived to win political control of the town and installed his brother-in-law as police chief.

He found a clever scam irresistable. Inspired by P. T. Barnum's sensational "Cardiff Giant," Smith came up with an allegedly petrified giant, whose nine-and-one-half-foot stone corpse was unearthed in one of Creede's numerous mines. After he had milked the credulity of Creede for what it was worth, Smith sold his hoax to a carnival.

A man of many parts, Soapy sent a weekly telegram of greeting to his mother in St. Louis and passed out Christmas turkeys to the needy. "He was the warmest-hearted man I ever knew," said one friend. Nonetheless, during the 1890s he was legally barred from Creede, Salida, Leadville, Aspen, Telluride, Silverton, and New Orleans.

He showed up in the Alaska gold rush in 1898 and was acclaimed for a time as the "Sultan of Skagway." His last notable scam involved setting up an enlistment office catering to volunteers for the Spanish-American War, a highly popular enterprise of 1898 (see *U.S. 40* itinerary). As the would-be enlistees stripped down for their "physical exams," Soapy's confederates emptied their pockets.

Smith was gunned down in July 1898 by a posse of vigilantes who had responded to a complaint from a prospector Smith had bilked.

Wagon Wheel Gap

Wagon Wheel Gap, **Milepost 13**, was another of the stage line stops on the route from wherever the railroad's end-of-track chanced to be in the San Luis valley to Lake City and the San Juans. In time Wagon Wheel Gap itself became the railhead of the Denver & Rio Grande, whose president at the time was none other than David H. Moffat. When Moffat bought into Creede's claim, the D&RG promptly built a ten-mile extension to the town of Creede.

According to legend, Wagon Wheel Gap takes its name from the vestige of a much earlier prospecting expedition. A wagon from Charles Baker's 1860 search for gold in the San Juans (see *U.S. 50-550* itinerary) is supposed to have broken a wheel at this point. The faulty wheel was discarded and discovered by subsequent travelers who named the site. An unlikely story, perhaps, since early prospector trails would rarely permit travel by anything more cumbersome than a burro, but the tale at least befits the dubious legacy of Soapy Smith.

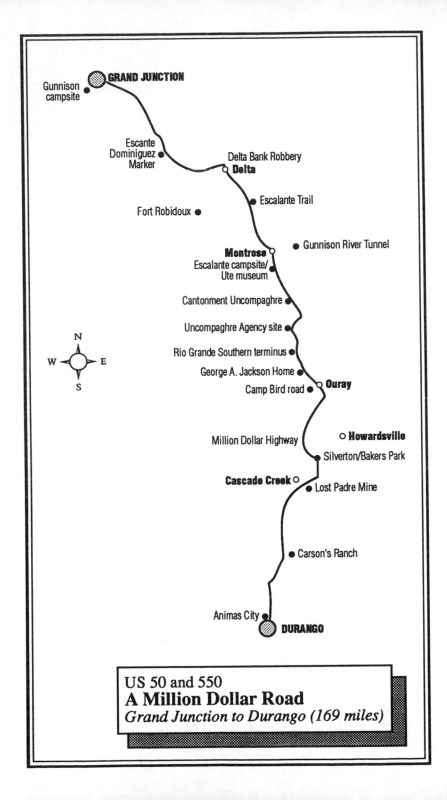

Gunnison
campsite

GRAND JUNCTION

Escante
Dominiguez
Marker

Delta Bank Robbery

Delta

Escalante Trail

Fort Robidoux

Gunnison River Tunnel

Montrose

Escalante campsite/
Ute museum

Cantonment Uncompaghre

Uncompaghre Agency site

Rio Grande Southern terminus

George A. Jackson Home

Camp Bird road

Ouray

Million Dollar Highway

○ **Howardsville**

Silverton/Bakers Park

Cascade Creek ○

Lost Padre Mine

Carson's Ranch

Animas City

DURANGO

N
W E
S

US 50 and 550
A Million Dollar Road
Grand Junction to Durango (169 miles)

US 50 and 550
A Million Dollar Road
Grand Junction to Durango (169 miles)

In September 1853, when U.S. Army Capt. John Williams Gunnison led his expedition through the valley of the river that now bears his name, his mission was to assess prospects for a transcontinental railroad through the midsection of the country. In less than a month, he was killed by an obscure band of Indians in Utah's Great Basin.

Near **Milepost 38** of U.S. 50, his successor, E. G. Beckwith, made this observation, which he later reported to the United States Senate: "No part of the route thus far from San Luis Valley . . . offers a spot of any considerable extent suitable for settlement." He would be surprised to learn that today there are five towns and cities along that route (see *U.S. 50W*) with a total population of fifty thousand people whose ancestors were lured here by prospects for mining and horticulture unmatched for hundreds of miles in several directions.

Twenty-eight years after Gunnison was killed by Indians, the imposing Ute nation occupying the Colorado lands through which Gunnison had passed was forced to leave as a consequence of the Meeker massacre (see *Colorado 13* itinerary). Their exodus to Utah took place on September 7, 1881. Observed Walker D. Wyman in a 1927 article in *Colorado Magazine*: "What a march of retreating civilization . . . could[be] seen! Here was the last defeat of the red man. Here the frontiers of the white man met, crushing the Utes in its mighty embrace."

The earliest white men to penetrate this empire of the Utes were Spaniards from Santa Fe, and the most famous of these were two Franciscan friars, Silvestre Vélez de Escalante and Francisco Atanasio Dominguez. Only days after Americans on the east coast had proclaimed their rebellion against Great Britian, these two ventured into the western wilds looking for a better route to Spain's California missions. A historical marker in the rest area at **Milepost 59** locates the mouth of Escalante Canyon, named by the Hayden Survey in 1875 for their Hispanic predecessor.

Escalante and Dominguez had been preceded by others in the 167 years since the founding of Santa Fe. The most recent was Don Juan Maria de Ribera who in 1765 carved a cross on a tree along the Gunnison River to the east of today's Delta, **Milepost 71**.

Another early sojourner in the vicinity was Antoine Robidoux, a St. Louis fur trader who established a trading fort about three miles south of **Milepost 64** around 1837. Called variously Fort Robidoux or Fort Uncompaghre, the post was a satellite to a more important Fort Robidoux at the mouth of the Uintah River in Utah. Traders traveling from the main trading establishment to or from Santa Fe and Taos usually stopped over here.

One reluctant visitor was Methodist minister Joseph Williams, who was obliged, to his dismay, to lay over at the post in 1842 on his return to the states from Oregon: "This place is equal to any I ever saw for wickedness and idleness. . . . Some of these people at the Fort are fat and dirty and idle and greasy. . . . [Moreover,] I tried several times to preach to them but with little if any effect."

Delta

Delta, **Milepost 71**, found itself in the 1890s to be perilously close to the Outlaw Trail, that legendary highway that carried rustlers and gunmen of various sorts from Montana to Mexico. It passed through the Powder River valley of Wyoming, where the famous Hole-in-the Wall had its resident gang, to Brown's Hole (see *Colorado 13* and *U.S. 40* itincraries), where Butch Cassidy maintained the Wild Bunch, to Robbers' Roost in southern Utah.

Among the desperadoes who rode the trail were the McCartys, the most notable of them Tom McCarty, a sometime comrade of Butch Cassidy. Two generations of

McCartys met their end in Delta on the morning of September 7, 1893, in a rather pathetic example of crime's absent reward.

Tom and his brother, Bill, walked into a Delta bank that morning to hold up cashier A. T. Blatchley and his assistant H. H. Wolbert. When one of them balked, Tom McCarty fired his pistol in intimidation. Collecting the money tendered them by the cashiers, the two brothers fled through the rear of the bank where Bill's son, Fred, held a string of horses for the getaway.

W. Ray Simpson, son and partner of the keeper of a hardware store across from the bank, heard the muffled sound of the shot, seized a Sharps repeating rifle, and stationed himself down the street in anticipation of intercepting the presumed robbers as they fled.

"He must have been a good shot," said Tom McCarty later, "for several bullets passed so near me that I felt the force of the balls. . . ."

Simpson's first shot struck Bill McCarty in the head, killing him in an instant. Fred, seeing his father fall, dismounted and returned to him. Another of Simpson's shots killed the son. Tom McCarty managed to escape, but he had a mere one hundred dollars of the loot.

Gunnison–Uncompaghre Junction

Escalante and Dominguez followed the Uncompaghre River toward its junction with the Gunnison as far as **Milepost 81**, observing that the trail downstream along the Uncompaghre (dubbed El Rio de San Francisco by the Franciscans) was "very wide and well-beaten." They left the river at this point and turned northeastward in search of a band of Utes of whom they had been informed. A few miles up the North Fork of the Gunnison River they were hailed by a party of five Sabuagana Utes, but not the ones they were seeking.

> We gave them wherewith to eat and smoke, but after a long parley—its subject being the quarrels they had been

having this summer with the Yamarica Comanches—we could not draw out of them anything useful for our plan, because theirs was to fill us with fear by exaggerating the danger to which we were exposing ourselves of being killed by the Comanches if we continued on our course. We . . . [told] them that our God, who is everyone's, would defend us if we should happen to run into these foes.

The party's modest defenses were underscored a few days later when they encountered the Ute band they had sought. Two civilian employees had been discovered trading with the Utes, in violation of their contract, in order to obtain arms.

> We had just been telling the Sabuaganas that we needed neither arms nor men because we placed all our safety and defense in God's almighty arm, and Andres our interpreter, and his brother Lucrecio, proved themselves to be such obedient and faithful Christians that they peddled what they secretly brought along and most greedily sought weapons from the infidels, telling them that they badly needed them because they were about to pass through the land of the Comanches.
>
> In this way, to our own sorrow, they betrayed their meager faith or lack of it, and how very unfit they were for ventures of this kind.

Uncompaghre Valley

By the early twentieth century, agriculture had developed to such a degree in the Uncompaghre valley that a more constant supply of water was required, a problem already common to other parts of Colorado (see *U.S. 34* and *U.S. 160* itineraries). In a notable feat of engineering, a tunnel was bored deep in the forbidding Black Canyon of the Gunnison to divert water to the upper reaches of the Uncompaghre.

The dauntless engineers of the Denver & Rio Grande Railroad had built a grade through about fifteen miles of the canyon's upper end, which was a half-mile deep at some points, but even they had to emerge and bypass the forbidding defile at Cimarron Creek (see *U.S. 50W* itinerary). The Black Canyon had defied even survey until the twentieth century, so the opening of a five-mile tunnel seven miles below Cimarron Creek was a major accomplishment. It was begun in 1904 by William W. Torrence, who became known as the "Father of the Gunnison Tunnel" when the project was finally completed in 1919. The diversion empties into the headwaters of Cedar Creek east of Montrose, **Milepost 93** on *U.S. 50*.

Ute Territory

The house and farm of famed Ute chief Ouray and his wife, Chipeta, were located west of **Milepost 126** on *U.S. 550*, near the present site of the Ute Indian Museum.

The Spanish padres, on August 26, 1776, camped near this site after descending the Uncompaghre Plateau to the west and striking the Uncompaghre River about four miles upstream. They were aware of the Utes' name for the stream (Uncompaghre means "Red Lake," an apparent allusion to the river's mineral-laden source) but chose to rename it El Rio de San Francisco. The campsite at this point was called La Cienaga de San Francisco ("the marshes of Saint Francis").

Here they met a wandering Ute and his family. Reminiscent of a later, famous Arapahoe chieftain (see *U.S. 36* itinerary), the Ute was named Left-Handed. "We tarried a good while with him, and after a lengthy conversation drew forth nothing more useful than that we had suffered from the sun's heat, which was indeed very fiery all the while the talk lasted, we continued our day's march. . . ."

Communities and mining camps had sprung up in the San Juan region since 1873, when the mineral-rich area was ceded by the Utes under the Brunot Treaty (see *Colorado 149* itinerary). In the hysteria following the Meeker massacre in September 1879, the federal government dispatched a number of troops into the area. Maj. Alfred L.

Hough, a commander of one of these units, made this observation in a reminiscence shortly after the event: "It will be the old, old story over again: while the government is talking, with a pretense of wanting to civilize the mass of the Indians, at the same time punishing none of the guilty ones, the frontiersman will seize their homes and thus give cause for further outrages which will be an excuse for harsher treatment. I was glad to get away from the muddle. . . ."

In July 1880 a supposedly temporary camp called Cantonment Uncompaghre was set up at **Milepost 121**. It was still there when the Utes left in September 1881 to be resettled on the Uintah Reservation in Utah, and it was rechristened Fort Crawford in 1886, marking it as a permanent military installation. In 1890 the post was deactivated and its reserve of land opened to settlement.

The Uncompaghre Ute Agency was located near **Milepost 115**.

Ridgway

The celebrated "Pathfinder of the San Juan," Otto Mears, built a railroad that meandered from Durango through the mining camps along the Dolores and San Miguel rivers (see *Colorado 62-145* itinerary) to Ridgway, **Milepost 103**. The 172-mile Rio Grande Southern, as he called it, joined the Denver & Rio Grande in Durango with the D&RG line that ran south from the mainline at Montrose to Ouray.

Ridgway also marks the southern boundary of the old Ute reservation that existed from the 1873 Brunot Treaty to the Ute Removal Act of 1880 (see *Colorado 149* and *Colorado 13* itineraries).

The man who in 1859 discovered Colorado's first important gold mine at today's Idaho Springs (see I-70W itinerary), George Andrew Jackson, decided eventually to retire in the fertile upper Uncompaghre valley. After making his famous strike, which was publicly announced in May 1859 by Horace Greeley, Jackson left Colorado in 1861 to serve as a lieutenant colonel under Confederate Gen. Stonewall

Jackson in the Civil War. In 1888, he brought his wife, the former Belle Hendricks of Kentucky, and daughter Nina, to settle in the vicinity of **Milepost 98**. He died in a gun accident in 1897 at the age of sixty-two.

Ouray

The town of Ouray, **Milepost 93**, was named for the Ute chief who was much acclaimed by early residents of the San Juan region for his willingness to accommodate to white demands in the interest, apparently, of maintaining peace between his people and white immigrants. One suspects that he met with white approval because he had also taken the trouble to learn English (see *Colorado 149* itinerary). Ouray negotiated the cession of the San Juan region in 1872 and 1873 with the chairman of the Federal Board of Indian Commissioners, Felix Brunot, a parley in which Ouray's friend, Otto Mears, played a minor but conspicuous role. The town was already named for him when Ouray died in August 1880, ten months after bringing his northern compatriots, headed by Chiefs Jack and Douglas, to heel following the Meeker massacre. He did not live to see his people removed from Colorado.

If the naming of Ouray signified the Ute legacy to white settlers, the history of the community typified the munificence of the San Juan mountains. The community began as a silver-mining camp known as Uncompaghre City in the mid-1870s. In 1882 Yankee Girl, a fabulously rich silver mine, was discovered in Red Mountain to the south. To the west, important silver mines had been found on Mount Sneffels.

"Pathfinding" in the San Juans

The ever-enterprising Otto Mears arrived to put Ouray on the map. He built two remarkable toll roads, one to each mining site. His first undertaking was incorporated under the name of the Ouray & San Juan Toll Road Company. At the request of the Ouray County commissioners Mears took

over a project that earlier road builders had dismissed as
financially unfeasible: to build a twelve-mile road through
the rugged Uncompaghre canyon to the Red Mountain mining district. Mears started in mid-June 1883, and, using a
technique pioneered by the Denver & Rio Grande Railroad
in the Black Canyon of the Gunnison, he had workmen
lowered down the canyon's walls to a point six hundred feet
above the canyon floor. They bored holes and placed dynamite charges with extra-long fuses that would allow them
time to be hoisted up before each explosion. A roadbed, one
quarter of a mile at a time was blasted out in this fashion. In
just three months the road itself was completed to **Milepost
81**, near the site of today's Idarado Mine.

That done, Mears turned to the task facing another road
company in which he held an interest, the Ouray & Canyon
Creek Toll Road Company, whose route lay from **Milepost
93** up Canyon Creek along today's *Colorado 361* to the
Mount Sneffels diggings. Construction was interrupted by
the onset of winter, so the completion of this road ran into
1884. Its remarkably moderate grades, despite the difficult
terrain, were deemed at the time an extraordinary engineering achievement, succeeding where five other companies
had failed over a period of eight years.

Dapper Otto Mears ar-
rived in the U.S. an or-
phaned Russian-Jewish
adolescent and became
the builder of impossible
wagon roads and rail-
roads in the rugged San
Juan mountains. *Colo-
rado Historical Society.*

In a squabble over high toll rates, Mears sold the road to the county as silver mining went into decline. He missed out on the bonanza that followed Thomas J. Walsh's discovery of gold at the upper end of Canyon Creek in the Camp Bird silver-mining claim. The Camp Bird mine produced $4 million in gold in the six years following its discovery in 1896. Purchased in 1900 by the British-owned Camp Bird Company and capitalized at approximately four million dollars, the mine averaged a profit of more than 16 percent over the next thirteen years.

Mears operated the Red Mountain toll road until 1891, the same year that his Rio Grande Southern Railway was completed to Ridgway. He sold this road to Ouray County as well, for the mere cost of its construction in 1883. He had not failed to make a profit on the enterprise in the time he was collecting tolls however, and to that must be added the income from a handsome resort hotel he ran at Bear Creek Falls, **Milepost 91.**

The benefits that Ouray derived from Mears's toll road soon became apparent to the town fathers of Silverton on the other side of Red Mountain. Yet they were reluctant to ask Mears to build a toll road from Silverton to the Red Mountain diggings. By now, Mears was powerful both financially, from his many businesses, and politically, because he sat in the Colorado General Assembly.

The Silverton *Democrat* complained that Republican Mears's "forte is in having contracts that will shrink and swell as the weather is wet or dry, and that seem one way by the sun and another way by the moon."

Grudgingly, perhaps, the San Juan County commissioners signed a contract with Mears on June 28, 1884, and he began construction of the toll road on July 8. The project was completed in late November. A delegation from Ouray came across Red Mountain on what was later to be called Mears's "million dollar highway" to participate in Silverton's inaugural celebration on December 5.

From 1870 to 1886 Mears built about 450 miles of toll roads, which he operated in partnership with Cuchara River merchant Fred Walsen (see *U.S. 160* and I-25S itineraries) under the aegis of six separate companies. In an audit of their financial condition in 1887 all but one of the companies had turned a profit and the average profit of all six was 13 percent.

After 1886 Mears concentrated on the building of railroads, not all of them in Colorado. In 1897, for example, he built the Chesapeake Beach Railway, which operated from Washington, D.C., to the beach resorts on Chesapeake Bay. In 1905 Mears became president of the Mack Brothers Motor Car Company, soon to be famous as a builder of big trucks but at that time a builder of motor rail cars. Mears returned to the place of his early triumphs, Silverton, in 1907. At the age of seventy, in 1911, he supervised the repair of fourteen miles of the Silverton Railroad's roadbed, which had been washed out in a flash flood.

Said the Silverton *Standard* on that occasion, "Otto Mears, the Pathfinder, is on the job. Confidence is restored and we all feel better."

Silverton–Baker's Park

The town of Silverton, **Milepost 70**, rests in a dramatically situated mountain hollow known originally as Baker's Park, named for a Virginian, Charles Baker, "a restless, adventurous, impecunious man who was always in search of something new." Baker had been grubstaked to prospect the San Juans in 1860 by S. B. Kellogg, who, with H.A.W. Tabor, had been one of the early exploiters of California Gulch near today's Leadville (see *U.S. 24W* itinerary).

Like so many of the early prospectors (see I-70W and I-25M itineraries), Baker was as much promoter as he was prospector. One pioneer purveyor to the mining camps, Canon City storekeeper Wolfe Londoner, recalled that ". . . a man named Baker . . . came up with glowing accounts of immense deposits of gold in the streams of the San Juan. He went around throughout the mining camps and told his story and got a great many converts. . . ."

Among those who responded to Baker's optimism was his

underwriter, Kellogg, who subsequently founded Animas City, the community that preceded Durango, fifty miles to the south of Baker's Park. But most who answered Baker's call were disappointed. So much so that at one point Baker was hailed before a kangaroo court of disgruntled prospectors and, under threat of mayhem, obliged to prove that gold could be found in Baker's Park. In the course of some earnest panning, Baker was able to turn up enough evidence of gold that his plaintiffs let him go and turned to panning for themselves.

The Durango-Silverton narrow-gauge train edges along the sheer face of a canyon wall above the Animas River. *Colorado Tourism Board.*

A short time later, Baker left to join the Confederate army in the Civil War. In 1868, the restless Baker returned to the San Juans and shortly thereafter was killed by Indians while prospecting along the Colorado River in today's Utah.

Finally in 1870 Adnah French, Dempsey Reese, and a third man discovered the first productive mines—the Little

Giant and the Mountaineer—in Baker's Park, launching a
bona fide gold rush that precipitated negotiation of the 1873
Brunot Treaty.

At the time French and his colleagues made their strikes
on the Ute reservation, the Indians supposedly controlled
nearly a third of Colorado Territory, over fifteen million
acres. The estimates of northern and southern Ute popula-
tions was eight hundred and twelve hundred, respectively.
Governor Edward McCook made this observation to the
Board of Indian Commissioners in 1870, "This great and rich
country is set aside for the exclusive use of savages. A white
man secures 160 acres by paying or preempting: but one
aboriginal vagrant, by virtue of being head of a family,
secures 12,800 acres without preemption or payment."

Along with French and his prospector colleagues, the San
Juans hosted some three hundred gold seekers similarly
without "preemption or payment," some of whom were
getting several hundred dollars a day in ore from diggings on
the reservation. Thus the 1873 Brunot Treaty ceding 3.5
million acres of Ute land to white settlement was another
inexorable consequence of "manifest destiny."

Although legally occupying the San Juan cession
for more than five years, local residents were greatly
alarmed when they heard about the September 29, 1879,
Ute killing of whites on the White River—the Meeker
massacre—225 miles away.

On the day of a county election, October 7, 1879, the
citizens of Howardsville, five miles northeast of Silverton,
were uneasy over the meaning of Indian signal fires that had
lighted up the surrounding hills in the course of the night.
Then came an ill-founded rumor that Animas City had suffered a massacre at the hands of the Utes. Forsaking the
franchise, electors abandoned Howardsville in panic.

Along Silverton's main street *Colorado 110* leads northeast to Howardsville, the headwaters of the Animas River,
and the divide that separates the Animas from the headwaters of the Lake Fork of the Gunnison River. Mears built
another toll road for the town of Silverton to serve the

mining camps along the forks of the Animas. There were other routes into Silverton but they amounted to little more than trails: one from Lake City via the Lake Fork of the Gunnison River to the headwaters of the Animas, another from Antelope Springs on the Rio Grande to Lost Trail Creek, a third from Durango along a trail closely following today's *U.S. 550* to the west of the Animas River valley, and lesser trails that joined Silverton to the mining camps on the Dolores and San Miguel rivers (see *Colorado 62-145* itinerarary).

Finally, on July 3, 1882, Silverton's first firm connection with the outside world arrived when the Denver & Rio Grande Railroad finished its right-of-way from Durango.

At **Milepost 51** the early trail from Durango to the north left today's highway to follow Cascade Creek, circling Engineer Mountain to approach Silverton from the west by way of Mineral Creek, where it joined another one leaving Silverton to cross over 11,743-foot Ophir Pass to the headwaters of the San Miguel River and the mining camps of Ophir and Ames. At Engineer Mountain the Durango-Silverton trail joined yet another running between Rico on the Dolores River and Silverton.

Lost Padre Mine

Legends of supposedly "lost" mines abound in the lore of the prospecting days. One notable, misplaced mine in the San Juans is the Lost Padre. Even the origin of its name is lost. A story survives, however, of the rediscovery and loss again of the Lost Padre.

The mine, if it existed, supposedly could be found a few miles east of **Milepost 48** near the Animas River town of Needleton. A reportedly "free-spending" prospector named Mike O'Leary showed up in the mid-1870s in Parrott City (see *U.S. 160* and *Colorado 62-145* itineraries) to announce that he had "rediscovered" the Lost Padre. To underscore his claim he frequented the saloons and gambling halls of Parrott City, Animas City, and Silverton, drinking and gambling wildly and "scattering gold indiscriminately."

Then he disappeared, never again to be seen in the San Juan
mining camps.

The Denver & Rio Grande Railroad had managed to lay
track to a railhead at Carson's Ranch, **Milepost 38**, before
winter halted operations in December 1881. From Carson's, the Meserole & Blake Stage Line operated into the
mountain mining camps, such as Rico, twenty-five miles to
the northwest.

Animas City–Durango

The first town in the lower Animas River valley was
Animas City, **Milepost 23**, founded by the veteran mining
entrepreneur, S. B. Kellogg, in May 1861. The town did
well until September 13, 1880, when surveyors employed
by a subsidiary of the D&RG showed up to plat a site just one
and one-half miles south of Animas City. The heretofore
unremarked Durango Land & Coal Company had bought
out six homesteaders and, with the advantage of selecting a
site for the D&RG depot, put Animas City out of business.
The result was another railroad creation, Durango City,
which would displace an existing community as had Salida
(see *U.S. 50W* itinerary) and Colorado Springs (see *U.S. 24E*
itinerary).

Colorado 62 and 145
Gallop of the Goose
Ridgway to Dolores (98 miles)

Ridgway

The railroad town has worked in Colorado history much in the manner that the black hole is thought to function in space. The railroad company or its land agent locates a depot and lays out a townsite where previously there was nothing and neighboring communities collapse into its vortex. In this fashion, Colorado Springs devoured Colorado City (see I-25M itinerary), Durango overcame Animas City and Parrott City, and Lamar did in Blackwell (see *U.S. 50E* itinerary).

So it was in 1890 with Ridgway and Dallas.

Named for a U.S. vice-president in office when Texas was admitted to the Union, Dallas Creek debouched into the Uncompaghre River on the doorsteps of a community known as Unaweep in the 1870s. Unaweep, appropriately, was a Ute word meaning "dividing of the waters," and both creek and community lay just within the southern boundary of the Confederated Ute Reservation, whose southern agency was located downriver just a few miles.

In 1879 Unaweep became Dallasville, as things Ute fell into disfavor following the Meeker massacre at the northern Ute agency on White River (see *Colorado 13, U.S. 50-550,* and *Colorado 149* itineraries). In 1885 it became Dallas City, a flag stop on the newly built Denver & Rio Grande Railroad line that was operating between Montrose and Ouray.

In 1890, the citizens of Dallas moved 2.7 miles south, for there the celebrated roadbuilder Otto Mears had launched his last grand enterprise in Colorado. He was building a railroad 172 miles through the mighty San Juan Mountains to connect Durango, an important station on the D&RG's southern line, with the Montrose-Ouray spur that fed into the D&RG's mainline at Montrose. The Rio Grande South-

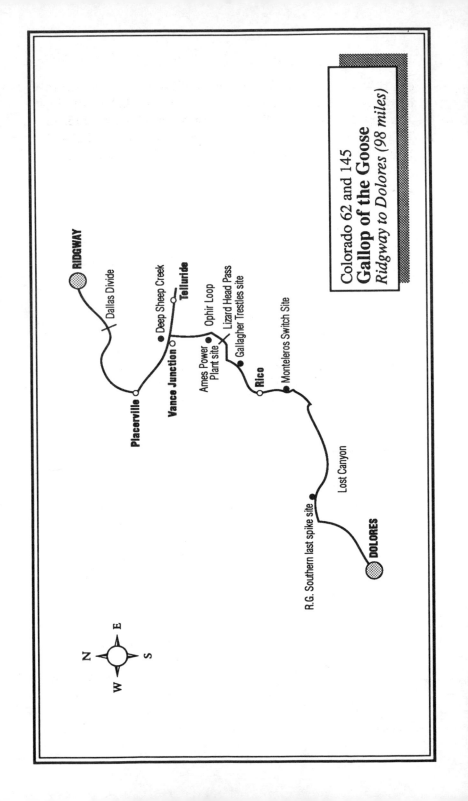

Colorado 62 and 145
Gallop of the Goose
Ridgway to Dolores (98 miles)

RIDGWAY

Dallas Divide

Deep Sheep Creek

Telluride

Placerville

Vance Junction

Ophir Loop

Ames Power
Plant site

Lizard Head Pass

Gallagher Trestles site

Rico

Monteleros Switch Site

R.G. Southern last spike site

Lost Canyon

DOLORES

N
W E
S

ern Railway would follow an existing Mears toll road from the Dallas railroad junction over 8,970-foot Dallas Divide, **Milepost 12**, to Placerville, **Milepost 83** on *Colorado 145*, to Telluride, three miles east of **Milepost 71**, over 10,222-foot Lizard Head Pass, **Milepost 59**, to Dolores, **Milepost 9**, and on to Durango.

Purchasing 490 acres for the townsite from three ranchers, Mears relabeled the merely functional Dallas Junction, **Milepost 23**, to honor the superintendent of the new railroad's northern division, R. M. Ridgway. In evident appreciation, superintendent Ridgway saw to it that twenty-six miles of track were laid in a mere ten days.

Over Dallas Divide by Automobile

Shortly after the turn of the century, a young Telluride lawyer, L. C. Kinikin, accompanied his friend John H. Adams to Montrose to pick up the first automobile to be brought into the northern San Juans. "We helped unload the light, no-top machine from the [railroad] car, put in gas and water and oil and drove uptown [in Montrose] for demonstration. We picked up two newlyweds, who sat in back of the car, and starting out about the same time we beat the train to Ridgway! The newlyweds got out, and we started for Telluride in high spirits."

The climb up Dallas Divide, **Milepost 12**, amounted to ascending two thousand feet in eleven miles. Adams gave Kinikin a can of powder with which to extinguish an engine fire, should need arise. At some point below the summit, however, the radiator went dry. They had to back down to the nearest farmhouse, because the road was so narrow they could not turn around.

"We started back up, chugg, chugg, chugging along, till we got on top, when John ran over a boulder too big to negotiate safely and it damaged the oil tank," Kinikin recalled. "To repair that took some two or three hours, and the train passed us up there on top of the world, with [our] uncertain transportation."

Down to Placerville, **Milepost 83**, and up the San Miguel

River they were without mishap until they reached the lime kiln at Deep Sheep Creek, **Milepost 74**, where they became mired in a mudhole.

"I walked a half-mile and got a man, a mule and chain, and in pulling us out of the mudhole the front axle was loosened. It took two or three hours and several feet of bailing wire to fix that, and with several fires extinguished up Key Stone Hill [**Milepost 71**] we reached my home in Telluride at midnight."

Placerville

Placerville is a settlement of uncertain origins. Prospectors began working the gravels where Leopard Creek joins the San Miguel River (**Milepost 84**) shortly after the Utes ceded the 3.5-million-acre San Juan region to white settlement in the Brunot Treaty of 1873 (see *Colorado 149* itinerary). Placerville shares its name with a California mining camp that sprang up in the gold rush of 1849. Many Forty-Niners came to Colorado a decade later when gold was discovered in the Rockies. The California camp was also known as Hangtown, but Placerville, Colorado, seems not to have been quite so notorious. A 1909 flood devastated the location on the bank of Leopard Creek. Cautious residents rebuilt a half-mile up the San Miguel River at the present site, **Milepost 83**.

Otto Mears's Rio Grande Southern Railway began to serve Placerville with scheduled trains in the early fall of 1890. The RGS turned up the San Miguel River from this point and on Sunday, November 23, reached Telluride. In July 1891, the spur was extended another two miles to serve the celebrated Smuggler Union mine at Pandora.

The mainline, meanwhile, had turned south five miles west of Telluride at the mouth of the Lake Fork of the San Miguel, **Milepost 73**, at a place that became known as Vance Junction.

Telluride

In late spring, 1884, an arrival of a more sinister sort had taken place in Telluride, three miles east of **Milepost 71**. A personable seventeen-year-old named George Leroy Parker showed up on a handsome horse and spent the next month training the animal as though to enter him in a race. In time he was joined by three others who purported to have been placer miners from McElmo Creek country around Cortez.

At ten o'clock in the morning of June 24, Parker, soon to be better known as Butch Cassidy, and two of the others, Tom McCarty and Matt Warner, entered the San Miguel Valley Bank and found the bookkeeper alone. With guns drawn the trio of desperadoes took $10,500 and fled to a point outside of Telluride where a fourth man, Bert Maddern, was holding a relay of horses one of them the racehorse Cassidy had been training.

The robbers fled south and lost the posse pursuing them somewhere in the vicinity of Lost Canyon Creek, a few miles south of **Milepost 29**.

In a remarkable moment of guilelessness the Telluride marshal, Jim Clark, revealed to the sheriff of a neighboring county: "The fellers who held up the bank were friends of mine. They told me their plans and said that if I made a point of being out of town at the time of the robbery they would give me a fair share of the take. . . . They were true to their word and left me this roll of bills amount[ing] to about $2200."

Clark was apparently never called to account for this or for his moonlighting ventures as a highwayman beyond Telluride's city limits. He had gained some early experience as a member of the outlaw gang that grew out of the Civil War Confederate guerrilla force led by William Quantrell.

Telluride came into being in January 1878, as the town of Columbia. Its first citizen was John Fallon, who filed a placer claim in what was known as Marshall Basin in October 1875. The next year James Carpenter and Thomas Lowthian found a lode which became the famous Pandora Mine. Their ore was packed on burros over a forbidding range to Ouray, freighted by ox-drawn wagons to the Denver & Rio Grande railhead at Alamosa, and hauled by rail from there to the Grant smelter in Denver.

At some point in the 1880s the U.S. Postal Service found an abundance of Columbias confusing so they asked the residents of this mining camp to choose another name. In token of a gold-rich fragment of telluride ore which had turned up in the San Miguel River at this site the citizens came up with the name Telluride.

A misdemeanor endemic in the mining camps, particularly where mines were owned and operated by large absentee corporations, was "highgrading."

"Highgrading is the practice engaged in by some of the workmen of sorting out and appropriating to their own use and profit many of the richest pieces of ore they can get away with," says John B. Marshall, a long-time resident of the San Juans. "In short it is stealing ore."

Telluride judge L. C. Kinikin noted that highgrading was a common practice in the San Miguel mines "with no special deterrent." He claimed that local businessmen—saloon and gambling house owners, jewelers, and merchants—often connived in the practice. More rigid rules were introduced to the Smuggler Union mine, however: "Miners were searched when entering and leaving the mines, belts were outlawed, and stealing limited to such free gold as could be carried under falseteeth, in openings between the teeth, in the hair of the head, or concealed somewhere in the timber to be returned to on a stormy, foggy day."

The Smuggler Union's new manager in 1901, Bulkley Wells, also persuaded the Colorado legislature to require state merchants to record amounts of ore, names of sellers, and purported origin of the ore in transactions where the precious metals were accepted as exchange. The law, however, was declared unconstitutional by the judiciary.

The Gold King Generator

The power lines that cross the highway at **Milepost 65** are a monument to a remarkable achievement, a world first. It came about in June 1891 as a consequence of a Telluride lawyer's initiative and the fortune of having a brother who was an electrical engineer. L. L. Nunn had been elected president of the Gold King Mining Company, whose diggings lay two miles northeast of **Milepost 65** on a site directly beneath these lines.

When Nunn took over the Gold King he was faced with a serious problem. Timber had been virtually cleaned from the vicinity of Alta Lakes where the mine was located. Coal had to be packed in on animals at prohibitive rates. Yet they needed power to run winches and pumps on the site. The answer was, of course, electricity. But in these remote mountains there was not a source of electricity within many miles.

Nunn decided to create his own source. He summoned his brother, Paul, and between them they planned a project that had yet to be done anywhere. They would build a water-powered generator to produce high-voltage alternating current and transmit it over the several miles from the river to the mine.

The 1891 "War of the Currents" was a battle between Thomas A. Edison, who advocated the use of direct current to supply communities with electrical power, and George Westinghouse, who argued in favor of the potential of alternating current. L. L. Nunn and brother Paul chose to try the so-far-untested alternating current system, which would have one notable advantage for use at the Gold King Mine—it could be transmitted greater distances than direct current, which was limited to little more than a mile. From the mine to Ames, the most likely place for a water-powered generator (at that point the Lake Fork of the San Miguel River dropped five hundred feet in less than a mile), the distance was three miles.

A team of engineers from Cornell University, aided by laborers from the San Juan mining camps, gathered in the early spring of 1891 to build the power system. Calling themselves the Pin Heads and their aggregation the Telluride Institute, the team installed a three-thousand-volt Westinghouse generator, strung the wires from river to

mine and got it all working two months before the world's
next high-voltage AC generator, which was put into operation in Germany. An integral part of the Telluride system
was a polyphase motor invented by a brilliant Croatian
emigré, Nikola Tesla, then residing in New York, but who
later moved to Colorado Springs. (see also *I-25 Middle*
itinerary.)

Ophir

Harsh winter weather in the upper San Juans stymied
progress on the RGS mainline after the Telluride spur was
completed in late 1890. Resumed in the spring, construction
on Yellow Mountain, south of Ophir, was handicappped by
some of the most formidable natural obstacles on the entire
route. The Ophir Loop, **Milepost 63**, and Highline were
built on high, curved trestles, which doubled back on themselves at one point and joined high rock shelves that had
been blasted from the side of Yellow Mountain.

Ophir itself, two miles east of the loop, was the site of
several important mines, earning the settlement its Biblical
name, after the site of King Solomon's famous mines. Developed in 1878, Ophir was a decidedly isolated settlement
until the Rio Grande Southern finally arrived. Mail and
other supplies came over 11,743-foot Ophir Pass from
Silverton—as the crow flies, just twelve miles or so due east
of the mining camp. In the early days private individuals
contracted with the federal government to carry the mail
into these remote communities.

"Of the three terrors," groused the Dolores *News* on
December 13, 1879, "Indians, Indian agents, and western
mail contractors, the latter is wholly a terror, and some of
them in particular are 'dead rank frauds.' "

Winter was the perilous time for the carrier who "straps
the mail sack on his back, puts on his Norwegian showshoes,
and, with a long guiding pole, starts on his eary [sic] climb
over the range." Respect for his derring-do was such, said
the *Colorado Graphic*, that "usually there is a crowd at the
post office to wish him good luck."

Swan Nilson left Silverton just before Christmas in 1883 on his way to Ophir with the mail. He disappeared in a December 23 avalanche.

"On August 13, 1885," the report went, "at the bottom of a snow bank the picks and shovels of the searching party uncovered the body of Swan Nilson, and still strapped to his back was the old pouch with Ophir Christmas mail. The lock was rusty, and the pouch had to be cut open. . . . Some of the mail was moldy, but a part of it could be read quite easily."

The Galloping Goose

In the summer of 1931, the Galloping Goose was introduced as the mountain mail carrier. It was a gasoline-powered vehicle fitted with trucks that permitted it to operate on the narrow-gauge tracks of the old Rio Grande Southern roadbed. Looking like misplaced old touring cars with enclosed truck beds attached, the vehicles were put together in the railroad's Ridgway machine shop, largely of parts from old Pierce-Arrow cars. The Galloping Goose attained Mark VII in its series of original models before it gave up in 1951.

The Galloping Goose sits outside the Telluride courthouse, a monument to the foundering Rio Grande Southern Railway.

Lizard Head Peak

In mid-1891, Rio Grande Southern track crews reached Lizard Head Pass, **Milepost 59**, at 10,222 feet the watershed between the San Miguel and Dolores rivers. Three miles to the northwest of **Milepost 57** Lizard Head Peak rises to 13,113 feet in the peculiar configuration that earned it its name. Mears's railroad used an artist's rendition of the peak as the centerpiece of the company's logo.

Two more mammoth trestles, known as the upper and lower Gallaghers, were required to get the RGS across the West Fork of the Dolores and back again, near **Milepost 56**, before the line could reach Rico, **Milepost 46**, from the north.

This view of Lizard Head Peak on the divide between the Dolores and San Miguel watersheds inspired the logo of Otto Mears's Rio Grande Southern narrow-gauge railroad.

Rico

Prospectors had shown an interest in the upper Dolores River valley long before the region was opened up to settlement in the 1873 Ute cession of the San Juans. What caught the attention of these gold-seekers was the presence of black oxide of manganese, usually a sign that gold is in the vicinity. Sheldon Shafer and Joseph Fearheiler, two prospectors on their way from Santa Fe to the Montana gold fields, stopped in July 1869 to try their luck. Fearheiler's luck was somewhat poor as it turned out—he was killed by Indians a year later.

R. C. Darling, commissioned to survey the boundaries of the Ute reservation, paused in 1870 to take some private measurements and stake out an illegal claim. When he returned in 1872, however, he could find only low-grade ore.

The belated discovery of rich lead carbonate of silver in California Gulch in the upper Arkansas River valley (see *U.S. 24W* itinerary) awakened other Colorado mining camps to new possibilities. Such was the case in Rico, where similar ore, discovered in 1879, prompted a boom.

The miners organized the Pioneer Mining District on July 17, 1879, with its membership limited to those who held claims in the area. Among the ordinances enacted were: "Each and every member is expected to act decorously under all circumstances. . . . Political and religious discussions will be strictly prohibited. . . . No . . . profane or obnoxious language during . . . meetings. . . ."

The most important rule was Article Thirteen: "Any member found guilty of 'salting' a mine or mines, erasing dates to gain priority or any other more than ordinary misdemeanor shall be expelled from the society and shall not be accepted as a member thereafter."

The mandate for decorous behavior failed to inhibit some. Anthony Boaro and W. L. Hall, for example, discovered a rich gold vein in the Johnny Bull mine, a few miles northeast of Rico. The claim was jumped by some neighboring miners, and ownership was fought out in the courts, frustrating any work in the mine until 1890.

The most remarkable story in Rico must be that of David and Laura Swickheimer. In 1881, Swickheimer held a third interest in a claim on Enterprise Hill, a flat-topped promontory in the locality. With his partners he sank a hole about thirty-five feet deep. Encountering no ore, Swickheimer and company sold their claim to George Barlow, who was working an adjacent claim with no more luck than Swickheimer. After a stint as sheriff, Swickheimer hired on at the Swansea mine down the mountain a short distance.

The Swansea was a successful operation, and from what Swickheimer observed in the mine, his hopes rose that his old claim, the Enterprise, might share the vein of silver ore being tapped in the Swansea. He used most of his savings to buy out Barlow's partner, and then he sold what he owned to finance the sinking of a shaft deeper into Enterprise Hill. Nothing showed.

His resources exhausted, Swickheimer was on the verge of defeat when suddenly his wife was declared a winner in the Louisiana state lottery. The money went into digging deeper into the Enterprise. Finally, on October 6, 1887, the final stick of dynamite was tamped into place to blast out rock to a depth of 262 feet, as far as Swickheimer could afford to take the diggings. Miraculously, the blast exposed the first evidence of a rich blanket vein of gold and silver ores.

When he eventually sold the Enterprise, Swickheimer was a millionaire. By 1890 he was a man of sufficient substance to be named president of the Rico State Bank. Unfortunately, as seems so often to have been the case in the history of Colorado mining, what goes up must eventually come down. The Rico State Bank failed in the Panic of 1907, and poor Swickheimer went with it.

Getting the equipment necessary to process the difficult lead carbonate ore was an early problem for Rico miners. In the late 1870s, when silver mining first showed its potential in the region, the nearest railhead was Alamosa, more than two hundred miles away.

In the summer of 1879, nonetheless, Jim McJunkins packed the machinery necessary for a saw mill from Alamosa to Animas City, the town that gave way to the later railroad town of Durango. He carted his equipment a few miles up the Animas River, then cut westward up the mountainous watershed that separates the Animas from the Dolores River, and went north along the Highline trail to the vicinity of Rico. Rico's eager citizens mustered at that point to build a fifteen-mile road—to be known as the McJunkins Road—to bring the saw mill the rest of the way into town.

A year later, on the Fourth of July, the Grandview Mining & Smelting Company received by much the same route a wagon train hauling the wherewithal to erect Rico's first smelter. The smelter shipment took sixty-six days. The freighter charged Grandview fifteen cents a pound—$300 per ton, using today's more inflated proportions. One can only speculate how many tons it takes to build a smelter.

Buried Treasure on the Highline Trail

In the expectant chill of a September morning in 1910, a youth was loading a string of burros with blocks of salt at a Rio Grande Southern siding on the La Plata River across from the Mayday mine. He earned his pay packing the salt into the mountains for use by livestock. On this occasion, he was approached by a tall stranger, whom he chose to call Long John, apparently a mine employee. Long John asked him to transport twelve seventy-pound bags across the mountains to Rico.

Long John accompanied the youth and the string of jacks—as the miners called the burros—on a three-day trek along the Highline trail, down Indian Ridge to timberline a few miles east of the old Monteloros switch of the RGS, **Milepost 44.** As they traveled, Long John admitted that the bags contained highgrade.

"It is the richest ore out of the richest mine in the La Platas," he confessed. "Me and my pardner have been a long time in getting it together, and now we don't want to lose it."

Long John's partner was waiting for them on the trail. He took Long John aside, and, after the two had spoken in confidence, they took the pack animals into the timber. A couple hours later they returned without the dozen bags. The young man was paid off and the three parted.

Several years later the youth encountered Long John in a Boulder sanatarium where the older man was dying of miner's lung disease. Recognizing his young collaborator, Long John said that his partner had warned him that morning in the mountains that the two were under suspicion, so they took their bags of highgrade and buried them a short distance into the forest, planning to return the next summer to retrieve them. Unfortunately, his partner was killed that winter in a mining accident in Arizona. When Long John returned a year later, he could not find the cache.

From [the place where we buried it] we could see the bluffs on a hillside across the Dolores river. South of the cache about 50 yards was a tall dead tree with a peculiarly twisted branch at the top. To the westward was a little spring. . . .

Kid, . . . that fortune is still there. Right where me and my partner buried it. We never told another soul about it, and it is worth going after, and it is yours if you can find it. My pardner is already gone and I soon will be, so it won't ever do us any good. It might pay you big to hunt for it, and I wish you the best of luck.

But if it ever was there, it is there still.

The Rio Grand Southern Railway

The construction crews of the Rio Grande Southern Railway's northern division, under the memorable R. M. Ridgway, and southern division, under Thomas Wigglesworth, met near **Milepost 28** on December 19, 1891, eighteen months from the time they had started. The southern division had worked its way from Durango via Mancos and Dolores. The last spike was seated in a snowstorm. The company sent out fifty dressed turkeys and four barrels of beer so that the construction crewmen could celebrate the occasion. The first train reached Ridgway from Durango on January 2, 1892, using for the most part narrow-gauge rolling stock discarded in 1890 by the Denver & Rio Grande and its Utah counterpart, the Rio Grande Western, when they refitted their mainline with standard gauge equipment (see I-70W itinerary).

Otto Mears was so pleased with his handiwork that he hired the famous Hayden Survey photographer, William Henry Jackson (see I-70W and *U.S. 160* itineraries), to record the achievement. A special train was outfitted in January 1893 to cruise the entire line, stopping as inspiration might strike the celebrated Jackson.

Then the roof fell in.

The Panic of 1893 had made itself felt to the point that President Cleveland, a Democrat, summoned Congress on June 30 to go into special session in order to repeal the Sherman Silver Purchase Act, a bit of legislation that had gratified the West, for it in effect had subsidized the production of silver.

By September 1 nearly half of Colorado's mines were shut down. Of a Colorado population of 450,000, 45,000 were unemployed. Hundreds of businesses failed.

The recently completed Rio Grande Southern went into receivership. The Pathfinder of the San Juan, Otto Mears, lost control of his creation, never to regain it (see *U.S. 50-550* itinerary). The line survived, however, and in 1895 the Denver & Rio Grande stepped in to take the RGS out of the hands of the courts.

The Rio Grande Southern skirted the margins of bankruptcy by various devices, including the invention of the Galloping Goose during the depression. But in 1952, sixty years after the RGS marked the passage of its first train, the last train completed the route of the Silver San Juan Scenic Line, picking up the rails as it passed. They had all been sold for scrap.

La Plata Mountains

Twenty miles east of Dolores, **Milepost 9,** the thirteen-thousand-foot peaks of the La Plata Mountains have tempted the prospector since before the American Revolution.

Pausing for a night near today's town of Dolores, Spanish Friar Silvestre Vélez de Escalante must have watched the rising sun etch their profile on the morning of August 13, 1776, and he may have recalled this note from a journal entry a few days before:

> [In] La Sierra de la Plata . . . there are said to be veins and outcroppings of metallic ore. However, although years ago certain individuals from New Mexico came to inspect them by order of the governor, who at the time was Don Tomas Velez Cachupin, and carried back metal-bearing rocks, it was not ascertained for sure what kind of metal they consisted of. The opinion which some formed previously, from the accounts of various Indians and from some citizens of the kingdom, that they were silver ore, furnished the sierra with this name [La Plata, meaning silver].

They were right. But just as *La Plata* means silver, *Dolores* means woe.

3. The High Plateaus

Colorado's last frontier lay in the high plateau country. A full generation passed —from 1858 to 1881—before much of the western third of the state was opened up to white settlement. Yet more than a century later, the high plateau country continues to be Colorado's new frontier. In a way, of course, the high plateau was also Colorado's first frontier, for the first serious exploration of the territory that is now Colorado was carried out by an expedition of Spanish friars who traveled from Santa Fe, New Mexico, in the same year America declared her independence from Britain—1776. They explored the plateaus in search of a route that would link the New Mexican with the California missions. The route they blazed became a part of the Spanish Trail that was used from about 1830 until the 1846-48 war with Mexico.

Being Colorado's first, last, and latest frontier makes the high plateau region something of a paradox. Indeed, it harbors Paradox Valley (see *Colorado 145-U.S. 666* itinerary), which is an honest geological paradox.

With a notable exception, the coveted gold fields of the Rockies were found mainly east of the Continental Divide. The Western Slope, as it is called, was for a considerable period simply conceded to the Indians. The indigenous Utes had ceded the 7,500-foot-high San Luis valley by treaty as early as 1868, retreating to the Pacific watershed of the

Rockies. After several years of confusion on the part of both whites and Indians, the easterly boundary of the Confederated Ute Reservation was determined to lie some miles west of the Continental Divide, along the 107th parallel. The hiatus resulted from topographers' problems in locating the prescribed line of longitude.

The effective northern boundary of the Ute reservation was for the Indians probably along the White River valley. The manifestly artificial boundary insisted on by white mapmakers, however, lay along what came to be the county line separating Rio Blanco from Moffat county at 40° 14' of latitude. The reserve, by federal reckoning, comprised well over fifteen million acres.

The boundary had little meaning for the aborigines, however, for they lived by the time-honored principle that one trod where one dared. They accepted the White River as a practical limit mainly because the territory north of the river was a sort of no-man's land where the Mountain Utes vied with the Sioux and Arapahoe of the plains for access to the huge herds of buffalo that lumbered through the grassy region.

By the mid-1870s, however, the Plains Indian tribes were either pacified (see I-76 itinerary) or, with the 1876 massacre of General Custer's command, retreating into Canada. The land north of the Ute reservation was being rapidly occupied by white ranchers whose cattle fancied the grasses it offered as much as the buffalo had.

The pivotal event on the Western Slope occurred on September 29, 1879, when the Utes rose up against the white employees of the Indian Agency at White River, killing the agent, Nathan C. Meeker, and eight other men and ambushing an approaching military column under Maj. Thomas T. Thornburgh, which caused thirty-six military casualties, including Thornburgh.

The outcry from white settlers resulted in the removal of the Utes from Colorado, except for a fifteen-mile strip reserved for Southern Ute tribes along the southwestern border with New Mexico.

Despite the outcry, two years passed before the Utes actually had to move. The reason? Their principal chief, Ouray, apparently had enormous influence with the U.S. government. Ouray spoke a modicum of English and probably better Spanish and was, as a consequence, employed by the federal government as an interpreter as early as 1856, according to one account. His annual retainer was a substantial five hundred dollars, doubled, as it turned out, when Washington sought to win Ouray's favor in obtaining the San Juan cession in 1873 (see *Colorado 149* itinerary). In addition, Ouray was instrumental in halting hostilities that resulted from the massacre at the White River Agency. Thus, the Utes were not moved from Colorado until after Ouray had died on August 24, 1880.

Alarms over misinformed reports of Indian raids persisted periodically through the 1880s, but in the meantime settlers flooded in to start ranches and orchards, build railroads, and search for energy resources that could fuel the United States' twentieth century industrial economy.

This was the last frontier, offering oil, uranium, and the stupendous but still costly oil shale deposits of the White and Colorado river valleys.

The president of the Colorado School of Mines in Golden, Victor C. Alderson, declared in 1919 that the state's oil shale resources comprised "the most valuable deposits of their kind in the world."

He has yet to be proved wrong.

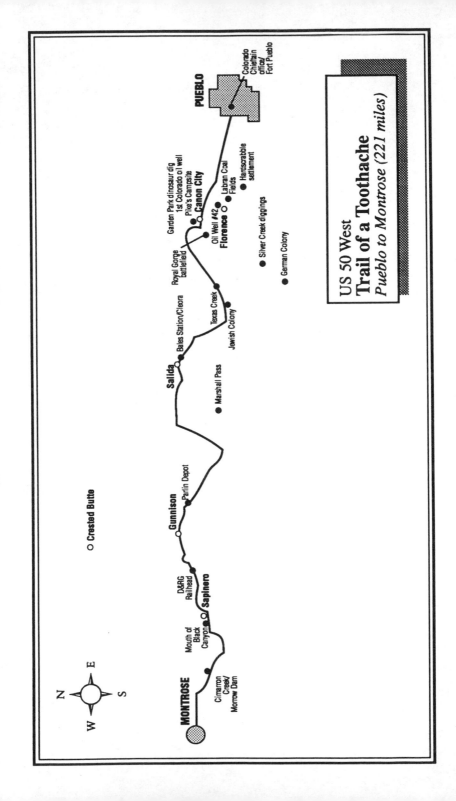

US 50 West
Trail of a Toothache
Pueblo to Montrose (221 miles)

PUEBLO

Colorado
Chieftain
office/
Fort Pueblo

Garden Park dinosaur dig
1st Colorado oil well
Pike's Campsite
Canon City
Hardscrabble
settlement
Labran Coal
Fields
Oil Well #42
Florence
Silver Creek diggings
Royal Gorge
battlefield
German Colony
Bales Station/Cleora
Texas Creek
Salida
Jewish Colony
Marshall Pass
Parlin Depot
Gunnison
D&RG
Railhead
Sapinero
Mouth of
Black
Canyon
MONTROSE
Cimarron
Creek/
Morrow Dam

○ Crested Butte

N
W   E
S

US 50 West
Trail of a Toothache
Pueblo to Montrose (221 miles)

Pueblo

The history of Pueblo, **Milepost 314**, is as colorful and even a bit longer than that of other cities along the Colorado Front Range. A hallmark of its past is a newspaper begun in 1868 as the *Colorado Chieftain*. Its co-founder was thirty-five-year-old Dr. Michael Beshoar, the Pennsylvania-born chief surgeon of the Confederate army during the Civil War. Beshoar also established the first drug store in Pueblo. Shortly after helping to set up the newspaper, he moved south to Trinidad (see I-25S itinerary), where he is memorialized in the suburban community of Beshoar Junction.

Beshoar's partner, Sam McBride, was the Arkansas valley Jeremiah. In a notable jeremiad, McBride railed against federal assistance to a colony of German immigrants who were making their way across the country from Chicago to settle in the Wet Mountain valley, south of **Milepost 252**. Irishman McBride's animosity was stimulated mainly by the person of Prussian-born Carl Wursten, the colony's organizer, but it was compounded by partisan politics. McBride and his paper favored the Democratic party while Wursten and his colonists appeared to have been generously treated by the Republican administration of Ulysses S. Grant and a Republican-controlled Congress, in the hope that they would bolster Republican party rolls in Colorado.

The colonists were given a military escort across the high plains, plus tents for each family and forty-two wagons. "The present administration appreciated our endeavors," professed Wursten, "and humanely and kindly assisted us. . . ."

In a speech in March 1870, as his colony began to put down roots, Wursten protested his welcome to the territory:

"I am no Carl I, as *The Chieftain* falsely asserts. We believe
that the majority should rule, and we will not tolerate one-
man power. I am not ashamed, however, to proclaim myself
a downright Republican, heart, body and soul. I will fight for
the banner to the last drop of my heart's blood. We are going
to vote the Republican ticket solid, and are bound to beat
our opponents. I apprehend that it was a knowledge of this
fact that caused *The Chieftain* to get so shaky."

On April 21, 1870, McBride wrote in *The Chieftain*: "Do
you not remember, dear Carl, that in less than a week after
the colony had arrived on the ground, and when a majority
of the society had become so disgusted with you as a leader
that they met and agreed to vote you out, that you, in the
presence of several gentlemen who are our informants,
exclaimed in very good English that you 'wished the
damned colony was in Hell'?"

The same day the two antagonists encountered each other
in the Pueblo post office, and in the altercation that ensued
McBride shot Wursten in the arm.

Pueblo's earliest enduring structure was an adobe fort
built in 1842 on an uncertain site now north of Union Station
along the Union Avenue Historic District. Erected by a
group of traders previously associated with the Bent
brothers at their famous Old Fort (see *U.S. 50E* itinerary),
the fort served as a center for trading with the Indians, for it
sat astride the Trappers' Trail that ran from Taos to Fort
Laramie on the North Platte River. The fort's founders, a
motley crowd of Americans, were men in the main married
to Taos women. A notable item of trade at the fort was a fiery
distillate known as Taos Lightning. Confected by a transplanted Missourian named Simeon Turley, Taos Lightning
was warehoused at Fort Pueblo for handier dispensation to
customers in the middle and northern Rocky Mountain
regions. Fort Pueblo waxed and waned and waxed again as a
community, but it prevailed as a structure for many years
beyond its habitation.

When Kit Carson led a party from Taos to the Platte River
valley in the summer of 1848, after hostilities had ceased in

the Mexican War, one of his companions noted "absolutely nothing living—only the empty Fort Pueblo and the deserted log houses of the Mormons." The so-called Mormon Battalion had established its post in this vicinity during the Mexican War, before moving on to [California].

Hardscrabble Creek

The charter inhabitants of Fort Pueblo had also moved on to start another community upriver, five miles south of **Milepost 289**, on Hardscrabble Creek. Curiously, one of their primary objectives was the cultivation of corn, a remarkably quiet occupation for men who had lived so precariously by their wits. But as Janet Lecompte notes in her *Pueblo-Hardscrabble-Greenhorn*, corn had become a prized commodity on the plains, for "it was not whiskey but corn that induced Indians to part with their [buffalo] robes" and corn was in markedly short supply in the mid-1840s.

One of the Hardscrabble settlers, George Simpson, the vagabond son of a St. Louis physician, noted: "A small number of trappers and traders had in the spring of 1844, combined for the purpose of farming on Hardscrabble, in a small way and a very small way it was—one American plow, procured from the 'States' by the writer the year before, with a half dozen hoes among nine of us, but it was a rather hard scrabbling to get in a crop—hence the name of the settlement."

Among others who joined the little colony of Americans, living illegally now in Mexican territory, were Lancaster P. Lupton, the founder of Fort Lupton on the South Platte River; the unprepossessing V. J. "Rube" Herring, who had survived a fatal duel (see I-25N itinerary); and John Poisal, whose wife was Snake Woman, the sister of the famous Arapahoe chief Left Hand (see *U.S. 36* itinerary). Virtually all of them packed up and left their little farming community to participate in the 1849 California gold rush.

Coal was the commodity to be coveted in the early 1870s. The Denver & Rio Grande Railroad nearly bypassed the growing town of Pueblo in its desire to exploit coal fields found near the now-defunct town of Labran, three and one-half miles south of **Milepost 285**. The persuasive William J. Palmer nonetheless managed to cajol the citizens of Pueblo to vote $50,000 in municipal bonds to underwrite the right-of-way from the D&RG's mainline up the Arkansas River valley.

Palmer's narrow-gauge had reached Pueblo from Colorado Springs on June 19, 1872. Four months later the thirty-six-mile spur to the Labran coal fields was built by a private contractor, who operated it under the name Canon Coal Railway Company until 1874, when finally the D&RG was able to pay off the contract.

Florence

The region abounded not only in coal, but in what was to become the fuel of the twentieth century—oil. Near Florence, two miles south of **Milepost 284**, is Well No. 42, thought to be the oldest continuously active oil well in the world. Drilled in 1889, the well had produced over a million barrels of oil by the early 1960s. It is only one of hundreds of perforations tapping into what is called the "Florence Pool."

Taking advantage of both native coal and an intersection with the D&RG Railroad, David H. Moffat, one of Colorado's pioneer railroad tycoons, built a narrow-gauge line from Florence north to Cripple Creek in 1894 to exploit the belated bonanza gold strike that occurred in that region (see *U.S. 24* itinerary).

Canon City

Oil Creek, five miles north of Canon City, **Milepost 280**, offered the first evidence that liquid fuel could be obtained in this area. Seepage from an oil spring prompted pioneer A. M. Cassiday, in 1862, to drill what would become the first oil well west of the Mississippi River.

Fifteen years later, in the same locality, scientists made a more esoteric discovery. The remains of some of the most dramatic of extinct dinosaurs were found for the first time. These included the fearsome carnivore, Tyrannosaurus, the enormous vegetarian, Brontosaurus, and the spine-plated Stegosaurus. The Garden Park Monument, commemorating the find, can be found six and one-half miles north of **Milepost 280.**

Capt. Zebulon Montgomery Pike perceived none of these remarkable features when, having given up his effort to scale the peak that now bears his name, he and his twenty-three-man brigade came up the Arkansas valley to camp near today's Canon City.

They came into this region in early December 1806. In his journal Pike noted: "It cleared off in the night and in the morning the thermometer stood at 2 below zero, being three times as cold as any morning we had yet experienced." The next day, he found "the weather moderating to 25 degrees but the men have no winter clothing; I wore cotton overalls but I had not calculated on being out in this inclement season of the year."

Pike and his men went due north from Canon City into South Park, where they became so confused regarding their location and course of march that, a month later, to their utter surprise, they found themselves back at this site, having marched in a wide circle (see *U.S. 285S* itinerary).

"I now felt at considerable loss how to proceed," he admitted. "I determined to build a small place for defense and deposit, and leave part of the baggage, horses, my interpreter and one man."

Pike's interpreter was Antoine Vasquez, a St. Louis fur trader who admired his leader to such an extent that he named his son Pike. The son, in his time, would dispatch the famous black frontiersman, Jim Beckwourth, to the 1859 gold camp at present-day Denver to set up one of its first mercantile stores (see *U.S. 285N* itinerary).

Pike, meanwhile, took thirteen of his company and headed south into the Wet Mountain valley intent upon crossing the intimidating Sangre de Cristo range (*see U.S. 285S* itinerary for the sequel to Pike's explorations).

Royal Gorge

One of the wonders of the West, Royal Gorge canyon, begins a mile upstream from **Milepost 277**. An anomaly of nature, the narrow, 1,053-foot-deep canyon was to provide the setting in 1878 for a bizarre circumstance in Colorado's railroad history. The Royal Gorge War pitted the indigenous narrow-gauge Denver & Rio Grande against the out-of-state, wealthier, standard-gauge Atchison, Topeka & Santa Fe in a violent but casualty-free struggle to see which would get right-of-way through the constricted bottom of Royal Gorge. There was room for only one set of tracks, whether standard or narrow.

It was an important prize, for beyond lay the upper Arkansas valley and the important silver mines of Leadville, where the Harrison Reduction Works alone offered a potential ore volume of twenty-four thousand tons per year. In the absence of rail service, the company was paying wagoneers eighteen dollars per ton to carry ore to Canon City and Colorado Springs.

The battle began between the two railroads in April 1878, when the D&RG was still smarting from having lost the right-of-way through Raton Pass (see I-25S itinerary) to the wily Kansans. A construction crew of the Santa Fe took up positions at the lower end of the canyon, in preparation to begin grading the roadbed. A crew of D&RG stalwarts, led by assistant chief engineer James R. DeRemer, slipped around to their rear, dispersed the Santa Fe crew, and threw their tools into the roiling waters of the Arkansas River. DeRemer and his men retreated to the upper end of the defile where DeRemer lettered "Dead-Line" on a cross tie and placed it across the would-be-right-of-way.

"The Santa Fe men," recalled a veteran D&RG engineer, William Walk, "never quite got up the nerve to cross it."

The situation became a stand-off. Both railroad gangs took up arms and settled themselves behind barricades, each waiting for the other to attempt something.

The stalemate was ratified by the courts: neither railroad was permitted to build in Royal Gorge pending a determination of which line held legal priority. A possible compromise granting both lines the right to build trackage in parallel was precluded by the canyon's narrow dimension.

Ever near the edge of financial disaster, D&RG president William Jackson Palmer found that delay had pushed his company once again to the brink. On October 9, 1878, he was forced to lease the D&RG's 337 miles of track to the more affluent Santa Fe at a fee of 43 percent of gross receipts. After much foot-dragging, Palmer finally got around to turning the D&RG over to the Santa Fe on Friday, December 13, a day that proved to be inauspicious for the leaseholders.

Finally, on April 21, 1879, the U.S. Supreme Court handed down its ruling: the D&RG had prior right to build through the Royal Gorge. Unfortunately for Palmer, however, he and his colleagues were no longer running the railroad, at least until the Santa Fe's lease expired. Palmer went back to court, this time seeking to have the lease declared null and void, on the grounds that the Santa Fe had breached one of several highly restrictive clauses in the lease.

Once again tension mounted and partisans took up arms. D&RG operatives sent telegrams from one D&RG outpost to another to prepare their supporters for the armed seizure of the Santa Fe's leased facilities. Santa Fe men retaliated by cutting telegraph lines, disrupting communications throughout the state.

At last, on June 10, 1879, Judge Thomas M. Bowen of Colorado's Fourth Judicial Court in Alamosa declared that the Santa Fe must turn operation of the D&RG back to its owners.

Palmer ordered roadbed construction to begin in the Royal Gorge. With a resourcefulness born of the need to pinch pennies, Palmers engineers devised a uniquely cantilevered bridge that hung for 175 feet, suspended from girders fixed to the sheer walls of the canyon where the swift waters of the river had to be crossed. Surprisingly, its cost was a mere $12,000.

Texas Creek

Texas Creek, **Milepost 252**, was christened by a Texas drover who suffered mishap while driving a herd of long-horns to Colorado mining camps. A marauding bear caused the herd to stampede during the night. The several days required to round up the cattle reinforced the Texans' memory of this site. The town came into being at the mouth of the creek around 1880.

The German Colony

Thirty miles south of **Milepost 252** on *Colorado 69* the short-lived German colony was planted by Gen. Carl Wursten. Wursten's autocratic mien, the colonists' lack of farming experience, and, finally, an early frost in 1870 undermined the organization. If spokesmen for the abstemious but successful Union Colony at Greeley (see I-25N itinerary) can be believed, there was yet another factor: "We understand that they established a Brewery early, which, of itself, is enough to ruin any colony."

Wursten resigned in September 1870 and moved to Canon City. His successor, Emil Nielson, gave it up two months later and moved with his family and twenty-five followers, to Pueblo.

Silver Cliff

A brooding, black cliff eight miles to the north of the abandoned colony proved in 1877 to be laden with silver, launching another mining boom that produced the town of Silver Cliff.

Cotopaxi

The assassination of the relatively liberal Czar Alexander II in 1881 and the accession of Alexander III led to pogroms against Russian and Polish Jews and a panicked immigration to—among other places—the United States. At the time an

American of Portuguese-Jewish ancestry, Emanuel H. Saltiel, was the operator of a silver mine near **Milepost 245**. He had organized the Cotopaxi Town Company with himself as president.

The news from Europe prompted him to go to New York to contact the Hebrew Emigrant Aid Society of the United States with a proposal for the creation of an agricultural colony of Russian-Jewish emigrants in the "fertile Wet Mountain Valley" of Colorado. The HEAS took him at his word, granted him a reported $10,000 for the project, and, on May 3, 1882, dispatched the first group of thirteen colonists to Saltiel's care in Colorado.

Sixty-three colonists had arrived by the end of summer. The HEAS had already sent an overseer and a lawyer from New York and, more important for the pious colonists, a Torah. Within six weeks of the first arrivals a synagogue had been set up.

Idel "Ed" Grimes was seventeen when he arrived at the barren site promoted by Saltiel, whose 1,780 acres proved to contain only a few hundred that were arable. "It was the poorest place in the world for farming, poor land, lots of rocks and no water, and the few crops we were able to raise were mostly eaten by cattle belonging to neighboring settlers." The colony had two plows and in the end only one successful crop—fifteen bushels of poor quality potatoes.

Some colonists took jobs in Saltiel's mines, working for $1.50 a day, until eventually Saltiel refused to pay them. Hampered by an uncertain grasp of English, they nonetheless found work digging trenches and cutting wood for the Denver & Rio Grande Railroad, which was building in Salida (**Milepost 221**) and Maysville (**Milepost 211**), a mining camp at the headwaters of the south Arkansas River below Monarch Pass (**Milepost 199**) on the Continental Divide.

Appeals to the Jewish community in Denver brought aid and an investigation. Denverites L. Witkowsky and George H. Kohn reported to the Hebrew Emigration Aid Society in New York, "We are at a loss to account for the sum of $8,750 said to have been expended up to October 23, 1882. We can assure you that the New York Society, and therefore the refugees, had paid more than twice as much for what they received as an honest administration of the fund would warrant. . . . We recommend . . . the immediate removal of the colony to some other place."

The HEAS accepted the recommendation and furnished one hundred dollars and cost of transportation to each family. The colonists left for Salt Lake City, California, South Dakota, and Denver. One man and his son even returned to Russia.

Cleora

In the fall of 1878, a confident Santa Fe management had pressed its advantage in the Royal Gorge War to the point of leasing the entire Denver & Rio Grande system. Anticipating court authorization to build through the Arkansas canyon and on to the mines of Leadville, they laid out a townsite on the route at **Milepost 223**. In tribute to a friendly local tavern keeper, Williams Bales, they named the place Cleora for his daughter.

By spring, 1880, however, it was apparent that the D&RG would win the battle of the courts. A D&RG official, the bumptious ex-governor of Colorado Territory, Alexander Cameron Hunt, had a townsite surveyed just above the mouth of the south Arkansas River, a mile or so removed from Cleora. Brushing aside protests of Cleora merchants, Hunt declared: "God Almighty makes a townsite, not men!"

Sensing that Hunt had a powerful ally, the Cleora business community decamped for the town that Hunt had christened Salida—"exit" in Spanish. The D&RG reached the mouth of the south Arkansas on May 1, 1880. Their first station was set up in a boxcar twenty days later.

Touting the presence of good water, central location, railroad facilities, and good climate—if not divine inspiration—Salida's city fathers failed, nevertheless, in their August 1881 bid to have Salida declared the state capital.

Marshall Pass

In the winter of 1873 a young Army topographer, Lt. William L. Marshall, suffered a misery so intense that it obliterated the slightest consideration that his moment in history was at hand. A member of the survey team of George M. Wheeler, Marshall was caught with his colleagues in the rude mining town of Silverton (see *U.S. 50-550* itinerary) as winter was settling in on the high country. And Marshall had a toothache.

His mouth was so swollen that his sole sustenance was gruel that could be sipped through immobilized jaws. The nearest professional help was several hundred miles away in Denver. The best known route to Denver was over Cochetopa Pass, whose reliability in winter was questionable (see *U.S. 285S* itinerary).

In his anguish, Marshall strained to recall the profile of the Continental Divide to the north of Cochetopa Pass, for a more direct line to Denver lay in that direction. He remembered the existence of an unrecorded depression, half-consciously perceived in his topographer's eye. Dave Mears, a packer with the survey team, volunteered to accompany him in attempting this desperate trip to the dentist's chair. Even at this early date, the annals of the Rockies abounded in tales of men who had perished in attempting a winter crossing of the Continental Divide.

The only established wagon road in the region was the toll road engineered by Otto Mears from Saguache over Cochetopa Pass to the Ute Indian agency on Los Pinos Creek. A more likely route for someone in Silverton, however, would have been due east to the headwaters of the Rio Grande and downstream through Wagon Wheel Gap to the newly established town of Del Norte (see *U.S. 160* itinerary). But the San Luis valley, which sheltered both Saguache and Del Norte, remained a long way and several high passes removed from Denver. Marshall and Mears seem to have chosen a more direct but riskier route that brought them to Tomichi Creek at **Milepost 189** where it is joined by today's Marshall Creek. At the head of Marshall Creek they discovered the pass that coincided with Marshall's half-remembered depression in the mountainous skyline. So elated was the suffering topographer that he remained a full day to take barometric and temperature readings and to make sketches of the terrain. Six days later, he kept the appointment with his Denver dentist.

When the existence of Marshall's new 10,846-foot crossing was made known, the soon-to-be famous roadbuilder from Saguache, Russian-born Otto Mears, built a road across it. The new road joined the other roads that Mears had built, connecting the Arkansas River valley with the Gunnison River valley by way of Saguache, in the San Luis valley, reducing the distance between the two points by many miles. In ten years Marshall Pass would become part of the Denver & Rio Grande Railroad's narrow-gauge mainline between Denver and Ogden, Utah.

Parlin

In their race to Gunnison, the Denver, South Park & Pacific Railroad and the Denver & Rio Grande met on either side of the Tomichi Creek at **Milepost 169.** The town of Parlin, which graces the site today, was in the early 1880s a portion of the dairy farm of James Parlin. Asked to sell one thousand acres to the DSP&P when it had descended Quartz Creek from Pitkin and the Alpine Tunnel (see *U.S. 285S* itinerary), Parlin gave the railroad a right-of-way through his land in exchange for a depot and the promise of a regular five-minute stop so that passengers could buy a glass of his milk.

Crested Butte

The valiant D&RG, having won its battle with the Santa Fe over rights to the Royal Gorge, started the branch that was to become the company's mainline, from Salida to Gunnison, in August 1880. The seventy-five-mile line was completed a year later. From Gunnison City Palmer's crews began immediately to build north to Crested Butte to exploit some more coal mines twenty-nine miles away on a headwater of the Gunnison River. Coal prospectors had turned up one of the few anthracite deposits in Colorado near Crested Butte. Colorado coal fields, though ample, are in the main compromised of bituminous, subituminous, and lignite, with this exception.

The Crested Butte spur was completed on November 24, 1881. On-site coal production for that year amounted to more than three thousand tons, compared with nearly 126,000 tons produced in 1881 by the well-established mines down the line at Canon City.

The boomtown architecture created in the 1880-1910 period in which Crested Butte was a mining town has won designation as a national historical district.

Gunnison

Gunnison City was named for U.S. Army Capt. John Williams Gunnison, a topographer commissioned in 1853 by Congress to participate in the search for a central railroad route to the Pacific. Gunnison's survey team crossed the Continental Divide at Cochetopa Pass on September 1, 1853. On September 6 they camped in the vicinity of **Milepost 157** and the site of the town that was to be named for him. On the morning of October 26, hundreds of miles west on the banks of Utah's Sevier River, Gunnison and a detachment of seven of his expedition died in a hail of Paiute arrows as they emerged from their tents.

On the eve of his death Gunnison exulted, "The great mountains have been passed and a new wagon road opened across the continent—a work which was almost unanimously pronounced impossible, by the men who know the mountains and this route over them. . . . [However,] for a railroad route, it is far inferior to the Middle Central, by Medicine Bow river, and Laramie plains"—the route eventually taken by the Union Pacific (see I-76 itinerary)

The town of Gunnison was not without violence in its mining heyday. An immigrant laborer employed on the

Alpine Tunnel of the Denver, South Park & Pacific Railroad
was jailed in late October 1881 following a fatal altercation
with one of the tunnel's construction contractors. Despite
the jailer's precautions, gunmen seized the accused in the
middle of the night and lynched him on the town's main
street.

In 1886 the now celebrated cannibal, Alfred Packer (see
Colorado 149 and *U.S. 285S* itineraries), following a re-
prieve of his original conviction, was retried in Gunnison
and sentenced to forty years in prison.

In their race to Gunnison the Denver & Rio Grande
Railroad beat the Denver, South Park & Pacific by about a
year. The South Park brought in its first train in September
1882 and, as the Rio Grande had done earlier, quickly put
its crews to work laying track to nearby mines. Averaging two
miles a day, they ran rails up Ohio Creek, one mile north of
Milepost 157, to diggings on the far side of Crested Butte's
twelve-thousand-foot Mount Axtell.

Sapinero

Sapinero, **Milepost 133**, commemorates a Ute sub-chief
whose band lived along the Gunnison River. It was Sapinero
whom Chief Ouray commissioned to carry his message to
the Northern Utes in October 1879 terminating hostilities
with the U.S. Army in the wake of the Meeker Massacre (see
Colorado 13 itinerary).

The Black Canyon Right-of-Way

Despite its numerous earlier engineering exploits, the
Denver & Rio Grande faced probably its biggest challenge
at **Milepost 130** in the spring of 1882. General Palmer and
his colleagues decided to build through the precipitous
Black Canyon of the Gunnison, which begins just north of
this point.

Palmer marshalled 1,045 men and 175 teams of horses to
tackle the canyon, whose murky chasm had been a source of

legend for both red men and white. The Utes long had believed that anyone who attempted to negotiate the fifty-mile length of the defile—a half-mile deep in many places—would never emerge alive. An American geologist was once lowered by rope one thousand feet down the sheer face of black schist from which nature has fashioned the canyon. When he was hauled back up he declared that "no man could go further and live."

Nonetheless, the D&RG grading battalion plunged ahead. Blasters were, like the geologist, lowered by scaffold to drill and place their dynamite charges in order to carve out a ledge for the narrow-gauge roadbed. In scarcely four months they had laid fifteen miles of track through the canyon. At Cimarron Creek, **Milepost 112,** they brought the right-of-way out of the canyon onto the plateau of the Western Slope. On August 13, 1882, the first D&RG passenger train came through the canyon to cross near this point. The last mile of trackage to this point was the most expensive, costing as much as the entire right-of-way through the Royal Gorge chasm.

One of the D&RG's early-day engineers, William Walk, reported that taking a train through the Black Canyon, marvel of engineering though it was, had its hazards. The principal risk involved falling or fallen rock. Walk and his comrades were obliged to carry dynamite with them with which to blast rocks from the path of their trains.

Eighty-nine years later another marvel of engineering was completed at approximately the same place in the canyon—the Morrow Point Dam. Finished in the spring of 1971 after eight years of construction, the dam was the first major double-curvature, thin arch concrete dam to be built in the United States. The dam, 469 feet high, features a free-fall spillway that dumps water 350 feet to a stilling basin. The reservoir behind the dam has depths of 450 feet at some points.

The National Park Service presents excellent exhibits of both the railroad and the dam along the Cimarron access road, **Milepost 112.**

Black Canyon of the Gunnison National Monument

The Black Canyon of the Gunnison National Monument was created in 1933. Under administration of the National Park Service, it embraces the most dramatic stretch, thirteen of the phenomenon's fifty-three miles. The south rim can be reached by following *Colorado 347* north from **Milepost 101.**

The foreboding Black Canyon of the Gunnison inspired a Ute legend that those who entered the 2,000-foot defile would never reappear. *Colorado Tourism Board.*

Montrose

Montrose, at **Milepost 93**, came into being the year that the D&RG emerged from the depths of the Black Canyon, in 1882. It was another station on the railroad's route to Salt Lake City. Town founder Joe Selig, even more of a romantic than A. C. Hunt, named the town for the duchess of Montrose, a character created by the Scottish novelist Sir Walter Scott.

US 40
Beyond the Troublesome
Empire to Utah (258 miles)

Empire

Gold prospects around the little town of Empire, **Milepost 256**, were as promising as its name was ostentatious from 1860 to 1866. Later on, silver was discovered up Clear Creek Canyon at Georgetown, but in the meantime, the mining camp had a particular allure for professional men and others of substance, attracted as much as anything, perhaps by the name.

Most of the diggings lay north of Empire on what was called Silver Mountain, where the Atlantic Mining & Milling Company was working the Conqueror Lode, the region's richest quartz vein. On the average, however, the gold diggings produced only low-grade ore, in which a single ton gave up only one-quarter to one-half ounce of gold.

As the population shifted to the more promising silver diggings down at Georgetown, federal Indian agents found it convenient to issue annuities to the high-country Utes at Empire. As many as fifteen hundred Utes would descend from Berthoud Pass each summer in the years 1865-67 to receive allotments of cattle, flour, and blankets. Camped across the West Fork of Clear Creek, the Utes would pass their nights with festivities that featured the dancing of warriors as women beat the drums.

In July 1869, the residents of Empire were treated to a different spectacle. Fire struck the forested slopes of Silver Mountain, and before it was contained many of the buildings at the Conqueror mine were destroyed. Even the mine's shoring timbers as far as fifteen feet into the shaft were charred. At least one mine supervisor died in the catastrophe, suffering a heart attack while battling the blaze. "For many nights afterward the smouldering fires in the tree

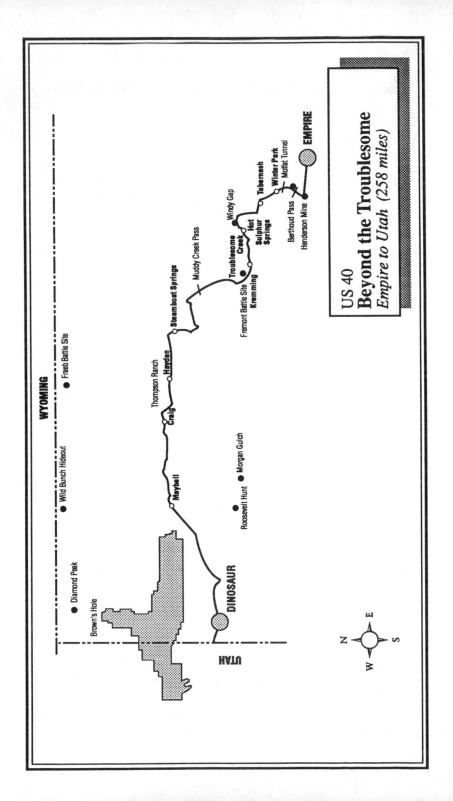

US 40
Beyond the Troublesome
Empire to Utah (258 miles)

tops looked like the lights of a distant city," wrote Emma Shephard Hill in a reminiscence.

Henderson Molybdenum Mine

Today, the AMAX Corporation's Henderson mine at **Milepost 249** represents one of the nation's largest operations aimed at extracting an important modern metal, molybdenum. Like the boom-and-fade fortunes of precious metals mining a century ago, however, the mining of exotic metals remains vulnerable to the whims of the world economy.

Berthoud Pass

Berthoud Pass, **Milepost 243**, takes its name from the man who discovered it in the summer of 1861. Captain E. L. Berthoud surveyed this 11,314-foot gateway to Middle Park as he was laying out a wagon route for the Central Overland California & Pike's Peak Express Company. That same year, the new territorial governor, William Gilpin, drew on Berthoud's findings to produce the first Colorado railroad survey.

Even after the 1862 Pacific Railroad Act had stipulated that routes for the transcontinental railroad could not have grades greater than 116 feet to the mile (2 percent), Berthoud Pass had its promoters. They were undismayed that the survey showed that a three-and-one-half-mile tunnel through solid granite would be needed for a train to negotiate Berthoud Pass. The sanguine John Evans, Gilpin's successor as governor and a railroad builder in his own right, even foresaw the possibility of finding gold in such a tunnel.

The Moffat Tunnel

Nearly seventy years would pass, however, before a railroad tunnel such as Evans envisaged would pierce the Continental Divide to connect Denver with the Pacific Coast. That would be the famous Moffat Tunnel whose west portal lies at **Milepost 232**. The brainchild of mine operator, financier, and railroad man David H. Moffat (see *U.S. 50W* itinerary), the tunnel became the object of his ambition as early as 1902 when, at age 63, he organized the Denver, Northwestern & Pacific Railroad to provide rail service west of Denver to Salt Lake City to connect with the established routes to the Pacific Coast.

The design of the tunnel called for a bore extending 6.2 miles through the mountains of the Continental Divide at an altitude of about nine thousand feet. The problem with the design from Moffat's standpoint, lay in its cost. So with the financial resources available to him Moffat chose an interim route that would cross Rollins Pass to the north of the preferred site, a route that already had served wagon freighters for thirty years.

In 1914 the city of Denver saw a number of advantages in supporting the development of the Moffat Tunnel. A bond issue was approved that would cover two-thirds of the cost of the tunnel, giving Denver not only a place on the transcontinental railroad map, but also an aquaduct that would divert sorely needed Western Slope water to the municipality. Unfortunately, amid a flurry of civil suits challenging the enterprise, the Supreme Court voided the action on the grounds that the state constitution precluded the city's joint venture with a private corporation.

The Colorado General Assembly eventually stepped into the breach, enacting a bill in 1922 to fund the tunnel. On February 18, 1927, President Calvin Coolidge pushed a button in the White House detonating the charge seventeen hundred miles away to remove the final obstruction in the lengthy bore. Regrettably, the tunnel's progenitor, David H. Moffat, was already dead.

The Denver Water Board leased the pioneer bore of the Moffat Tunnel and refurbished it to bring 28,813 acre-feet of water from the Pacific watershed to the thirsty metropolis.

Tabernash

Unlike the railroad, the Rollins Pass wagon road joined the present highway, then the Berthoud Pass wagon road, much farther north, at **Milepost 223**, the site of Tabernash, a community that commemorates an incident foreshadowing the tragic Meeker Massacre of 1879 (see *Colorado 13* itinerary).

As the meadow grass along the Fraser River bottom ripened in the summer of 1879, a nearby rancher fenced off a sizable portion to provide winter feed for his stock. A small band of Utes arrived and turned their horses loose in the enclosure. When the rancher protested, the Utes rebuffed him with the warning, "One sleep. You go."

When the rancher appealed to the sheriff at Hot Sulphur Springs, **Milepost 202**, a posse arrived to force the Utes to leave. As the Utes, angry at their summary eviction, mounted to leave, a hot-tempered member of the posse, "Big Frank," shot and killed one of the band whose name was Tabernash. The Indians then demanded that the sheriff turn the culprit over to them for retribution, but he refused.

The next morning, after bypassing Hot Sulphur Springs on their way back to the reservation in the western part of the state, they waylaid a rancher on the Williams Fork of the Colorado River, due south of **Milepost 196**, as the unsuspecting cattleman emerged from his cabin to fetch firewood.

The murder prompted formation of another posse, which pursued the band back to their reservation. The guilty Indians could not be found, despite the apparent willingness of tribal leaders to cooperate with the posse. An Indian who guided the posse back to Middle Park observed, however, that the murder of the Williams Fork rancher was compatible with the principles of aboriginal justice—the life of one innocent for that of another.

Familiar with the old story, a Moffat Road engineer named the site for the murdered Ute when the railroad reached the place of the contested meadow.

Windy Gap

Excavations for another water diversionary project in the

summer of 1981 uncovered an eight-thousand-year-old secret that was as revolutionary in its implications as the archaeological findings on the Lindenmeier Ranch in the mid-1920s (see I-25N itinerary). The discovery at Windy Gap, **Milepost 209**, revealed evidence that someone had built structures at this point five millenia before the raising of Egypt's pyramids. The structures were made of fired mud and wattle and were used seasonally for perhaps 3,500 years.

"It tells us," said one state archaeologist, "that someone was smart enough to think: 'If I add something to clay, it will stick together better. If I heat it, it will stay together better.' And as importantly, 'I need to build it because I either am going to stay or I will be back again.' That's pretty sophisticated thinking."

Hot Sulphur Springs

Hot Sulphur Springs, at **Milepost 202** was a favorite Ute camping site and spa. It was also the inspiration for a Ute legend in which a wise old medicine man sought long ago to forestall the aboriginal proclivity for war with rival tribes. Extolling the benefits of peace, the old shaman was overruled by a hot-blooded young warrior who urged his comrades to seek honor in war. As a consequence, the perennial hostilities with tribes of Plains Indians, such as the Arapahoes, Cheyennes, and Sioux, persisted until the arrival of the white man. Meanwhile, the medicine man ruminated sadly into an Indian twilight zone, his perpetual campfire burning by the side of the river, heating it constantly to produce these hot springs.

Although seekers of gold were the first to settle in Colorado, the entrepreneurs of real estate and tourism seemed never to have been far behind. The town site of Hot Sulphur Springs was platted as early as May 1860 by some enterprising gentlemen from the Cherry Creek settlements who hoped to develop the springs into a spa, which they would have called Saratoga West, in emulation of Saratoga, New York. For reasons that are not difficult to divine, the project failed to materialize.

In 1863, the town was called Grand City by virtue of its place on the banks of what was then called the Grand River. In 1921, the Colorado legislature officially changed the river's name from Grand to Colorado.

Most of the town and, more importantly, its springs came into the possession of William N. Byers, pioneer land agent and publisher of the region's first newspaper, the *Rocky Mountain News* (see I-25N & M and *U.S. 285N* itineraries). The narrows stretching downriver for two miles from **Milepost 201** are called Byers Canyon.

Troublesome Creek

Troublesome Creek crosses *U.S. 40* to empty into the Colorado just south of **Milepost 189**. North, that is upstream on the Troublesome, at least two persons noteworthy in the history of Colorado had ranches at various times. One was the mysterious Frenchman Adolphe François Gérard, alias Louis Dupuy, who established the Hotel de Paris in Georgetown (see I-70W itinerary). The other was Maj. James Blair Thompson, at one time a special agent to the Utes, who manifested their respect for Thompson by dubbing him "One-Talk."

Thompson came to Denver from Peoria, Illinois, in 1869, when President. Ulysses S. Grant appointed his father-in-law, Gen. Edward M. McCook, territorial governor. Named McCook's private secretary, Thompson took on the day-to-day handling of the governor's ex officio responsibility as federal supervisor of Indian affairs. Thompson became a close friend of the famed Ute chief Ouray (see *U.S. 50-550* itinerary).

Thompson made what was a daring innovation in local Indian policy. He gave the Mountain Utes permission to descend to the prairies to hunt buffalo. The eastern plains had been perilous grounds for the Utes because of the domination of their historic enemies, the Plains Indian tribes. But in 1869, the last battle had been fought with the tribes of the Colorado high plains when the 5th U.S. Cavalry defeated the Cheyenne Dog Soldiers at Summit Springs (see I-76 itinerary). Even though the Plains Indians were gone, however, the white settlers who had endured their depredations still feared the sight of an Indian band. But there were no serious incidents. "This privilege was highly regarded by them and proved one of the most potential agencies in keeping them straight . . .," reported Thompson. "They were instructed by both Ouray and myself that they must never beg or steal from settlers, nor molest the white people in any way."

In the fall of 1874, Thompson was directed to visit the Utes in northwestern Colorado along the White River to investigate reports that a Ute band, under Captain Jack, had access to illegal whiskey and was causing trouble. Declining an escort of army troops, Thompson hired a buckboard and driver and rode the several hundred miles into the desolate rangeland. In dramatic manifestation of the moral authority he enjoyed with the Utes, Thompson was able to apprehend the bootlegger who was supplying whiskey and to quell hostilities.

Muddy Pass

On the return leg of his expedition to California in 1844, Capt. John Charles Fremont led his men over Muddy Pass, **Milepost 157**, from the headwaters of the North Platte River. They came down Muddy Creek, following the present route of *U.S. 40*. Near the mouth of Muddy Creek on the Colorado River, **Milepost 184**, they encountered a war party of Arapahoes, up from the eastern plains on a marauding mission against the Utes.

"All whom they met on the western side of the mountains," observed Fremont, "[the Arapahoes consider] to be their enemies." Fremont and his men were not given the option. "We had no time to build a fort, but found an open place among the willows which was defended by the river on one side and the overflowed bottoms on the other," Fremont wrote in his *Memoirs*. "We had scarcely made our few preparations when about two hundred of them appeared on the verge of the bottom, mounted, painted, and armed for War. We planted the American flag between us, and a short parley ended in a truce. . . ."

John Charles Fremont explored parts of the future state of Colorado on four different occasions in the 1840s, looking each time for a suitable railroad route across the Rockies. *Colorado Historical Society.*

Steamboat Springs

In the years prior to 1908 travelers approaching the town of Steamboat Springs, **Milepost 131**, were often duped into thinking that the modest torrents of the Yampa River had been opened to commercial navigation. They heard, floating across the prairie, the chugging sound like that of a Mississippi River steamboat.

Perhaps this very sound lured the town's first settler, appropriately enough a Missourian named James H. Crawford. Leaving Sedalia and traveling the Smoky Hill Road (see I-70 itinerary) by way of Deer Trail, Crawford and his wife and two children arrived in Denver on June 4, 1872. Crawford was attracted to the Yampa River country as a consequence of an article he had read in the *Rocky Mountain News*. After spending a couple of winters, first at Empire and then at Hot Sulphur Springs, Crawford had managed to scout the vicinity of Steamboat Springs and was resolved to settle there.

During the winter of 1874-75 he grew fearful that someone might preempt the land he had staked out. Before the snows had melted in the spring, he raced off on skis from Hot Sulphur Springs to build a one-room log cabin and, as evidence of "proving up" his claim, plant a small garden. Then he returned to fetch his family. They officially took up their modest abode in July 1875.

In 1908, David H. Moffat brought his ambitious railroad, the Denver, Northwestern & Pacific, to Steamboat Springs. And with it, sadly, the steamboat sounds of the springs vanished, silenced in the grading of the right-of-way required by the train.

Battle Creek

The earliest white visitors to the Rocky Mountains were the legendary fur traders and trappers who earned the name "mountain men." Among the earliest in this section of the Rockies was a flinty German immigrant named Henry Fraeb, who trapped the headwaters of the North Platte and Yampa rivers. He first appeared in the region in 1829 at the head of a company of free trappers. The following year he became a partner in the Rocky Mountain Fur Company, whose principals included Thomas "Broken Hand" Fitzpatrick and Jim Bridger.

In 1837, Fraeb joined another St. Louis trader, Peter A. Sarpy, in establishing a trading post, Fort Jackson, on the South Platte River (see I-25N itinerary). When that enterprise foundered a couple of years later, he rejoined Jim Bridger and, in 1841, helped to erect Fort Bridger, a waystation on the newly developed Oregon and California immigrant trails, located in today's southwestern Wyoming on the Black Fork of the Green River.

In order to provision the new fort, Fraeb led a hunting party of white trappers and Shoshone Indians on a buffalo hunt along the Little Snake River, a tributary of the Yampa that runs parallel to the Wyoming border before dropping to join the Yampa near the eastern boundary of Dinosaur National Monument.

Thirty-five miles north of **Milepost 108**, at the mouth of Battle Creek on the Little Snake River not far from the current Wyoming border, Fraeb and his twenty-two-man party were attacked by five hundred Sioux, Cheyenne, and Arapahoe warriors. "The Arapahoes didn't do much fighting," recalled Jim Baker, one of Fraeb's men, "but they urged the others on."

As the hostile Plains Indians charged repeatedly, Fraeb instructed his men to fire sparingly so that some would always be available with a load in their weapons. Dead horses and tree stumps provided breastworks for the defenders. The attackers charged perhaps forty times, racing up to within ten or fifteen paces of the defenders. Baker estimated that a hundred warriors were killed. Only three defenders died, but one of them was Henry Fraeb.

"He was the ugliest looking dead man I ever saw . . . ," said Baker. "His face was all covered with blood, and he had rotten front teeth and a horrible grin. When he was killed, he never fell, but sat braced against the stump, a sight to behold."

Battle Creek takes its name from the incident. When the Plains Indians finally ceased their attacks, the defenders retreated to a mountain south of the site where the Indian wives of the mountain men had taken refuge. In consequence, the heights now bear the name Squaw Mountain.

Routt County

The year after James Crawford settled in at Steamboat Springs Colorado became a state, in 1876. Along with earning designation as the "Centennial State," Coloradans gained the right to elect their governor.

John Long Routt, the last territorial governor to be appointed, was the first state governor to be elected. The 2,330-square-mile county of which Steamboat Springs is the seat is named for him.

Maj. James B. Thompson, erstwhile special agent to the Utes and bosom friend of Chief Ouray, set himself up as a rancher in this vicinity. Three years later, alerted by Ute friends that trouble was brewing over the hard-nosed policies of Indian agent Nathan C. Meeker (see *Colorado 13*), Thompson abandoned his ranch and left the region.

"The country north of the Colorado Reservation [today's Moffat and Routt Counties] is very desirable for farming and grazing purposes, and is thickly settled," noted an 1879 commentary on the Meeker massacre. "For three or four years past the Indians have been in the habit of intruding into this district as well as into North and Middle parks, which practice has caused considerable annoyance to settlers, particularly on [Little] Snake, Bear [Yampa] and Grand [Colorado] Rivers."

Morgan Gulch

Morgan Gulch, named for a family of ranchers who came into the area in the 1870s, lies six miles south of **Milepost 72**. In a 1954 reminiscence, cowboy J. L. Tagert recounted a somewhat unseemly sidelight to another Ute war scare in 1887. European royalty was fascinated with the American West in the nineteenth century (see I-70 and *U.S. 36* itineraries). One ghoulish and unnamed nobleman, visiting Frank Morgan's ranch, let it be known that he would prize the acquisition of a Ute scalp.

"It was after dark and our horses were in the corral," said Tagert, "so one of our boys, Tom Skerritt came over to where I was at the camp fire and said, 'Kid, let's get that fellow an Indian scalp.'

" 'How can we do it, Tom?'

" 'Come with me.'

"Skerritt cut a section of the tail from a corralled black colt. '[We] set up all night by the camp fire to tan the scalp. Next morning, the Count purchased the scalp. My cut," noted Tagert, "was $15.00."

Powder Wash Creek—Outlaw Waystation

A waystation on the notorious Outlaw Trail that, in the 1890s, ran from Hole-in-the-Wall, Wyoming, to Mexico lay about thirty miles north of Maybell, **Milepost 60**, on another minor tributary of the Little Snake River called Powder Wash Creek. There the celebrated Butch Cassidy set up headquarters for his own gang, the Wild Bunch, and an assortment of other robbers and rustlers over which he presided in 1897. Joining him there in late summer were seventy-five members of the Hole-in-the-Wall gang, led by "Flat Nose" George Curry, who had been flushed from their Wyoming hideout by law officers.

Cassidy, a mild-mannered ne'er-do-well, was born George Leroy Parker to a prominent Mormon family of Circle Valley, Utah. He took his "professional" alias from his early mentor, Mike Cassidy, a ranchhand who moonlighted as a rustler. The bogus Cassidy was thirty years old in 1897 when he served as outlaw chief of the Wild Bunch. It would be another twelve years before he died in a hail of police bullets in the jungles of Bolivia.

When the United States declared war on Spain in April 1898, members and alumni of Butch Cassidy's outlaw brigades secretly arranged to meet in Steamboat Springs to consider organizing themselves into a volunteer fighting unit, along the lines of Teddy Roosevelt's Rough Riders. They would call themselves—what else?—"The Wild

Bunch." The fever of patriotism was cooled, however, when some of the veterans of the Outlaw Trail envisaged the legal pitfalls that might be encountered on their way to the battlefront.

Brown's Park

Fifty miles from Maybell on *Colorado 318* one enters Brown's Hole, now more decorously known as Brown's Park, another outlaw refuge patronized by Cassidy and his friends. A pleasantly sheltered Shangri-la watered by the Green River before it plunges down the rapids of Lodore Canyon to a rendezvous with the Yampa, Brown's Hole takes its name from an early-day French-Canadian voyageur of the Hudson Bay Company, Baptiste Brown, who left the Oregon Territory in 1827 to settle with his Indian wife in this valley of the Green River.

In the next decade so many trappers came to spend their winters as Brown's neighbors that two Americans, Philip Thompson and William Craig, thought it would be profitable to establish a trading post in the valley to purvey sundries to residents and transients. They called it Fort Davey Crockett. The trading post, a cottonwood stockade embracing a single small cabin, fell into disuse and decay after 1840 when its owners moved on to more promising locations. Trapper and army scout Jim Baker, having survived the Fraeb battle with the Indians, found the living easy in the valley and settled there permanently.

Teddy Roosevelt's Lion Hunt

To celebrate his election as vice-president of the United States, Theodore Roosevelt in 1901 headed for a five-week mountain lion hunt in Colorado. On arrival he picked up two friends from Colorado Springs, Dr. Gerald C. Webb and Phillip B. Stewart.

Roosevelt would pen a lengthy article on the hunt for *Scribner's* magazine, entitled "With the Cougar Hounds."

It appeared a month after its author had succeeded to the presidency following McKinley's death on September 14, 1901, from an assassin's bullet.

Although a New York City native, the forty-three-year-old Roosevelt was an avid hunter. He had written two books about hunting in places spread from North Dakota to Texas to Washington state. By the time of his Colorado trip he counted himself an unqualified expert in the sport.

In the *Scribner's* article Roosevelt was unstinting in his praise of his Colorado guide, John B. Goff, and Goff's hounds. "In cougar hunting the success of the hunter depends absolutely upon his hounds. . . ," noted Roosevelt, "and upon the man who trains and hunts the hounds. Goff was one of the best hunters with whom I have ever been out, and he had trained his pack to the point of perfection for its special work which I have never known another such pack to reach. . ."

The dogs were necessary, he explained, because "no animal, not even the wolf, is so rarely seen or so difficult to get without dogs" as the mountain lion. While "very much afraid of man" the lion, he declared, "habitually follows the trail of the hunter or solitary traveller, dogging his footsteps, itself always unseen."

The vice president and his companions hunted for two weeks at the Keystone ranch in Moffatt County's Coyote Basin about fifteen miles due south of **Milepost 58**. Later Roosevelt moved on to the Mathes brothers' ranch in Scenery Gulch on the southeastern slopes of Colorow Mountain.

In a 1934 reminiscence, J.R. Mathes recalled that his bucktoothed guest "was an all around good fellow, jolly and agreeable. Talked a good deal about when he used to be in the cattle business in Montana [actually in North Dakota]. He enjoyed going out in the corral with the kids and roping the calves; laying down on the bed in the bunkhouse telling stories with the rest of us men; or sitting down to the table to eat with his coat off—and he could eat."

Roosevelt clearly enjoyed himself. "The keen, cold air, the wonderful scenery, and the interest and excitement of

the sport," he exulted, "made our veins thrill and beat with
buoyant life."

He kept a meticulous record of the game they killed,
carefully noting sex, color ("blue" or "red" for the mountain
lions), length, weight, and the date bagged. His party took
fourteen mountain lions and ten bobcats.

Upon his return to Washington for his inauguration as
vice president on March 4, 1901, Roosevelt turned his game
trophies over to an official of the U.S. Department of Agriculture's Biological Survey department.

The bantam sportsman-politician also boosted the then
innovative craft of wildlife photography. His magazine article included a dramatic closeup of a bobcat glaring down
from a tree.

The Great Diamond Hoax

The Great Diamond Hoax of 1872 had its focus in the
extreme northwest corner of Colorado, about forty-eight
miles north of **Milepost 11**. Some of the canniest investors in
the country were duped, including such notables as Gen.
Grenville Dodge, a major official of the Union Pacific Railroad, and Gen. George McClellan, a key Union army commander in the Civil War.

The confidence game began when two prospectors, Philip
Arnold and John Slack, pretended to take a San Francisco
bank clerk into their confidence. They showed him some
diamonds they claimed to have found and swore him to
secrecy. Flouting his pledge, as evidently Arnold and Slack
knew he would, the clerk showed the gems to officers of his
bank. They promptly formed the New York & San Francisco
Mining & Commercial Company and brought the seemingly
reluctant Arnold and Slack into the enterprise. Tiffany's of
New York assessed their rough diamonds as gems of value.

At this point a bona fide curtain of secrecy fell over the
operation. Elaborate ruses were used to suggest that the
diamond mine was hundreds of miles from its presumed
location. As it happened, however, Clarence King was con-

ducting a federally commissioned topographical survey on a one-hundred-mile band north of the fortieth parallel (see *U.S. 36* itinerary). From clues dropped by the diamond mine promoters he deduced that the site was within the bounds of his survey.

Reviewing survey data, King and some colleagues located the probable site. Reaching the scene, they found footprints in the vicinity of some anthills on the mountainside. They sifted the soft dirt of the anthills and uncovered rubies, a gem well-known to accompany diamond deposits.

One of King's associates, Samuel Franklin Emmons, noted later, "But when we found one with no footsteps near, no holes but at the top, no ruby rewarded our search, and our explanation was that some one must have pushed in a ruby or two on the end of a stick. We dug in the gulch again, and found the rubies decreased as we left the rock, until at a certain distance, sift the sand as we would we got none at all."

Using King's official letter demonstrating that the alleged diamond quarry had been salted, the army chief of engineers later reported the hoax to Congress.

Curiously, in the early 1980s at least two companies continued to prospect for diamond deposits along the Colorado-Wyoming border, 165 miles east of Diamond Peak, and once again the activity was shrouded in secrecy. Diamonds, of course, are not as rarely found as some might think, but to have commercial potential a deposit must yield at least ten carats of diamonds for each hundred tons of ore.

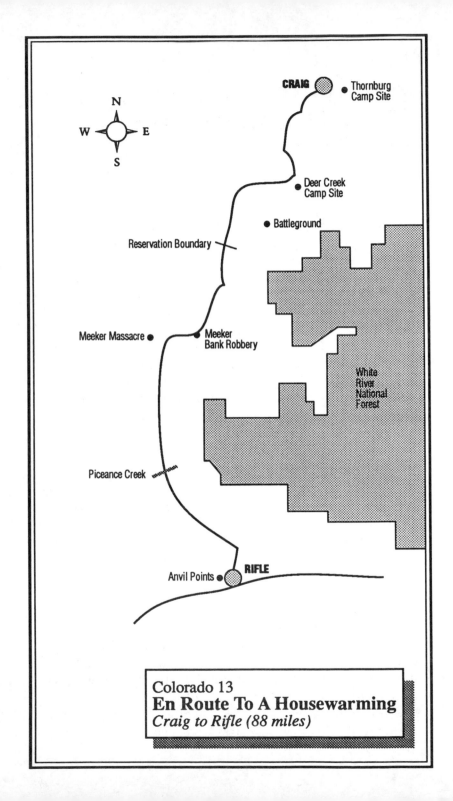

CRAIG ● Thornburg Camp Site

● Deer Creek Camp Site

● Battleground

Reservation Boundary

Meeker Massacre ● ● Meeker Bank Robbery

White River National Forest

Piceance Creek

Anvil Points ● RIFLE

Colorado 13
En Route To A Housewarming
Craig to Rifle (88 miles)

Colorado 13
En Route
To A Housewarming
Craig to Rifle (88 miles)

Craig

The community of Craig, **Milepost 88** on *Colorado 13*, is the creation and namesake of a Protestant minister of the 1880s, the Reverend Bayard Craig. Originally the trade center for ranch families dotting the area, Craig became the terminus of the Denver, Northwestern & Pacific Railroad when David H. Moffat built the line in the first decade of the twentieth century (see *U.S. 40* itinerary).

In 1925, important oil discoveries were made in the vicinity, which helped make Colorado a significant oil-exporting state. With the added production from Craig, the state attained for the first time an annual production of one million barrels. Today Colorado wells produce about thirty million barrels in an average year.

Elkhead Creek

Elkhead Creek empties into the Yampa River about six miles upstream from **Milepost 86**. Opposite the mouth of the creek a military detachment camped one night late in September 1879 on a fateful mission from Fort Fred Steele, near Rawlins in Wyoming Territory. Maj. Thomas T. Thornburgh, commandant of Fort Fred Steele, was on his way to the reservation of the White River Utes, whose agency was thirty-five miles to the south.

The Indian agent who had summoned Thornburgh was sixty-two-year-old Nathan C. Meeker, the unbending founder of abstemious Union Colony No. 1, whose town was named for Meeker's benefactor and former boss, Horace Greeley (see *I-25N* itinerary). Eighteen months earlier, Meeker, at odds now with the Union colonists, had persuaded Colorado Senator Henry M. Teller to back his appointment as agent to the northern Ute tribes.

Duly named to the post on March 3, 1878, at an annual salary of only $1,500, Meeker moved promptly to the remote agency, bringing his sixty-year-old wife, Arvilla, and nineteen-year-old daughter, Josephine. Once there he was not long in informing Teller, "When I get around to it in a year or so, if I stay as long, I shall propose to cut every Indian down to a bare starvation point if he will not work."

The Utes, unfortunately, seemed disinclined toward the work ethic and were also inveterate gamblers, priding themselves especially on their swift horses. Meeker sought to plow up a horse pasture favored by Chief Douglas, and the two came to blows on September 10, 1879. Frightened, Meeker quickly sent for help to Fort Steele, 150 miles away.

On September 26, Thornburgh's contingent of nearly two hundred soldiers and civilians took notice of five Utes who rode into their camp at the mouth of Elkhead Creek. Chief Jack and a subchief named Colorow protested Thornburgh's plans to enter the Ute reservation. Jack said there was no reason to enter, for all was peaceful at the Agency.

Thornburgh Mountain

Two days later, Thornburgh and his men camped just outside the reservation on Deer Creek, a few miles south of **Milepost 75**. Colorow reappeared, alone this time, to warn the major not to cross the reservation boundary line at Milk Creek. But early the next morning, Monday, September 29, Thornburgh's force came down Milk Creek and about a mile into the reservation entered narrow Red Canyon, whose two-hundred-foot bluffs brooded over the slowly moving column of troops.

From the heights of the canyon nearly three hundred warriors opened fire on the soldiers. A body of Utes charged at one point, breaking through the extended flanks of the column to separate one contingent from the rest. Thornburgh led twenty men in a futile charge to close the breach. He and nine men were killed in the sally. By day's

Charles Adams, German immigrant, militia general, and Indian agent, is shown here with Ute Chief Ouray and his wife, Chipeta. *Colorado Historical Society.*

end thirteen soldiers had been killed, twenty-three wounded, and 250 horses and mules destroyed. Scout Joe Rankin slipped away under cover of darkness and rode for twenty-eight hours to seek help at Rawlins.

The battle site lies at the southern foot of what is now called Thornburgh Mountain, about twelve miles south and east of **Milepost 67** where Milk Creek crosses *Colorado 13*.

Even as the troops were ambushed, things remained quiet at the Agency. Ignorant of the armed clash scarcely twenty miles away, Meeker sent a messenger to meet Thornburgh. Escorted by two supposedly friendly Utes, Wilmer Eskridge, the agency sawyer, was summarily murdered by his companions just two miles from the agency. At that moment the mayhem began. All nine white men employed at the agency were killed, and three women, including Meeker's wife and daughter, and two small children were abducted by the Utes.

Encircled for four days, the Thornburgh survivors had reason to doubt that aid was coming. But that night, under cover of darkness, a forty-three-man detachment of the 9th Negro Cavalry joined the beleaguered unit. The black troopers, under Capt. Francis S. Dodge, had been on patrol in Middle Park (see *U.S. 40* itinerary) in the weeks following the murder of a white rancher by Utes who had retaliated for the killing of one of their number, Tabernash (see *U.S. 40* itinerary).

Finally, after a week-long siege, an 850-man relief force under Col. Wesley Merritt arrived to rout the Indians. In the meantime, Chief Ouray had sent a plea from his village in southwestern Colorado to halt the hostilities (see *U.S. 50-550* itinerary). Chief Jack sued Colonel Merritt for peace on October 11.

Not until October 23 did special envoy Gen. Charles Adams (see I-25M and *Colorado 149* itineraries) succeed in negotiating the release of the white women and children who had been taken by the Utes.

The White River National Forest

The White River, **Milepost 43**, drains from the Flat Tops Wilderness, much of which is embraced in the White River National Forest, whose boundary lies about thirteen miles east of this point. The White River Forest was the first nationally authorized timber reserve in the state, and only the second in the nation (the first was Yellowstone Forest Reserve, since divided into the Teton and Shoshone national forests). A one-million-acre area was formally set aside by President Benjamin Harrison on October 16, 1891. The White River National Forest now comprises two million acres.

Meeker

A gang of teenagers inspired by the legend of Butch Cassidy and the Wild Bunch (see *U.S. 40* itinerary) arrived in Meeker on October 13, 1896, bent on emulating their heroes. Dubbed the Junior Wild Bunch, the four youths were all residents of Brown's Park, a sometime hideout of the actual Wild Bunch. They had come to rob the Bank of Meeker. The bank was a modest establishment, to say the least, for it was attached to the general store.

Three of the aspiring desperadoes entered the bank, guns drawn. An ill-advised shot of intimidation alerted townsmen who quickly surmised what was happening. As the boys emerged from the bank with their loot, local citizens were stationed to cover the bank's exits. The three bandits were gunned down. The fourth, who had been minding a string of fresh horses at the outskirts of the village, fled to report the fatal incident to the victims' relatives in Brown's Park, an otherwise idyllic valley of the Green River in the extreme northwestern corner of Colorado.

The citizens of Meeker kept the boys' corpses on display for several days. For a long time after that photographs of the decedents were kept prominently posted in the town to discourage similar adventures.

White River Indian Agency

A historical monument commemorating the Meeker massacre overlooks the site of the old White River Agency (now private property), two miles west of **Milepost 39** on Colorado 64.

Ranching and Rustling on the High Plateau

The 1870s and 1880s marked the high point of the Colorado cattle industry, with the high plateau of the White River country hosting much of it. Ranchland bordered the northern extremity of the Ute reservation, which coincided with today's boundary between Moffat and Rio Blanco counties, **Milepost 58**. Rising with the growth of stock raising was another industry—rustling. Rustling was, of course, one of the early indulgences of such dedicated organizations as Cassidy's Wild Bunch. There were also some full-time ranchers who were not reluctant to undertake some occasional rustling.

Confined to their reservation, extensive as it was —stretching 140 miles south from **Milepost 58** and 115 miles east from the Utah border—the Utes depended in large measure upon government annuities. These allotments of goods were granted by treaty in exchange for Indian land concessions. The annuities included many of the necessities of life, among them livestock, following the decimation of the buffalo. In 1879, the year of the massacre of Nathan Meeker and his colleagues, the Utes were robbed of an estimated twelve hundred head of cattle.

Ute annuity livestock was branded "I.D." for Indian Department. A favorite "running iron" brand employed by rustlers, as a consequence, was the Double Box, two squares that could be neatly superimposed on the I.D. brand. The rustling of Ute cattle was not the least of the causes that underlay the Meeker massacre, in the view of some historians.

The murder of the White River Indian agent precipitated a revision of the Ute treaties of 1868 and 1873. Congressional legislation in 1880 obliged most of the Utes to cede all of their land in west-central Colorado. Two years after the Meeker incident, in September 1881, the Utes were removed from Colorado to a reservation in Utah.

When the White River reservation land was opened up, ranchers quickly moved in. With the spread of the cattle industry into vacated Ute lands, its shadow industry, rustling, naturally followed. Among the ranching families that moved to former reservation land along the Piceance Creek, **Milepost 19**, a tributary of the White River, was the Reigan family. By some means the Reigans seemed to possess information about rustlers and their activities in the area, and unfortunately they were so indiscreet as to talk about it. In the spring of 1885 a dynamite bomb exploded in a cabin occupied by three Reigan men. Only one escaped with his life.

When not afflicted with human violence, the rancher often faced natural disaster. The fabled winter of 1888-89, for example, resulted in livestock losses of 60 to 75 percent, according to one estimate. "You could pretty near walk on dead cattle from . . . White River City clear up [Piceance] Creek . . . ," noted one old cowboy.

Piceance Creek—Oil Shale

The cattle country of Colorado's high plateau region proved to have a hidden resource. "Moses performed a miracle in the eyes of the children of Israel, when he tapped the rocks of Kadesh for water," noted an observer in 1919. "But our scientists, to the automotive world, have achieved a far greater wonder, for they have discovered where we can draw an almost boundless measure of oil from stone."

Federal scientists and long-range economic forecasters in the 1950s began to reckon with the potential of a rock that early explorers had called marlstone. Permeated with kerogen, a petroleum-like substance, the rocks proved to be flammable.

The United States had been largely self-sufficient in liquid petroleum up to that point, but the reservoirs of easily tapped crude oil were rapidly diminishing, just as America's post-World War II society was becoming increasingly mobile—especially "automobile." The long-term answer to the country's mounting appetite for crude oil could be found in the enormous reserves of marlstone—or, in today's terms, oil shale—found in deposits in a triangle formed by

Utah, Colorado, and Wyoming—and in marked concentration along Piceance Creek.

An early estimate put the extent of oil shale land in three Colorado counties—Garfield, Mesa, and Rio Blanco—at 2,592 square miles, consisting of deposits on the average five hundred feet thick. Twenty-two thousand acres were identified in the Piceance Creek valley alone. Geologists calculated that each ton of oil shale heated in retorts could produce from twenty-five to thirty gallons of liquid kerogen. One trillion barrels of oil were estimated to be contained in one sector of fifteen hundred square miles. Extrapolating from such figures, the oil shale reserves of the United States constitute, therefore, more than the entire world's known reserves of liquid crude.

Readily accessible and extremely cheap oil from the Arabian peninsula distracted the U.S. oil industry from the difficult and costly task of processing oil shale and obscured the need for national self-sufficiency in oil until the 1973 Arab oil embargo caused the price of oil to multiply tenfold.

Anvil Points

A federal research center, Anvil Points, nine miles west of Rifle, **Milepost 1**, was activated in 1964 to study methods for the extraction of kerogen from shale. Needed was a process that would make shale oil competitive with liquid crude. Research and development costs were high, and environmental concerns, such as acquisition of large quantities of water in a naturally arid region, continued to keep commercially produced shale oil just beyond the market price of oil. Industries sought federally guaranteed loans. By the early 1980s, as American demands for petroleum subsided, world crude oil supplies rose and prices fell, making oil shale processing even less feasible.

Rifle

Regardless of the shortcomings of today's oil shale technology, there was a time of unquestionable innocence in the past when rock was rock, and marlstone was not an unattractive example of it. One mercifully nameless Rifle pioneer built an imposing log cabin, appointing it with a splendidly constructed fireplace of native stone. Inviting his friends and neighbors, he lit a fire for the occasion and had what one newspaper reckoned to be the most spectacular housewarming the state has ever seen.

The town of Rifle, at the beginning of *Colorado 13*, came into existence like most of the other communities west of the Gore Range—after the removal of the Utes in September 1881. Its name is supposed to have been derived from an earlier incident when soldiers were laying out mileposts for a road between the Colorado and White rivers following the 1879 Meeker massacre. One of the soldiers, as the legend goes, forgot his rifle by the banks of the creek that empties at this point into the Colorado River. When he returned to find it, the stream was dubbed Rifle Creek. The town that eventually followed adopted the name.

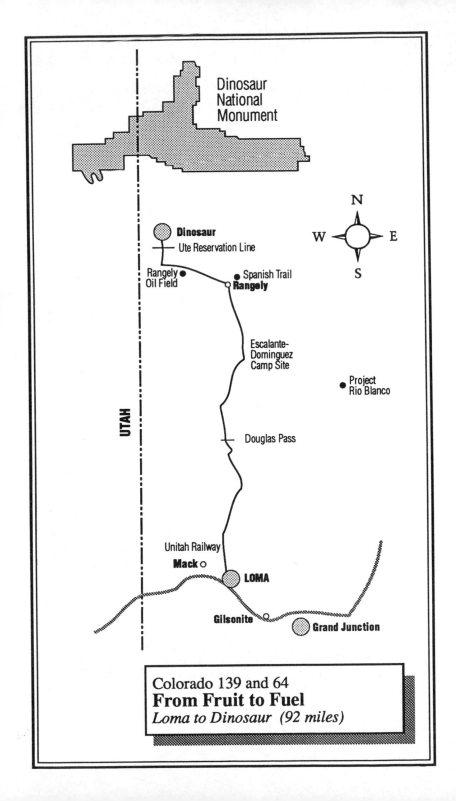

Dinosaur National Monument

N
W   E
S

Dinosaur

Ute Reservation Line

Rangely Oil Field

Spanish Trail
Rangely

Escalante-Dominguez Camp Site

Project Rio Blanco

Douglas Pass

UTAH

Unitah Railway

Mack   o

LOMA

Gilsonite

Grand Junction

Colorado 139 and 64
From Fruit to Fuel
Loma to Dinosaur (92 miles)

Colorado 139 and 64
From Fruit to Fuel
Loma to Dinosaur (92 miles)

Gilsonite

An oil refinery sits across the Colorado River opposite **Milepost 17** of I-70 just two miles east of the little town of Loma. The site is called Gilsonite because the refinery originally processed a form of asphalt by that name in a nearly forgotten area industry.

Gilsonite takes its name from a gentleman in Salt Lake City, S. H. Gilson, and it refers to a natural form of asphalt that seems to be found only in Utah. Entrepreneurs in Mack, Colorado, three miles west of Loma, found deposits of this naturally refined tar at the Dragon Mines near Watson, Utah, sixty-five miles distant. To obtain the gilsonite the Uintah Railway Company operated a narrow-gauge railroad that wound northward through West Salt Creek, paralleling *Colorado 139*, which ascends the valley of East Salt Creek ten miles to the east.

The tiny, narrow-gauge Uintah Railway train labors through a tight curve on its way over Baxter Pass on the route between Mack, Colo., and the Utah gilsonite deposits. *Colorado Historical Society*.

The little Uintah railroad overcame 7.5 percent grades and sixty-six-degree turns to surmount Baxter Pass, at 8,347 feet, and to descend through the valley of Evacuation Creek to the site of the deposits. Their unique cargo was hauled back to Mack for thirty-seven years, ending in 1939.

Douglas Pass

Douglas Pass, **Milepost 33**, marks the headwaters of East Salt Creek. It is named for a northern Ute head chief who played an ambiguous role in the 1879 massacre of Indian agent Nathan C. Meeker and his colleagues at the White River Indian Agency (see *Colorado 13* itinerary). The pass shares its name with Douglas Creek, which heads on the north side of the pass and runs northward with the highway to join the White River thirty-eight miles away at Rangely.

As Gen. Philip H. Sheridan said after the massacre, Nathan Meeker was "a good man but not a practical one, [who] endeavored to put into force by ironclad methods industrial theories good enough, perhaps, for a partly civilized people, but unsuited to savages who as yet knew nothing but war and the chase."

Chief Douglas appears in retrospect to have headed the Ute faction that chose to collaborate with the inexperienced White River agent, despite his faults. A decade earlier Meeker had founded the highly successful agricultural colony at Greeley, Colorado (see I-25N itinerary), but a falling out with his colleagues at Greeley led the cantankerous Ohioan to seek the agent's post on this remote reservation. Meeker's rather arbitrary changes at the agency were opposed by an Indian faction headed by Chief Jack and a lesser figure named Colorow, a contest that brought death to Meeker and disaster to the Utes.

Project Rio Blanco

Three nuclear devices with a combined equivalent of ninety kilotons of TNT were detonated at 10 a.m. on May 17, 1973, twenty-two miles east of **Milepost 50** in a remote gulch of the Piceance Creek basin. Authorized by President Richard M. Nixon and the Atomic Energy Commission as a part of Project Plowshare, the blasts took place more than a mile underground in an experiment to release natural gas trapped in limestone. The explosion registered 5.3 on the Richter scale but, despite fears of conservationists and of oil men whose interests were vested in neighboring oil shale formations, no serious side effects resulted from the experiment (see I-70W itinerary).

The political fallout, however, was something else. Because the Republican party had been identified with Project Rio Blanco—named for the county in which the test took place—the GOP caught the backlash in the 1974 Colorado elections. By a three-to-one margin Colorado voters backed a referendum that required citizen approval of any future nuclear tests in the state. Democratic gubernatorial candidate Richard D. Lamm defeated the Republican incumbent, John D. Vanderhoof, and challenger Gary Hart, also a Democrat, ousted Senator Peter H. Dominick.

The Spanish Trail

On September 8, 1776, two Spanish friars emerged at **Milepost 55** from the canyon of East Douglas Creek. Fray Francisco Atanasio Dominguez and Fray Silvestre Vélez de Escalante were on a lengthy journey of exploration in search of a route from their own base in Santa Fe, New Mexico, to the Spanish missions of Monterey in California. Part of the route they pioneered would become known as the Old Spanish Trail.

"On this side of [East Douglas] Canyon," wrote Escalante, "already near its exit, there is an exposed vein of metallic ore, but we are ignorant of its nature or quality, although one companion took one of the rocks fallen off the vein, and Don Bernardo Miera, showing it to us, said . . . it is an indication of gold ore. We neither decided nor shall we vouch for this, for not having mining expertise and because a more thorough testing is always required than what we could do at the time."

They moved on, little realizing that the gold in this region, as we shall see, is black.

In the fall of 1833 a youthful Kit Carson followed the Escalante-Dominguez trail from Taos to its junction with the White River at **Milepost 20** of *Colorado 64*, just east of Rangely, on his way with fur trader Stephen Lee to Fort Uintah on the Green River in present Utah. There they found Fort Uintah's proprietor, Antoine Robidoux, so-called kingpin of the Colorado River fur trade, and twenty trappers. Robidoux operated between the Green River and Taos, maintaining an intermediate trading fort near present-day Delta, Colorado (see *U.S. 50-550 itinerary*).

Nine years later, Rufus B. Sage, an itinerant journalist of the frontier, also passed through here in the company of Robidoux en route to Fort Uintah. Much of Robidoux's trade in 1842 was with the resident Utes and Snakes, or Shoshone, Indians who occupied much of Utah and Idaho at the time.

"The Utahs and Snakes afford some of the largest and best finished sheep and deer skins I ever beheld," observed Sage. "These skins are dressed so neatly as frequently to attain a snowy whiteness, and possess the softness of velvet. They may be purchased for the trifling consideration of eight or ten charges of ammunition each, or two or three awls, or any other thing of proportional value."

In the late spring of 1844, Kit Carson came through Fort Uintah once again, this time as guide to Col. John Charles Fremont on the return leg of the latter's second expedition in exploration of the West. Fremont later reported to the world that Fort Uintah had been razed, apparently by angry Indians. The cause of their ire, as Sage suggests, might have been one too many "trifling considerations."

The White River Valley

The Fremont expedition of 1844 passed through this corner of Colorado, about forty-five miles north of here at Brown's Hole (see *U.S. 40 itinerary*). The following year, Fremont took his third expedition through much of the valley of the White River on its way to the Green River.

When Escalante and Dominguez reached the mouth of Douglas Creek they named the parent stream el Rio de San Clemente, an appellation that failed to stick. They camped that night of September 10, 1776, near **Milepost 10** on Colorado 64 in a waterless arroyo, a site that they dubbed El Barranco—the Ridge. The ridge running southeast-to-northwest through here is called Raven's Ridge.

Rangely—the "Oil Basin"

Oil men in 1902 drilled some shallow wells in this area and came up with some highly promising high-gravity crude. By 1920 the wells were producing about sixteen thousand barrels a day. Then the California Company decided to try drilling ten to fifteen times as deep as the earlier wells. Raven No. 1 well pierced the Weber formation to tap into an enormous oil pool. Due to the remote location nothing was done about developing this remarkable find until the middle of World War II. By the end of the war 182 wells had been drilled into the field around Rangely.

"The 'Oil Basin,' as Rangely was known, was remote, 100 miles over crumbling blacktop, through mud and dust from the nearest railroad," recalled geologist Howard R. Ritzma. "It was wartime with its tangle of allocations, rationing and shortages of everything but red tape. Often a bankroll couldn't buy a hamburger for there was none to be had. . . . Re-capped tires failed, gas coupons ran out and the milk of human kindness and decency soured in the frenzy and frustration."

And it did not stop with the war's end. From 1945 to 1948 the number of wells increased to 473.

The Ute Reservation

The Rio-Blanco–Moffat County line at **Milepost 2**, also marks the northern boundary of the old fifteen-million-acre Ute reservation that existed from the Treaty of 1868 when the Utes gave up rights to lands east of the Continental Divide, until June 15, 1880, when lameduck president

Wind-twisted junipers frame Whirlpool Canyon some two-thousand feet above the Green River in Dinosaur National Monument. *Colorado Tourism Board.*

Rutherford B. Hayes signed the Ute Removal Bill, legislation prompted by popular indignation over the Meeker massacre. As late as 1887, however, area ranchers were alarmed over rumors that hostile Ute renegades had left their reservation fifty miles away in Utah to wreak havoc in this region (see *U.S. 40* itinerary).

Dinosaur National Monument

In August 1909, a scientist commissioned by steelmaker-turned-philanthropist Andrew Carnegie was poking around a hill just across the border in Utah. Paleontologist Earl Douglass recognized the green and purple shale of the Morrison formation, a common repository for fossils (see I-70W and *U.S. 50W* itineraries). Douglass was searching for some suitable specimens for Pittsburgh's Carnegie Museum, and he found some: eight tail bones from a Brontosaurus. In time fossils of thirteen species of dinosaur came to light, and 350 tons of rock were sifted through to uncover them.

The find was so important that in 1915 President Woodrow Wilson signed a bill declaring the site a national monument. Most of its 211,085 acres lie just north of Dinosaur, Colorado.

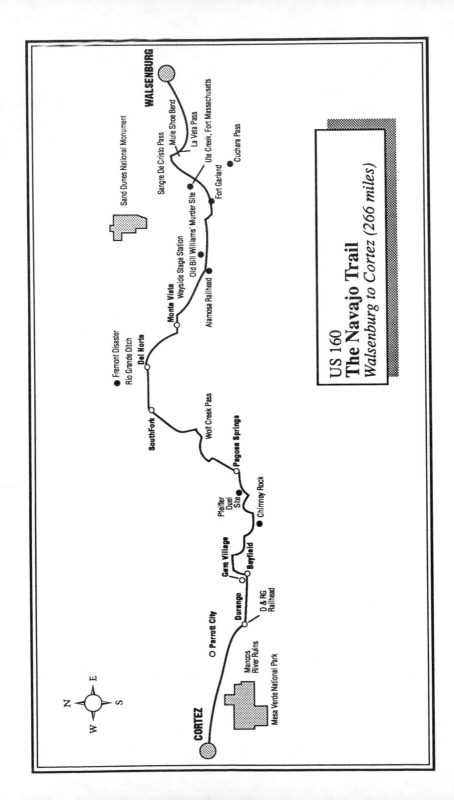

WALSENBURG

Mule Shoe Bend
La Veta Pass
Ute Creek, Fort Massachusetts
Cuchara Pass
Sangre De Cristo Pass
Fort Garland
Old Bill Williams' Murder Site
Wayside Stage Station
Sand Dunes National Monument
Monte Vista
Alamosa Railhead
Fremont Disaster
Rio Grande Ditch
Del Norte
South Fork
Wolf Creek Pass
Pagosa Springs
Pfeiffer Duel Site
Chimney Rock
Gem Village
Bayfield
Durango
D & RG Railhead
Parrott City
Mancos River Ruins
Mesa Verde National Park

CORTEZ

N
E
S
W

US 160
The Navajo Trail
Walsenburg to Cortez (266 miles)

US 160
The Navajo Trail
Walsenburg to Cortez (266 miles)

Walsenburg

Originally a village settled by natives of New Mexico, Walsenburg, at **Milepost 305**, experienced an influx of Anglo-Americans, many of German ancestry, in the years immediately following the Civil War. One of them, Fred Walsen, a storekeeper, left the community his name. About the same time, however, a grizzled mountain man decided also to settle here to live out the remainder of his years, completing a lifetime that nearly spanned the entire nineteenth century.

John David Albert entered the world at Hagerstown, Maryland in 1806. His father had been killed—one of only twenty-one Amercian casualties—in Andrew Jackson's epic, if tardy victory over the British at New Orleans in the War of 1812. A short time later Albert's mother also died.

In 1833, after working his way from New Orleans to St. Louis in a keelboat, he joined the American Fur company. His next three winters were spent trapping in the mountains.

In the spring of 1837, as his thirty-first year approached, he arrived at Bent's Old Fort on the Arkansas (see *U.S. 50E* itinerary), and took the mountain route to Santa Fe and Taos, where he married and settled down. He found employment in the distillery of Simeon Turley, the creator of the frontier whiskey known as Taos Lightning (see *I-25S* itinerary).

Albert was still working for Turley ten years later when, on January 19, 1847, the Taos Massacre took place. Reacting to the American military occupation of New Mexico, Mexicans and Indians rioted in Taos, killing Americans they found in the town, including visiting Governor Charles Bent. After sacking Taos, they stormed twelve miles north to Turley's mill in the Arroyo Hondo, besieging Turley and his American employees, including Albert. A handful of the besieged managed to escape.

Alone, Albert went north over the Taos Trail toward Fort Pueblo on the Arkansas River. He had to cover more than two hundred miles on foot without heavy clothing to ward off the chill of the mountain winter. Halfway to his destination, in the blustery snow of 9,400-foot Sangre de Cristo Pass, **Milepost 277**, Albert—exhausted, starving, and frozen—managed to kill a deer. Feasting on the venison, he also skinned the creature and used its hide for protection against the elements. When he finally stumbled into the settlements around Fort Pueblo, still wrapped in the blood-caked deer hide, he was momentarily mistaken for a monstrous apparition.

His report was the first word received on the American frontier about the Taos tragedy. William Bent, brother of the assassinated governor, was notified at his trading fort, downriver from Fort Pueblo. Albert joined the expedition that hurried to Taos to help put down the rebellion.

Tom Tobin and the Espinosas

In the spring of 1863 two brothers, Felipe and Julian Espinosa, launched a vendetta against "gringos" who were arriving in mounting numbers in Colorado Territory. The two had seemingly been wronged in some manner so that they felt their bloody rampage amounted to a holy vengeance.

A series of brutal slayings took place over a period of two months. Killed were a blacksmith at Hardscrabble Creek, some miners in South Park, and others in California Gulch on the upper Arkansas. When a stagecoach holdup was botched near Tarryall, a posse was organized in South Park. The Espinosas were tracked to Cripple Creek. In a shootout, Felipe was killed, but Julian escaped.

A diary discovered on Felipe's body indicated that they were sworn to kill six hundred gringos. After shooting up his hometown of Conejos in the lower San Luis Valley, Julian Espinosa left a letter for Territorial Governor John Evans in which he claimed that he and his deceased brother had already killed twenty persons. Evans offered a $2,500 reward for Julian's capture, dead or alive.

Espinosa continued to elude both posses and the U.S. Army, whose detachment at Fort Garland had been mobilized to track him down. On September 5, 1863, Julian and his nephew accosted a man and a woman who were driving a carriage through Sangre de Cristo Pass in the mountains above Fort Garland. The pair escaped to the fort.

To bring the Espinosas to justice, the Fort Garland commander enlisted the services of Thomas Tate Tobin, a one-time mountain man and veteran army scout. The thirty-eight-year-old Tobin led a small patrol of soldiers into the Sangre de Cristo mountains in a three-day search for the fugitives.

Late one night Tobin, accompanied only by his young nephew, found the two fugitives seated around a fire near the summit of Cuchara Pass, about twenty-two miles south of **Milepost 294** on *Colorado 12*. From ambush Tobin shot them both dead. The next day he rode into Fort Garland and deposited a sack containing the heads of the two outlaws at the feet of the fort's commanding officer.

Tobin operated a ranch on Trinchera Creek until he died in 1884 at the age of fifty-nine.

La Veta Pass

Although Sangre de Cristo Pass, joining the Rio Grande watershed with the Huerfano River watershed, served for the pack animals of the Taos merchants and trappers to cross from the New Mexican high parks to the Colorado high plains, its near neighbor, La Veta Pass, connecting the Rio Grande basin to the Cuchara River watershed, has come to serve modern transportation.

In June 1877, the pass, at 9,382 feet, marked a high point in railroad history. Negotiating the tortuous Mule Shoe

Bend, **Milepost 281,** a Denver & Rio Grande train crossed over the imposing Sangre de Cristo range to arrive at Fort Garland in the San Luis valley. In doing so the little narrow-gauge had climbed one thousand feet higher than any train in the world. (U.S. 160 crosses North La Veta Pass, 9,413 feet, about two miles north of the railroad pass, which can also be reached by car. The D&RGW has moved its right-of-way to yet another Veta Pass ten miles south.)

The feat brought railway engineers from other continents to Colorado's mountain fastnesses to learn how it had been done. Their pilgrimage paid tribute to the achievement of a forty-year-old Philadelphia Quaker, who had already managed to reconcile pacifism with a militancy that won him a Union general's star. An apprenticed railroad builder at the age of seventeen and an executive at thirty, William Jackson Palmer had helped to build the Kansas Pacific west to Denver (see I-70 itinerary) and the Denver Pacific south from Cheyenne (see I-25N itinerary) when he got the urge to build one on his own.

"I had a dream," he told his fiancée in January 1870, ". . . how fine it would be to have a little railroad a few hundred miles in length, all under one's own control with one's

Two Denver & Rio Grande engines build up steam at the summit of La Veta Pass, the world's highest railroad right-of-way in 1877. *Colorado Historical Society.*

friends . . . to be able to carry out unimpeded and harmoniously one's views in regard to what ought and ought not to be done."

The few hundred miles of that dream shortly became about 850 miles when Palmer decided to build from Denver to the valley of the Rio Grande, which heads in the San Luis valley, and thence to El Paso, Texas. From there his dream envisioned another nine hundred miles of track to Mexico City. But after the remarkable cresting of the 14,000-foot Sangre de Cristo Mountains, the D&RG never got farther down the Rio Grande River valley than Santa Fe, New Mexico.

At the outset, in 1870, the financial obstacles facing Palmer were at least as formidable as the physical obstacles. Palmer had eschewed federal subsidy of his enterprise, in contrast with the other railroad companies then operating in the West, which were granted twenty sections of public land for each mile of track. Privately, from friends in Philadelphia and in England, Palmer managed to raise a million dollars with which to launch the Denver & Rio Grande Railroad.

From innovative financing Palmer went immediately to innovative engineering. He opted for narrow-gauge track and rolling stock, the first to do so in the American West. Popular in England, narrow-gauge offered some attractive features for someone in Palmer's situation. Economy was the first consideration: narrow-gauge gradings, tunnels, and bridges cost half that of standard gauge. Its lighter rolling stock could manage tighter turns and steeper inclines, both of which were important in conquering the rugged Rockies. The proof came, of course, in surmounting La Veta Pass.

There was another reason that was rumored to have prompted the fastidious Palmer to choose narrow-gauge. Insensitive booking agents on standard-gauge lines insisted on putting perfect strangers in the same sleeping berths. More befitting the Victorian age, the narrow-gauge sleeping car allowed room for only one to a berth.

Spanish Fort

About five miles northeast of Sangre de Cristo Pass is the

site of a Spanish fort, an outpost of Santa Fe that was erected after the 1819 Adams-Onis Treaty that confirmed Spain's claim to the southern bank of the Arkansas River, most of today's southeastern corner of Colorado. The post was probably abandoned after the 1821 Mexican Revolution when the new Mexican Republic faced more pressing concerns.

There are unverified indications that the fort, before it was abandoned, was overrun by an Indian war party. Spanish documents indicate that in the summer of 1819 the Spanish governor of New Mexico, Facundo Melgares, ordered that a fort be erected east of Sangre de Cristo Pass. In a letter written in October 1819, Melgares reported that one hundred men "dressed as Indians" had attacked the post. He directed that a three-hundred-man contingent be dispatched from Santa Fe to reinforce the threatened outpost.

Enroute to their exploration of the Front Range of the Rocky Mountains in the spring of 1820, the U.S. Army expedition headed by Maj. Stephen H. Long spent some time with the Pawnee tribes of the Platte River valley, more than five hundred miles from Sangre de Cristo Pass. The expedition's chronicler, Edwin James, was told of the experience of a Pawnee war party in previous months that might be the other side of Melgares's story: "One of their parties encountered a party of Spaniards, who, my informant asserted, sought safety in flight. But it seems highly probable that a battle took place, and that many were killed, inasmuch as the victors returned with much clothing, merchandize, very handsome figured blankets, many horses, and some silver money. . . . The party had certainly brought with them some scalps which were not those of Indians. . . . "

Fort Garland

Until they were displaced by American settlements, ratified in an 1868 treaty of cession, the Utes claimed mastery of the San Luis valley. Ute Creek descends the slopes of Blanca Peak and crosses *U.S. 160* at **Milepost 258** at Fort Garland. But long before there was an American military presence here an incident occurred, recounted by Janet Lecompte in *Pueblo-Hardscrabble-Greenhorn*, that illustrates the hazards of frontier life. It involved one of the founders of Fort Pueblo, George Simpson, and his New Mexican wife as they followed the trail to Taos in the fall of 1844:

> . . . A Ute village [was] moving up Ute creek with a large number of cattle and sheep. Without a word George handed Juana his belt containing a pistol and hunting knife. She buckled the belt around her waist, having discussed with her husband many times what she should do if faced with worse-than-death captivity among the Indians. They hid in the willows by the stream until nightfall. Then they crept out of their hiding place and rode twenty-five miles in darkness and silence to the Culebra River. At the village of Rio Colorado the next day they learned that the Utes they had seen had killed several herders of that village and three travelers on their way to Taos.

The first military post in what is now Colorado, Fort Massachusetts, was built in June 1852, six miles up Ute Creek from **Milepost 258**. The new installation was an outpost of Fort Union, 165 miles south in New Mexico. Fort Massachusetts accommodated 150 men, half cavalry and half infantry. One visitor, Gwin Harris Heap, questioned the value of the post's nicely groomed but cornfed horses. "They would soon break down on a march in pursuit of Indians mounted on horses fed on grass. . . ."

Six years later Fort Massachusetts was decommissioned and a new post, Fort Garland, was erected at **Milepost 258**. A correspondent of the New York *Times*, William H. Rideing, remarked on the desolation of Fort Garland even in 1875: "Nevertheless not an item of discipline was omitted. The reveille was beaten (and the) guard was mounted and relieved in the fullest and neatest dress, and to inspiring music, even though six men were all the post could muster. Reports were submitted and received with the same pomp

A life-sized tableau depicts a parley between army officers at Fort Garland and Ute Indians of the San Luis Valley. *Colorado Tourism Board.*

and circumstances as one observed in the largest army, and the sentries challenged with unremitted vigilance all who pass the gates."

Great Sand Dunes National Monument

The thirty-nine-thousand-acre Great Sand Dunes were made a national monument on St. Patrick's Day, 1932, and placed under the administration of the U.S. Department of the Interior. Located fourteen miles north of **Milepost 248** on *Colorado 150*, the dunes are among the world's largest inland accumulations of sand, cresting at seven hundred feet above the floor of the valley.

When Zebulon Pike crossed Medano Pass early in 1807 and encountered the phenomenon on Medano Creek, he likened the dunes to a stormy, dun-colored sea. Archeological excavations in the area suggest that primitive hunters of the Folsom period, such as those who left their mark on the Lindenmeier site in northern Colorado (see I-25N itiner-

ary), might have been found here as well ten thousand years
ago.

The Demise of "Old Bill" Williams, M.T.

An incident that underscored the need for a military post
in this vicinity resulted in the death of one of Colorado's
most colorful mountain men, William Sherley "Old Bill"
Williams, M.T. (Master Trapper, as he styled himself). He
was shot on March 21, 1849, somewhere between **Milepost
248** and the Rio Grande at **Milepost 233**. The deaths of
Williams and Dr. Benjamin J. Kean marked the tragic
sequel to an already disastrous expedition undertaken by
John C. Fremont in yet another attempt to find the ideal
passage for a transcontinental railroad.

Williams was born on June 3, 1787, in Rutherford County, North Carolina. At the age of eight he went with his
family to Spanish Louisiana. Eight years later he left home
to become a trader with a band of Osage Indians, where,
with two Indian wives, he remained until 1828. That year
Taos became his base for trading with the Mountain Utes of
Colorado, and in 1830 he began a decade of trapping and
guiding other trappers throughout the Rocky Mountains.

In 1840 Williams led a motley band of Americans, New
Mexicans, Canadians, and Indians on a raid into Mexican
California where they managed to steal three thousand
horses, half of which they lost in driving them east through
the mountains. At Bent's Old Fort Willams sold his share
rather casually for a barrel of whiskey.

Fremont encountered Williams at Fort Pueblo in August
1845 and hired him to guide his third expedition up the
Arkansas River and on to the west. At the Great Salt Lake
Williams argued with Fremont and left the expedition. In
succeeding years he continued to roam from one end of the
Rockies to the other. In November 1848 he set the stage
for his demise.

He encountered Fremont at Pueblo once again and was
persuaded to join the ill-fated fourth expedition to seek a

route across the southern Rockies that would permit winter-time travel by rail. The endeavor failed, with several of the party dead of starvation and freezing. When the survivors had been evacuated, Williams and Kean returned to the place, high in the La Garita mountains, where the party had abandoned its scientific instruments and other equipment. Having fetched the gear, the two were overtaken by their attackers on their way to Taos. They were presumed to have been killed by Utes.

Alamosa

A stagecoach station called Wayside was located at the point where *U.S. 160* crosses the Rio Grande del Norte, **Milepost 233**, until the Denver & Rio Grande Railroad arrived in July 1878. A major stockholder and executive official of the D&RG, former Governor A. C. Hunt, laid out a townsite at the new railhead and, betraying a certain fascination with Spanish words, named it Alamosa—"cottonwood grove." In 1913, Alamosa became the seat of Colorado's sixty-third and last county—Alamosa County.

By 1878, when the D&RG arrived, the perils faced by travelers in the San Luis valley had been updated. Instead of marauding Indians, the stagecoaches that picked up train passengers to carry them on to other valley destinations and beyond to the San Juan Mountains frequently were intercepted by highway men.

Billy LeRoy, a markedly diminutive desperado from Kansas City, stopped the stage one evening by putting a log across the road and bracing willow shoots against it so that, in the dusk, they looked like rifle barrels leveled at the oncoming stage. Carrying on a one-sided colloquy with his imaginary companions, LeRoy managed to convince driver and passengers that he was strongly backed by gunmen. The sheriff's investigation the next day uncovered the ruse, but the lawmen remained baffled. They thought Le Roy's size four boot prints were made by a woman.

Another holdup artist proved too clever for his own good. Ordinarily a liveryman for the stage line, he moonlighted on one occasion behind a mask and assisted some comrades in the holdup of a stage. Unfortunately one of the stagecoach horses started acting up. Seeking to calm the animal the part-time bandit called him by name.

Rio Grande Irrigation Canal

The Rio Grande Irrigation Canal, **Milepost 202**, was built in 1883 at the substantial cost of $300,000. Irrigating 200,000 acres of the arid but fertile San Luis valley, where nature provides only eight inches of rain annually, the ditch set the stage for the development of the valley's now extensive vegetable industry (see *U.S. 285S* itinerary). One San Luis valley farmer, R. A. Chisholm, set the world record in 1916 for potato yield—847.5 bushels per acre.

Tragedy on Mesa Mountain

Embargo Creek empties into the Rio Grande one mile north of **Milepost 194**. At the creek's head, fifteen miles north-northwest, high on the shoulders of Mesa Mountain, one encounters the site of a famous disaster. The controversial but colorful John Charles Fremont, fresh from a court-martial conviction and his forced resignation from the U.S. Army, had set out to prove that the southern Rocky Mountains were passable in winter. His hope was to find a suitable route through this sector of the Rockies for a transcontinental railroad.

After departing from the already abandoned Fort Pueblo in November 1848, passing up Hardscrabble Creek into the Wet Mountains, and then crossing the Sangre de Cristos, Fremont's party, which included Old Bill Williams, skirted the Great Sand Dunes and arrived in the San Luis valley.

There, for the second time in his association with Fremont, Williams argued with his boss. He objected to Fremont's plan to take an untried route through the mountains in the depths of winter. Tested fair-weather trails existed to the north at Cochetopa Pass (see *U.S. 285S* itinerary) and to the south over the Old Spanish Trail via Abiquiu, New Mexico.

But Fremont was adamant that they should plunge into the unknown regions between the two.

The Fremont brigade—thirty-three men and 120 mules—went up the Rio Grande past today's Del Norte to Alder Creek, **Milepost 186**, north to Wanamaker Creek, and eastward around the base of 12,944-foot Mesa Mountain, where they encountered their moment of frozen frustration. Stymied by deep snows, with both men and animals starving, Fremont was forced to send a squad of four men back down the mountain for help. Williams was one of them. When they came to a camp of Utes, Williams recognized the band and refused to approach the Indians for fear of retaliation for his past misdeeds against them. Moreover, he had participated in a U.S. Army punitive campaign against the Utes and Apaches in northern New Mexico just a few months earlier.

By now at the end of his endurance, the squad leader, Henry King, died of starvation and exposure. Despairing of the rescue squad's prospects, Fremont and the others overtook them. By this time all 120 mules were dead and the entire expedition was on foot. Only twenty-three of the original thirty-three managed to reach the New Mexico settlements alive, all either ill or crippled.

The Utes eventually managed to accomplish what Old Bill Williams had feared. On March 21, 1849, they overtook and killed the old mountaineer and his companion as they were returning with the expedition's abandoned equipment (see above).

Pagosa Springs

Across the Continental Divide at Wolf Creek Pass lies Pagosa Springs, **Milepost 143**, the site of one of several spas enjoyed by the Ute Indians in what is now Colorado. Among the others are Hot Sulphur Springs (*see U.S. 40* itinerary) and, at the base of Pike's Peak, Manitou Springs, (see *U.S. 24E* itinerary). Pagosah means "healing waters" in the Ute tongue. Nomadic Utes wintered at this site.

A U.S. Army topographical expedition in search of a route for a military road to Utah first reported the existence of the forty-by-fifty-foot thermal pool in July 1859. Capt. John N. Macomb and his men were guided to this place by a veteran Army scout, Albert H. Pfeiffer, Sr., who was then Indian agent to the Utes.

When the region was later ceded to white settlement by the Utes, Pfeiffer made a curious claim of ownership of the thermal springs. The place was his, he declared, because he had helped the Utes to withstand an earlier Navajo challenge to its possession. In a quaintly medieval manner the rival tribes had elected to let the outcome of a one-on-one duel decide ownership. The Utes chose Pfeiffer as their champion, and the white man managed to dispatch the Navajos' gladiator without difficulty. The duel is said to have taken place in a meadow in the vicinity of **Milepost 136**.

A native of Prussia, Pfeiffer was afflicted with some sort of skin ailment, possibly a form of acne. The malady apparrently responded to the effects of bathing in hot springs, so Pfeiffer took advantage of the opportunities that came his way.

According to Louis B. Sporleder, Sr., a Cuchara valley native who knew him, Pfeiffer nearly lost his life indulging in the baths on one occasion. Assigned to a fort in Apache territory, Pfeiffer took his wife and a servant girl to a hot springs some ten miles from his post. As he bathed, an Apache war party attacked, killing his wife and their servant. Warriors pursued the naked Pfeiffer as he ran barefoot back toward the fort. Feet lacerated from cactus and stone and with an arrow in his back, he managed to reach the safety of the fort.

After leaving the army in 1867 as a captain, he retired to Del Norte, **Milepost 202**, where he died on April 6, 1881, at the age of fifty-nine.

Immigrants began to arrive in 1876, but, despite the 1873 Brunot Treaty ceding the San Juan region, the Utes continued to be restive. In 1878 Fort Lewis was established at

Pagosa Springs to protect settlers. The town was platted in 1883 and finally, in 1891, incorporated.

Chimney Rock

Chimney Rock looms over **Milepost 126**, perpetuating the memory of the Ancient Ones—the Anasazi. These mysterious Indians built and occupied their honeycomb, multi-dwelling adobe apartment houses throughout southwestern Colorado about the time that William the Conqueror was subduing the Anglo-Saxons in 1066. Some of these dwellings lie to the south of Chimney Rock on Chimney Rock Mesa, which can be reached by an access road about four miles south on *Colorado 151*.

Archeological excavations begun in 1921 suggest that as many as two thousand people occupied the site in the tenth to the twelfth centuries. An apparently prolonged drought forced them to leave.

Named a national historic site in 1974, Chimney Rock ruins are administered by the United States Forest Service through the ranger district office in Pagosa Springs.

Gem Village

A Bayfield gem merchant, Frank Morris, established a colony of artists and artisans at **Milepost 100** in 1942 to encourage the working of decorative pieces of semiprecious stones. Today Gem Village is a rendezvous for rock hunters.

Durango

Durango, now the principal city of southwestern Colorado, at **Milepost 83**, was the product of another railroad power play, much in the manner of Colorado Springs (see I-25M itinerary). Animas City, whose site is on the northern limits of modern Durango, came into being in 1861, nearly a generation prior to Durango's founding. It was the creation of S. B. Kellogg, a gold-prospecting entrepreneur who had grubstaked Charles Baker, the first successful prospector in the San Juan mountains (see *U.S. 50-550* itinerary). Kellogg followed his protégé to this region from Leadville and decided to settle here.

Fourteen miles to the west, meanwhile, in the spring of 1874, a San Francisco, California, land development firm, Parrott & Company, bought a township, thirty-six square miles, from Ute Chief Ignacio and arranged to have Parrott City proclaimed the seat of La Plata County, then an entity of seven thousand square miles.

In 1880, however, the Durango Land & Coal Company bought out six homesteaders and surveyed a new townsite. Witnessing the event, the editor of the Animas City *Southwest* told his readers: "The Bank of San Juan has issued a circular in which it is stated that a branch office will be opened at the 'new town of Durango on the Rio Animas.' Where the 'new town of Durango' is to be or not to be God and the D. and R.G. Railroad only know. If they are in 'cahoots' we ask for a special dispensation."

A year later the D&RG arrived, erected its station a couple miles from the Animas City *Southwest's* office, and watched the residents of the earlier town move south. A few months later most of the citizens of Parrott City also transferred to the new town of Durango, bringing their county seat with them.

Despairing of John C. Fremont's thirty-five-year-old hope for a railroad through the San Juans, the D&RG went south from Alamosa, **Milepost 232**, to Antonito (see *U.S. 285S* itinerary), crossed Cumbres Pass, and picked up the Old Spanish Trail near Chama, New Mexico, over which it built its right-of-way to Durango. As the D&RG arrived so did the San Juan & New York smelter, built by John A. Porter and J. H. Ernest Waters but eventually taken over by the American Smelting & Refining Company in the late 1890s (see I-25S itinerary).

In 1881 outlaw gangs roamed the valleys of the San Juan and terrorized Durango citizens. Henry Moorman was

lynched one Sunday in April for the murder of James K. Polk
Prindle. The noose was thrown over the branch of a pine
tree across from the bank on Ninth Street.

Ike Stockton and Harg Eskeridge, the outlaw leaders,
were excoriated by Mrs. Romney, the plucky lady who three
months earlier had launched the daily Durango *Record* in a
tent. The two threatened Mrs. Romney, and for ten days her
printers wore pistols as they put the *Record* to bed each
morning. Finally, the Committee of Safety—the same vigilantes who had disposed of Moorman—backed Mrs. Romney and issued warrants for the capture of the gang, forcing
the outlaws to flee the region.

A famous vestige of the country's plucky narrow-gauge
railroad fraternity continues to run from Durango to Silverton, the site of Charles Baker's gold strike in the San Juans
(see *U.S. 50-550* itinerary). The station is located at 479
Main Avenue, Durango.

Parrott City

Parrott City, La Plata County's seat from 1874 to 1881,
had its site three miles north of **Milepost 72** on the banks of
La Plata River.

Shortly after its founding, a twenty-five-year-old miner
arrived from Leadville. His name reportedly was Lon Wolf,
but, because of his taciturn, unsocial character, he was
quickly dubbed Lone Wolf. The mystery surrounding him
became of intense interest in Parrott City one day in 1878 when
Wolf showed up with two burros carrying bags of remarkably
high-grade gold ore, which he apparently had found on the west
slope of Parrott Mountain just behind Parrott City.

Wolf took the ore to the D&RG railhead at Alamosa and
dispatched it to the already prosperous mining entrepreneur H.A.W. Tabor, whom he may have known in Leadville. A timely grubstake had just resulted in the bonanza
Little Pittsburg silver mine for Tabor. Wolf notified Tabor
that he wanted $25,000 for his Parrott Mountain claim.
Tabor sent a mining engineer to examine the mine. Confirming its value, Tabor's envoy presented the sullen young

prospector with a check for $25,000. Wolf refused; he wanted cash or nothing.

In 1908 the same mining engineer returned, by chance, to the La Plata valley and told his story to an old prospector, George Brauner, who was familiar with the area that the engineer described. Brauner searched the west slope of Parrott Mountain, matching the clues that the engineer had given, and in time found some old diggings that possessed some richly gold-flecked ore. Hurrying back to town, Brauner lined up a partner who would help him finance and work the diggings. As Brauner was guiding his colleague to the site, however, he was stricken with a fatal heart attack.

So the Lone Wolf mine was misplaced for a second time.

Mesa Verde National Park

William Henry Jackson, the celebrated photographer of the Hayden Survey, once called the Mancos River, **Milepost 57**, "a street a thousand feet deep." Jackson was the first to record the fabulous and mysterious cliff houses of the Anasazi, in 1874. "The entire construction of this little human eyrie," he wrote in his diary, "displays wonderful perseverance, ingenuity, and some taste."

Many of the elaborate adobe apartment dwellings had been seen by Charles Baker and other gold prospectors of the San Juan as early as 1860, but they all apparently overlooked the truly spectacular ruins that now constitute Mesa Verde National Park. Jackson missed these as well, although he took forty photos that awed the world. Jackson and his party circled what is now the reserve of Mesa Verde, whose sensational ruins were not discovered until 1888 when a couple of cowboys in search of strays chanced upon them. The park, whose entrance lies at **Milepost 48.5**, was estabished in 1906, eighteen years after cowboy Richard Wetherill rode up to the edge of a mesa, looked across the intervening canyon, and saw nestled under a rock overhang the multi-tiered two-hundred-room remains of a city, abandoned for six hundred years. He quickly called to his partner, Charles Mason, to view what is now called the Cliff Palace.

Square Tower House in Mesa Verde National Park is a striking example of the architecture of the Anasazi whose best works eluded discovery until 1888. *Colorado Tourism Board.*

In the generation that followed, archeologists, along with the curious and the greedy, rushed to the site, many guided by Wetherill himself, whose name was given to one of the mesas in the park. At one point a local banker reportedly underwrote the dismemberment of the ruins in exchange for a share of the profits.

A Colorado woman's group organized the Colorado Cliff Dwellings Association, whose two hundred members obtained a lease from the Weminuche Utes to protect the site. They financed a road from Mancos, **Milepost 56**, to Cliff Canyon and lobbied for twenty-five years for the establishment of a national park at the site. Ironically, when the legislation for the park had finally been written in Congress, the Cliff Dwellings Association found that the official survey had left Wetherill's Cliff Palace outside the park boundaries. Fortunately, this bureaucratic fumble was duly recovered.

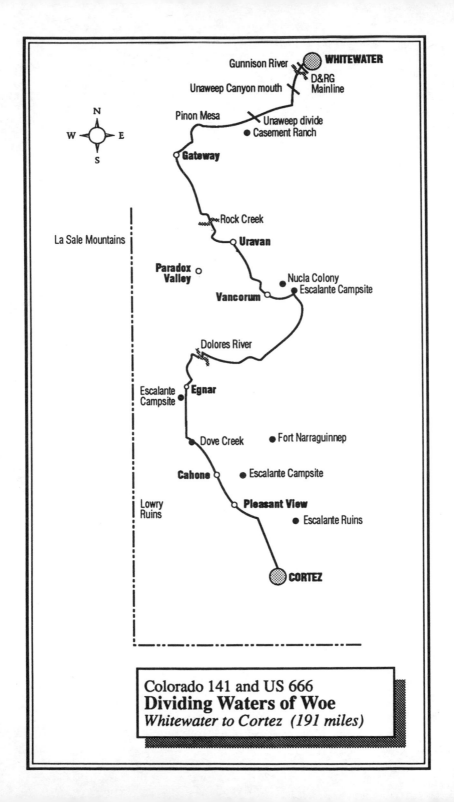

Colorado 141 and US 666
Dividing Waters of Woe
Whitewater to Cortez (191 miles)

Colorado 141 and US 666
Dividing Waters of Woe
Whitewater to Cortez (191 miles)

Whitewater

The town of Whitewater at the junction of *Colorado 141* and *U.S. 50* began as a community serving a fruit industry that flourished immediately after the Ute reservation was opened for settlement in September 1881 (see *Colorado 149* and *Colorado 13* itineraries). The delta region where the Colorado, Gunnison, and Uncompaghre rivers converge was hailed as one of the best regions in the country for fruit tree cultivation.

The town takes its name not from the turbulence of the major rivers in the vicinity but from the alkali deposited by the creek that descends from Grand Mesa to the east.

D&RGW Mainline Route, Denver–Ogden

The Denver & Rio Grande Western Railroad crosses the highway at **Milepost 154**. This was the mainline of the famous Colorado-based narrow-gauge railway when it came through here in the fall of 1882 on its way to Grand Junction and union with the Rio Grande Western, which was building from Ogden, Utah. The line, completed on June 1, 1883, joined Ogden with Denver by way of the Gunnison River valley, Marshall Pass, Canon City, and Pueblo (see *U.S. 50W* itinerary). In 1890, the D&RG changed over to standard gauge, thanks to the development of more powerful locomotives that could negotiate the steep grades of the Rockies, and the D&RG mainline shifted from the Gunnison River valley to that of the Eagle and Colorado rivers (see I-70W itinerary).

Ironically, thirty years earlier an Army Topographical Corps survey team, passing through this locality, dismissed it as unsuitable for a transcontinental railroad route. The group, headed by the ill-starred Capt. John W. Gunnison, reached this point in late September 1853. Before he was killed by Indians near Lake Sevier in Utah a few weeks after passing through this vicinity, Gunnison concluded that the so-called Thirty-eighth Parallel Route, much favored by powerful Missouri Senator Thomas Hart Benton, would not serve the requirements for the cross-country rail line.

The Gunnison River, **Milepost 154**, is, of course, named for the slain topographer.

Unaweep Canyon

The Unaweep Canyon opens at **Milepost 152** and continues for forty miles. Unaweep is a word from the Ute language meaning "dividing of the waters." Like several other features of southwest Colorado's topography, it is an anomaly. It has all the appearances of a major river channel, but the canyon is host merely to two modest creeks. One of them empties into the Gunnison River and is appropriately called East Creek. The other runs the opposite direction to the Dolores River at the west mouth of the canyon, which earns it the designation of West Creek. The divide between the two watersheds lies incongruously near the midpoint of the canyon, **Milepost 130**.

Geologists speculate that, in another geological era, the canyon was the channel of the present Colorado River, which now flows thirty miles to the north in a direction roughly parallel to that of the Unaweep Canyon.

Dan Dillon Casement was a Princetonian and scion of a family that supervised construction of the Union Pacific from Omaha to Promontory Point, Utah. In the mid-1880s he became a pioneer rancher in Unaweep Canyon. During his first visit in 1883, Casement recalled; "We climbed to the summer range on Pinon Mesa [north of **Milepost 122**] by an Indian trail strewn with broken tepee poles and other evidence of its recent use by the banished Utes. We found the forage on top luxuriant, the water abundant, the nucleus of the herd fat and contented."

The Casement ranch was at Fall Creek, **Milepost 126**, just a few miles west of the divide within the canyon. Several generations of Casements operated the ranch over a period of fifty-eight years.

During these years [on] the Unaweep Cattle Range . . . [We started] on the open range with a breeding herd and the three-year-old beef steer as its normal product, [after which we] ran through the whole scale of commonly accepted practices and ended by marketing registered Herefords, bulls produced by a small herd of select cows confined to home meadows.

[We] twice experienced exhaustion of the open range by overstocking resorted in desperation to illegal fencing, grazed [our] stock under government permit after the creation of the [Uncompaghre] National Forests [in 1905] and finally shrank within the boundaries of the comparatively small area to which [we] had undisputed title.

Casement was part of the initial wave of white settlement that followed the eviction of the Utes in 1881 from their twelve-million-acre reservation to Indian lands in Utah. He acquired still another tie to that pivotal period in Colorado history. In 1897 he married Olivia Thornburgh, daughter of army major Thomas T. Thornburgh, who was killed in a clash with Utes on September 29, 1879—an incident that set the stage for the Meeker Massacre (see *Colorado 13* and *U.S. 40* itineraries). The subsequent murder of Indian agent Nathan C. Meeker and his companions at the White River Agency prompted the evacuation of the Utes from western Colorado.

Roc Creek

A Montrose photographer who moonlighted as a prospector, Thomas M. McKee, was instrumental in 1896 in the discovery of a new mineral, carnotite. The samples procured by McKee that led to its identification came from a mine on Roc Creek, **Milepost 89.**

In the summer of 1896 McKee developed a friendship with a young French scientist, Charles Poulot, who had been hired by a Michigan mining syndicate to assay ore samples at the Cashin mine near Bedrock, fifteen miles up the Dolores River valley from the mouth of Roc Creek. For a year McKee had been puzzling over the nature of the lemon-colored ore samples. He had already established that the ore contained no gold, sliver, copper, or iron. As it turned out, Poulot could not identify the stuff either, so he sent several pounds, given him by McKee, to Paris for more comprehensive analysis.

When McKee encountered Poulet some weeks later, he learned that experts in Paris had identified the ore as a compound of uranium. In token of their scientific expertise, evidently, they also appropriated the privilege of naming it, much to McKee's dismay. The name honored Adolphe Sadi Carnot, a scientist who was French inspector-general of mines. "I was dumbfounded and very much disappointed," said McKee, "because it had not been named in honor of Colorado or Montrose County."

The phenomenon of radioactivity was still in its most primitive stages of study at the time. The X-ray had been discovered by Wilhelm Roentgen only the year before, and the radioactivity of such metals as uranium was only vaguely appreciated in the scientific world and probably not at all in rural southwestern Colorado. Curiously, McKee himself had been using a nitrate of uranium since 1880 in processing his photographic prints. By chance, he stored some carnotite ore samples in his darkroom and suffered, without realizing the cause until some years later, the irradiation of some of his photographic plates.

It was not until 1903 that Madame Marie Curie published her discovery of the element radium in pitchblende, another uranium ore. By that time the irrepressible McKee was conducting his own experiments using the ore he introduced to the scientific world (and which he preferred to call "montroseite" instead of carnotite) to create images on photographic plates in the manner of the clinical x-ray.

Uravan

Uravan, **Milepost 76**, is the 1936 creation of the United States Vanadium Corporation. Vanadium, as it turned out, is another component of the ore identified as carnotite. As a

trace element it serves two known purposes: it helps sea
squirts to process oxygen and humans to harden steel. As a
consequence, it became important to humans in World War
II. In 1943, the Colorado carnotite deposits delivered an
estimated 75 percent of the world's production of vanadium.

Vancorum

Another company town, Vancorum, at **Milepost 62**, is a
slightly corrupted acronym for Vanadium Corporation of
America. The town was created as a bedroom community in
support of the VCA's operations down the road at Naturita,
Milepost 60.

VCA established Vancorum as a housing development in
1930, and the timing of this investment tends to underscore
the three ages of carnotite. The first, of course was the age of
radium, initiated in Madame Curie's turn-of-the-century
discovery of the element. A process for separating carnotite
into its components was developed and, in 1906, patented
by two Denver men, Justin H. Haynes and Wilber D.
Engle.

From that time radium from Colorado carnotite ores was
much in demand. In 1910, for example, $1.1 million in ore
was produced in the area. By 1912 three companies had built
reduction plants in the vicinity and investments in radium
extraction reached $10 million, a sizable sum for the time.

In 1923 H. E. Bishop, manager of the Radium Company
of Colorado, estimated that 90 percent of the world's production of radium, valued at $20 million, had come from the
ore deposits of this region. That same year the market for
Colorado radium collapsed. Extensive ore deposits were
discovered in the Belgian Congo and their exploitation
proved to be less costly than those in America.

That brought Colorado into the age of vanadium. World
War II's demands for high-grade steel enhanced the importance of this component of carnotite. On the eve of Pearl
Harbor, in the years 1940-41, there were reports that substantial amounts of vanadium concentrate had been stolen
by employees of the mining and processing companies and

secretly sold to eager steelmakers. Employee thefts of refined metal, called "highgrading" and common in gold and
silver mining (see *Colorado 62-145* itinerary), amounted to
an estimated $33,000 in the months prior to U.S. entry into
World War II. Highgrading of vanadium prompted a federal
investigation. Local rumor held at the time that much of the
stolen vanadium concentrate had been smuggled to Nazi
Germany and Japan.

The war's end, punctuated with the detonation of the
world's first atomic bombs over Japan, introduced the age of
uranium. In place of the old pick-and-shovel prospectors
leading their "jacks," those ubiquitous burros of the Southwest, uranium seekers drove jeeps and used Geiger coun-
ters.

Paradox Valley

Ore was processed around company-created towns such
as Uravan and Vancorum, but much of the mining took
place west of Vancorum on *Colorado 90* in aptly named
Paradox Valley. The twenty-five-mile-long valley unac-
countably sits at right angles to the Dolores River, which
bisects it. In the valley, near Bedrock, is the famous Cashin
mine, where Thomas McKee's French friend, Charles
Poulot, made his headquarters. The Cashin, whose heyday
was 1896-99, also produced silver, gold, and copper ores.

Just above Paradox Valley are the La Sal Mountains in
which the celebrated outlaw, Butch Cassidy, had one of his
early hideouts, perhaps his jumping-off point for the 1889
robbery of a Telluride bank (see *Colorado 62-145* itinerary).

The La Sal Mountain lair offered relatively direct access
both to the railroad towns of the Colorado and Gunnison
valleys and to the mining towns of the San Juan Mountains.
The outlaws could flee through Paradox Valley over a rather
intimidating stretch from the San Miguel to the Dolores
River.

"This section of the valley is really a desert," reported
Thomas McKee, "no water after leaving the San Miguel,
except a well . . . and one other place in some sandstone

rocks, where the pot holes filled with rain water during the raining season and snow water during the spring. From there to the Dolores there was no more water, and it sure was a hard trip . . . hot, dusty and a long day's travel."

Nucla

On *Colorado 97*, four miles north of **Milepost 60**, lies the town of Nucla, a name supposedly derived from the word "nucleus" but having no allusion to the uranium atom. The town came into being about the time carnotite was undergoing identification and naming in Paris. A cooperative colony founded the town in a spirit of highmindedness represented in the name of the society's publication, *Altrurion*.

Organized in Denver in February 1894 amid the reverberations emanating from the federal government's abandonment of the silver support price, the Colorado Cooperative Company sought to provide its members with a simpler style of life. Nominally a corporation capitalized at $100,000, the society limited each of its members to a single one-hundred-dollar share.

B. L. Smith toured the state on behalf of the organizers in search of a suitable agricultural site. Colorado, by this time, had become host to numerous agricultural colonies (see I-25N, *U.S. 50W*, I-76 and *U.S. 285S* itineraries), some that succeeded and many that failed. Nucla, despite its share of difficulties, proved to be a winner.

Among the difficulties was Smith's inability to locate a suitable site until, one day, as he lay ill in Placerville (see *Colorado 62-145* itinerary), someone stopped to tell him about Tabeguache Park, situated on a mesa overlooking the San Miguel River. When he had recuperated, Smith moved his family to the place. They settled initially at Naturita, then merely a stop on the stage line.

When others had rallied to the colony, they organized a temporary camp at the mouth of Cottonwood Creek, about ten miles to the east of Naturita on what is now *Colorado 90*. There they set up a sawmill, a cash enterprise that supplied the fruit growers of the Uncompaghre River valley with boxes, builders with lumber, and miners with flumes. Society members worked for credits on joint enterprises such as the sawmill and the cooperative's irrigation ditch. Associates received coupon books in token of their work credits, which in turn became a form of scrip that was negotiable at the society's commissary.

By 1905 the irrigation canal was completed, the farms of the cooperative came to life, and Nucla was born.

The far-ranging Spanish friars, Silvestre Vélez de Escalante and Francisco Anatasio Dominguez, passed through the eventual site of Nucla in their historic journey of 1776. They camped between the San Miguel River and today's *Colorado 90* about one mile north of **Milepost 57** before following Cottonwood Creek to its headwaters on the Uncompaghre Plateau. The lightly armed expedition of the Franciscan fathers blazed the route of the Spanish Trail, which would run from the missions in New Mexico to those in California (see *U.S. 50-550, I-70* and *Colorado 64-139* itineraries).

Dolores River

The Dolores River, **Milepost 21**, heads in the mineral-rich San Juan Mountains and courses more than two hundred miles to a rendezvous with the Colorado River to the north. The Utes recall the legend of an ancient city of cliff dwellers whose remarkably advanced and peaceful urban community was nestled somewhere along the valley of the Dolores, a river named, incidentally, by Escalante and Dominguez in honor of Our Lady of Sorrows (*Nuestra Señora de los Dolores*). Unidentified invaders from the north came suddenly to destroy the city in a single day, killing all its inhabitants.

The legend inspired a 1907 poem by A. C. King, a former miner blinded in a mine accident, which concludes:

But the river still mourns for her people,
With weird and disconsolate flow,
Dolores, the River of Sorrow,
Dolores—the River of Woe.

Egnar

The town of Egnar, **Milepost 9**, is a relatively late and oddly perverse establishment. Founded with the commissioning of a post office in 1917, the surrounding community of ranchers chose to give recognition to that which was important to them by naming the town Range—and then spelling it backwards.

A few miles south of Egnar and west of *Colorado 141*, in the vicinity perhaps of **Milepost 5**, the traveling Franciscans spent the nights of August 14 and 15, 1776, at a waterhole that had been covered, evidently by the Utes, either to conceal it from others or to protect it from evaporation in the hot August sun. At Camp Agua Tapada, as they called it, they took time to allow Dominguez to recover from an illness. Escalante recorded the following:

This afternoon [August 14] we were overtaken by an Indo-Caucasian half-breed and an Indian of Mixed Plains [Indian] parentage from Abiquiu [New Mexico] the first Felipe and the second Juan Domingo by name. So as to wander among the heathens, they had run away without permission of their masters of that pueblo, with the desire of accompanying us as their excuse. We had no use for them, but, to forestall the mischief which either through ignorance or through their malice they might do by wandering any further among the Yutas [Utes] if we insisted on their going back, we took them on as companions.

Prior to being overtaken by the two runaways from Abiquiu, they had camped on the Dolores River, opposite the mouth of Narraguinnep Creek, four miles east of **Milepost 52** on *U.S. 666*.

The concern of the pious fathers for mischief that might come to the heathen Utes was plainly sincere. A couple of weeks after passing through here, for example, they encountered a band of Utes, among whom was one Red Bear:

On learning that they called him Red Bear [Padre Dominquez] instructed them all by explaining to them

the difference existing between men and brutes, the purpose for which either of them were created, and the
wrong thing they did in naming themselves after wild
beasts—thus placing themselves on a par with them, and
even below them.

Promptly he told the [Indian] to call himself Francisco
from then on. When the rest saw this, they began repeating this name, although with difficulty, the [Indian] joy-
fully pleased for being so named.

Narraguinnep Fort

Ten miles above the mouth of Narraguinnep Creek at
the upper end of Narraguinnep Canyon one can find the
site of an impromptu fort created in one of the last clashes
between white settlers and Indians. Narraguinnep Fort,
built by ranchers in 1885, was a breastwork of pine logs laid
to a height of about nine feet and fitted with loopholes. Its
construction was the closing act in a series of fatal incidents
that summer.

In June 1885, stockmen operating in the shadow of Narraguinnep Mountain had experienced the loss of a number
of cattle, which they determined to have been killed and
butchered by Indians. The boundary of the Southern Ute
reservation was scarcely thirty miles south. The ranchers
accosted a band of Indians and, in what was locally called the
Beaver massacre, killed eleven. Indians retaliated by attacking and killing a number of settlers in the Montezuma
valley, the depression lying between today's Cortez and
Mesa Verde National Park.

The Narraguinnep Fort was built and occupied for about
two weeks before hostilities subsided.

Lowry Indian Ruins

A nine hundred-year-old pueblo of the Anasazi Indians
was discovered nine miles west of **Milepost 46** at Pleasant
View by a homesteader named George Lowry. Originally
three stories tall and attended by an exceptional example of a

Great Kiva that apparently served as a regional ceremonial site, the Lowry Ruins are carried on the National Register of Historic Places.

Similar Anasazi ruins were discovered six and one-half miles east of **Milepost 37** along *Colorado 184* by Escalante and Dominguez when they climbed the Dolores River bluffs above their August 13, 1776 campsite: "Upon an elevation on the south side of the river there was a small village long ago, of the same type as those of the Indians of New Mexico, as we note from an inspection of the ruins," wrote Escalante.

The U.S. Department of the Interior's Bureau of Land Management has built an impressive exhibit at the site, which emphasizes the passage of two ancient cultures long since engulfed by modern America.

Bibliography

Books

Arps, Louise. *High Country Names*. Denver: Colorado Mountain Club, 1966.

Atherton, Lewis. *The Cattle Kings*. Lincoln: University of Nebraska Press, 1961.

Bancroft, Caroline. *Famous Aspen*. Boulder: Johnson Publishing Company, 1967.

Barney, Libeus, *Letters of the Pike's Peak Gold Rush*. San Jose: Talisman Press, 1959.

Bartlett, Richard A. *Great Surveys of the American West*. Norman: University of Oklahoma Press, 1926.

Beebe, Lucius, and Charles Clegg. *Narrow Gauge in the Rockies*. Berkeley: Howell-North, 1958.

Bird, Isabella. *A Lady's Life in the Rocky Mountains*. Sausalito: Comstock, 1960.

Brown, Dee. *The Gentle Tamers*. New York: Bantam, 1958.

Byers, William N. *Encyclopedia of Biography in Colorado*. Chicago: Century, 1901.

Cafky, Morris. *The Colorado Midland*. Denver: Rocky Mountain Railroad Club, 1965.

Chronic, Halka. *Roadside Geology of Colorado*. Missoula: Mountain Press, 1980.

Commager, Henry S., ed. *Documents of American History*. New York: Appleton-Century-Crofts, 1959.

Crum, J.M. *Rio Grande Southern Story*. Durango: Railroadiana, 1957.

Danielson, Clarence L. and Ralph W. *Basalt: Colorado Midland Town*. Boulder: Pruett, 1965.

Davis, Richard Harding. *The West From a Car-Window*. New York: Harpers, 1903.

DeArment, Robert K. *Bat Masterson*. Norman: University of Oklahoma Press, 1979.

Dunn, William R. *War Drum Echoes*. Colorado Springs: Century One, 1979.

Eichler, George R. *Colorado Place Names*. Boulder: Johnson Publishing Company, 1977.

Feitz, Leland. *A Quick History of Creede*. Colorado Springs: Little London Press, 1969.

Fetter, Richard L., and Suzanne. *Telluride.* Caldwell, Caxton, 1979.

Fisher, John. *A Builder of the West*. Caldwell. Caxton, 1939.

Foscue, Edwin J., and Louis O. Quam. *Estes Park: Resort in the Rockies*. Dallas: University Press, 1949.

Fremont, John C. *Memoirs of My Life*. Chicago, 1887.

Garrard, Lewis H. *Yah-To-Yah and the Taos Trail*. Norman: University of Oklahoma Press, 1955.

Goetzmann, William H. *Army Exploration in the American West*. Lincoln: University of Nebraska Press, 1959.

Goodykoontz, Colin B., ed. *Colorado: Short Studies of its Past and Present*. Boulder: University of Colorado Press, 1927.

Greeley, Horace. *An Overland Journey*. New York: Knopf, 1969.

Gregg, Josiah. *Commerce of the Prairies*. New York, 1844.

Grinnell, George B. *The Fighting Cheyennes*. Norman: University of Oklahoma Press, 1956.

——. *Two Great Scouts and Their Pawnee Battalion*. Cleveland: Clark, 1928.

Hafen, LeRoy R. *Broken Hand*. Denver: Old West, 1973.

——, ed. *Mountain Men and The Fur Trade of the Far West*. 10 vols. Glendale: Arthur H. Clark, 1964-1972.

——, ed. *Pike's Peak Gold Rush Guidebooks of 1859*. Glendale: Arthur H. Clark, 1941.

Hagood, Allen. *Dinosaur: The Story Behind the Scenery*. Las Vegas: KC Publishing, 1971.

Hall, Frank. *History of Colorado*. Chicago, 1895.

Horgan, Paul. *Lamy of Santa Fe*. New York, Farrar, Straus & Giroux, 1975.

Horner, John W. *Silver Town*. Caldwell: Caxton, 1950.

Inman, Henry, and William F.. Cody. *The Great Salt Lake Trail.* Topeka: Crane, 1913.

James, Edward T. (ed.). *Notable American Women, 1607-1950.* Cambridge: Harvard University Press, 1971.

James, Edwin. *An Account of an Expedition from Pittsburgh to the Rocky Mountains.* Philadelphia, 1823.

Kelly, Charles. *The Outlaw Trail.* New York: Devon-Adair, 1959.

Kemp, Donald C. & Langley, John R. *Happy Valley, A Promoters Paradise.* Privately published, 1945.

Kushner, Ervan F. *Alferd G. Packer, Cannibal!—Victim?* Frederick, Colorado: Platte 'N Press, 1980.

Langer, William L. *An Encyclopedia of World History.* Boston: Houghton Mifflin, 1972.

Lavender, David. *The Great West.* New York: American Heritage, 1982.

Lecompte, Janet S. *Pueblo, Hardscrabble, Greenhorn: The Upper Arkansas, 1832-1856.* Norman: University of Oklahoma Press, 1978.

Lee, Wayne C. *Trails of the Smoky Hill.* Caldwell: Caxton, 1980.

Long, Priscilla. *Mother Jones, Women Organizer.* Cambridge, Massachusetts: Red Sun Press, 1976.

Marcy, Col. Randolph B. *Thirty Years of Army Life on the Border.* New York, 1886.

Marshall, John B., and Temple H. Cornelius. *Golden Treasures of the San Juan.* Denver: Sage, 1961.

McMechen, Edgar C. *Walter Scott Cheesman, A Pioneer Builder of Colorado.* Denver: privately published, undated.

Mills, Enos A. *The Story of Estes Park.* Estes Park: Self, 1917.

Morgan, Dale L. *Pioneer Atlas of the American West.* New York: Rand McNally, 1956.

Mumey, Nolie. *Creede: History of a Colorado Silver Mining Town.* Denver: Artcraft, 1949.

Murray, D. Keith. *Guide to Energy Resources of the Piceance Creek Basin*. Rocky Mountain Association of Geology, 1974.

Murtagh, William J. *The National Register of Historic Places*. Washington: Government Printing Office, 1976.

Oliver, John W. *History of American Technology*. New York: Ronald, 1956.

Pabor, W. E. *Greeley in the Beginning*. Greeley: Greeley Museum, 1973.

Parsons, E. *Guidebook to Colorado*. Boston: Little, Brown, 1911.

Quaife, Milo M., ed. *Kit Carson's Autobiography*. Lincoln: University of Nebraska Press, 1959.

Rohrbough, Malcolm J. *Aspen*. New York: Oxford University Press, 1986.

Sage, Rufus G. *Rocky Mountain Life*. Dayton, 1857.

Schoolland, J. B. *The Switzerland Trail*. Boulder: Boulder Historical Society, 1960.

Sell, Henry B., and Victor Waybright,. *Buffalo Bill and the Wild West*. New York: Oxford University Press, 1955.

Sheedy, Dennis. *Autobiography*. Denver: privately published, 1922.

Shoemaker, Len. *Saga of a Forest Ranger*. Denver: University of Colorado Press, 1958.

Smith, Joseph. *The Book of Mormon*. Salt Lake City: Deseret Publishing, 1977.

Steinel, Alvin T. *History of Agriculture in Colorado, 1858-1926*. Fort Collins: State Agricultural College, 1926.

Tierney, Luke. *History of the Gold Discoveries on the South Platte River*. Pacific City, Iowa, 1859.

Ubbelohde, Carl, Maxine Benson, and D. A. Smith. *A Colorado History*. Boulder: Pruett, 1982.

Van Doren, Charles, and Robert McHenry. *Webster's Guide to American History*. Springfield: Merriam, 1971.

Warner, Ted J., ed. *The Dominguez-Escalante Journal, 1776*. Provo: Brigham Young University Press, 1976.

Watrous, Ansel. *History of Larimer County*. Fort Collins: Courier Printing and Publishing, 1911.

Webb, Ardis. *The Perry Park Story*. Privately published, 1974.

Articles

The official publication of the Colorado Historical Society, *Colorado Magazine*, afforded a broad and comprehensive look into the circumstances and personalities associated with historical sites in the state. In the sixty-plus years that the society has been publishing a journal—from *Colorado Magazine* to the current *Colorado Heritage*—its pages have carried thousands of scholarly investigations, interviews, and personal reminiscences. The information gained from at least 150 of these articles is reflected in the narrative of this book. Lack of space, however, has precluded listing them individually.

Among other periodicals and newspapers consulted in my research are the *Westerners Brand Books*, annual publications prepared in Denver and Chicago; *True West; Munsey; Survey; Empire Magazine*, the Sunday supplement of the Denver *Post; Colorado Heritage News; Journal of the West;* the New York *Times;* the *Rocky Mountain News;* and the Denver *Post*.

The Denver & Rio Grande Western and the Colorado Southern Railroads furnished brochures, prepared by their public relations departments, that gave summarized accounts of the histories of these corporations, their antecedents, and subsidiaries.

Manuscripts

Manuscript documents, such as the D&RGW Railroad's annual reports from its early years, were examined at the Colorado Heritage Center's reference library in Denver. Unpublished interviews with Colorado pioneers were also surveyed in the archives of the Western Historical Department of the University of Colorado's Norlin Library in Boulder.

Maps

Of great importance, of course, were vintage and manuscript maps, such as the Rio Grande Southern's 1891 chief engineer's map held by the Heritage Center; the Crown Collection of American Maps of the Norlin Library; Colton's 1879 map of Colorado; and the Rand McNally *Pioneer Atlas of the American West*, published in Chicago in 1869.

For data to acquaint modern motorists with these historical sites, the detailed maps of the U.S. Forest Service, covering a third of the state, were exceptionally valuable. The United States Geological Survey maps in scales from 1:50,000 to 1:250,000 provided important data, as did the several Colorado county maps based upon them. Finally, maps produced by the Colorado Department of Highways for travelers and for internal administrative uses facilitated the accurate siting of mileposts in relation to locations mentioned in the narrative.

Index